Operational Risk Management: Analysis and Operations

Operational Risk Management: Analysis and Operations

Baldev Singh Chhikara

venus

Venus Books

Publishers & Distributors

NEW DELHI (INDIA)

Operational Risk Management: Analysis and Operations

ISBN 978-93-5111-662-2

First Published 2017

VENUS BOOKS

4376-A/4B, Gali Murari Lal, Ansari Road
Darya Ganj, New Delhi-110 002, INDIA
Phone : +91-11-43580356, +91-11-23289044
e-mail: venusbooksinfo@gmail.com

Reprinted 2025

Type Setting by : Friends Media, Delhi-110089
Digitally Printed at : Replika Press Pvt. Ltd.

Preface

Operations management is an area of business concerned with the production of goods and services, and involves the responsibility of ensuring that business operations are efficient in terms of using as little resource as needed, and effective in terms of meeting customer requirements. It is concerned with managing the process that converts inputs into outputs.Operations traditionally refers to the production of goods and services separately, although the distinction between these two main types of operations is increasingly difficult to make as manufacturers tend to merge product and service offerings. More generally, Operations Management aims to increase the content of value-added activities in any given process. Fundamentally, these value-adding creative activities should be aligned with market opportunity for optimal enterprise performance.

The term Operational Risk Management (ORM) is defined as a continual cyclic process which includes risk assessment, risk decision making, and implementation of risk controls, which results in acceptance, mitigation, or avoidance of risk. ORM is the oversight of operational risk, including the risk of loss resulting from inadequate or failed internal processes and systems; human factors; or external events.

The most important types of operational risk involve breakdowns in internal controls and corporate governance. Such breakdowns can lead to financial losses through error, fraud, or failure to perform in a timely manner or cause the interests of the bank to be compromised in some other way, for example, by its dealers, lending officers or other staff exceeding their authority or conducting business in an unethical or risky manner.

Banks, business organisations, practitioners of operational risk discipline and students pursuing courses on Risk Management and Finance Management will find this book useful.

I would like to thank my team for standing beside me throughout my career and writing this book.My special thanks go to "Venus Books" who have published the book.

– Baldev Singh Chhikara

Contents

1

Operations Management

Operations management is an area of business concerned with the production of goods and services, and involves the responsibility of ensuring that business operations are efficient in terms of using as little resource as needed, and effective in terms of meeting customer requirements.

It is concerned with managing the process that converts inputs into outputs.Operations traditionally refers to the production of goods and services separately, although the distinction between these two main types of operations is increasingly difficult to make as manufacturers tend to merge product and service offerings.

More generally, Operations Management aims to increase the content of value-added activities in any given process. Fundamentally, these value-adding creative activities should be aligned with market opportunity for optimal enterprise performance.

The U.S. Department of Education, Operations Management, the physical and/or technical functions of a firm or organization, particularly those relating to development, production, and manufacturing.

Instruction in principles of general management, manufacturing and production systems, plant management, equipment maintenance management, production control, industrial labour relations and skilled trades supervision, strategic manufacturing policy, systems analysis, productivity analysis and cost control, and materials planning.

CONCEPT OF PRODUCTION AND OPERATIONS MANAGEMENT

INTRODUCTION

The Subject of Production Management is studied under different Headings-such as Production Planning and control, Production and Inventory control, production and operations control and many more. What ever may be the title of the subject, the contents of the subject are more or less one and the same. Before we discuss about production management, let us discuss about product, production and management. This will give us a rough idea about production Management and with what a production manager has to deal with.

PRODUCT

Though many authors define the product with Consumer orientation, it is better for us to deal with different angles, because it will be helpful for us to understand the subject of production and Operation Management:

- *For a Consumer*: The product is a combination of or optimal mix of potential utilities. This is because every consumer expects some use or uses from the product. Hence he/she always identifies the product in terms of the uses. Say for example-Soap can be identified by complexion, cleanliness of body, freshness, fragrance or health.... etc. Because of this, many producers advertise that they are selling health, or they are selling Cine star Complexion or they are selling freshness and so on.
- *For a Production Manager*: Product is the combination of various surfaces and processes. This is because the production Manager is solely responsible for producing the product. He has to think of the various surfaces by which the product is made of, so that he can plan for processes by which a particular surface can be made and plan for required capacity of the facility by which the surface is produced. While planning he has to see that the required surface is produced by the best and cheapest method, so as to make the product to face competition in the market.
- *For a Financial Manager*: For him the product is a mix of various cost elements as he is responsible for the profitability of the product.
- *For a Personnel Manager*: For him the product is a mix of various skills, as he is the person who selects and trains the personnel to meet the demand of the skill to produce the product. In general we can define the product as a bundle of tangible and intangible attributes, which along with the service is meant to satisfy the customer wants.

PRODUCTION

Production means application of processes. The raw material to add the use and economic values to arrive at desired product by the best method, with out sacrificing the desired quality.

We have three ways of Production, they are:

- *Production by Disintegration*: By separating the contents of Crude oil or a mixture the desired products are produced. For example the crude oil is disintegrated into various fuel oils. Similarly salt production is also an example for product produced by disintegrated. We can use Mechanical or Chemical or both technologies to get the desired product, so that it will have desired use value.

- *Production by Integration*: In this type of Production various Components of the products are assembled together to get the desired product. In this process, Physical and Chemical Properties of the materials used may change. The examples are: Assembly of Two wheelers, Four wheelers and so on.
- *Production by Service*: Here the Chemical and Mechanical Properties of materials are improved without any physical change. The example for this is Heat Treatment of metals. In real world, a combin-ation of methods is used. In general production is the use of any process or procedure designed to transform a set of input elements into a set of output elements, which have use value and economic value.

MANAGEMENT

Management can be explained as an art or science, of getting things done by the people, by planning, coordinating, organizing, directing and controlling the activities to meet specified goals, with in the frame work of agreed policies. The explanation put emphasis on getting things done, Planning, Organizing, Coordinating, and controlling and specific objectives and agreed policies. Today's manager needs scientific base as well as personal tactics to manage the people under him to achieve the desired goals. Production and management will help us to understand what exactly the Production Management or Production, and Operations Management.

CRITERIA OF PERFORMANCE

Three aims of performance of the Production and Operations Management system may be identified.

They are,:

- Effectiveness,
- Customer satisfaction,
- Efficiency.

The case of Efficiency is productive utilization of resources is clear. Whether the organization is in 'private sector' or in the 'public sector', is a 'manufacturing or 'non-manufacturing' organization or a 'profit' or a 'non-profit' organization, the optimal utilization of resource inputs is always a desired objective. The effectiveness has more dimensions to it. It involves optimality in the fulfillment of multiple objectives with a possible prioritization within the objectives. Modern production and operations management has to serve the target customers, the people working within, as also the region, country or society at large. Thus Production/Operations Management system, has not only to be profitable and/or efficient, but must necessarily satisfy many more customers. This effectiveness has to be again viewed in terms of the short and long-term horizons depending upon the operations system.

Optimum, Good, Better operations management can improve:

- Efficiency of operation system to do things right and broader concept.
- Effectiveness of operation system refers to doing right things that is seven rights, they are: Right operation, Right Quantity, Right Quality, Right Supplier or Right Vendor, Right Time, Right Place and Right Price.

Basically, efficiency and effectiveness of the operations system can be measured by four dimensions, they are:

1. Cost,
2. Quality,
3. Dependability and
4. Reliability.

In fact these directly relate to the competitiveness of the organization, both nationally and internationally. Modern developments in better tools and techniques, methods and systems like Automation, Flexible manufacturing, CAD, CAM, CIM at management, CADD, CIMS, Use of Robotics, TQM, OR Techniques etc, are taking place to achieve improvements in Cost, Quality, Dependability, Reliability and Flexibility and thus to help for better management.

OPERATIONS MANAGEMENT: A FRAMEWORK FOR MANAGING OPERATIONS

Managing operations can be enclosed in a frame of general management function. Operation managers are concerned with planning, organizing, and controlling the activities which affect human behaviour through models.

PLANNING

Activities that establishes a course of action and guide future decision-making is planning. The operations manager defines the objectives for the operations subsystem of the organization, and the policies, and procedures for achieving the objectives. This stage includes clarifying the role and focus of operations in the organization's overall strategy. It also involves product planning, facility designing and using the conversion process.

Organizing

Activities that establishes a structure of tasks and authority. Operation managers establish a structure of roles and the flow of information within the operations subsystem. They determine the activities required to achieve the goals and assign authority and responsibility for carrying them out.

Controlling

Activities that assure the actual performance in accordance with planned performance. To ensure that the plans for the operations subsystems are accomplished, the operations manager must exercise control by measuring actual outputs and comparing them to planned operations management. Controlling costs, quality, and schedules are the important functions here.

Behaviour

Operation managers are concerned with how their efforts to plan, organize, and control affect human behaviour. They also want to know how the behaviour of subordinates can affect management's planning, organizing, and controlling actions. Their interest lies in decision-making behaviour.

Models

As operation managers plan, organise, and control the conversion process, they encounter many problems and must make many decisions. They can simplify their difficulties using models like *aggregate planning models* for examining how best to use existing capacity in short-term, *break even analysis* to identify break even volumes, *linear programming and computer simulation* for capacity utilisation, *decision tree analysis* for long-term capacity problem of facility expansion, *simple median model* for determining best locations of facilities etc.

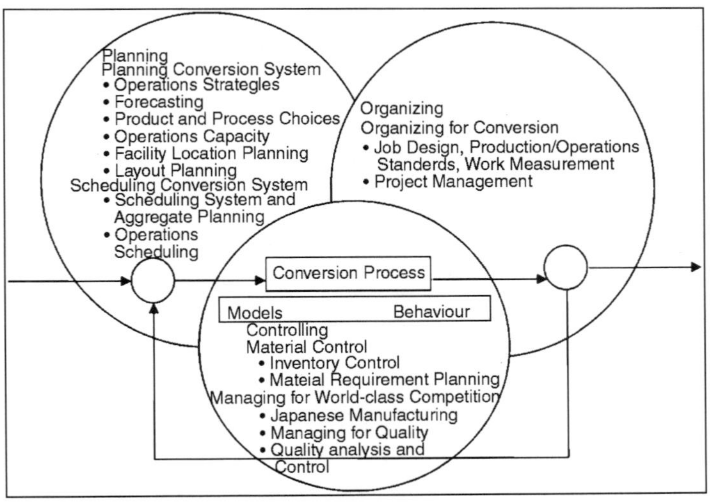

Fig. General Model for Managing Operations

OBJECTIVES OF OPERATIONS MANAGEMENT

Objectives of operations management can be categorised into customer service and resource utilisation.

Customer Service

The first objective of operating systems is the customer serivce to the satisfaction of customer wants. Therefore, customer service is a key objective of operations management. The operating system must provide something to a specification which can satisfy the customer in terms of cost and timing. Thus, primary objective can be satisfied by providing the 'right thing at a right price at the right time'.

These aspects of customer service—specification, cost and timing—are described for four functions in Table. They are the principal sources of customer satisfaction and must, therefore, be the principal dimension of the customer service objective for operations managers.

Principal Function	Principal Customer Wants	
	Primary Considerations	Other Considerations
Manufacture	Goods of a given, Requested or Acceptable Specification	Cost, i.e., Purchase Price or Cost of Obtaining Gooda. Timing, i.e., Delivery Delay from Order or Request to Receipt of Goods.
Transport	Management of a Given, Requested or Acceptable Specification	Cost, i.e., Cost of Movement. Timing, i.e., 1. Duration or Time to Move. 2. Wait or Delay from Requesting to its Commencement.
Supply	Goods of a Given, Requested or Acceptable Specification	Cost, i.e., Delivery Delay From Order or Request to Receipt of Goods. Timing, i.e., Delivery Delay from Order or Request to recipt of Goods.
Service	Treatment of a given, Requested or Acceptable Specification	Cost, i.e., Cost of Movements. Timing, i.e., 1. Durationor time Required fo Treatment 2. Wait or Delay From requesting Treatment to its Commencement

Fig. Aspectsof Customer Service

Generally an organization will aim reliably and consistently to achieve certain standards and operations manager will be influential in attempting to achieve these standards. Hence, this objective will influence the operations manager's decisions to achieve the required customer service.

Resource Utilisation

Another major objective of operating systems is to utilise resources for the satisfaction of customer wants effectively, *i.e.*, customer service must be provided with the achievement of effective operations through efficient use of resources. Inefficient use of resources or inadequate customer service leads to commercial failure of an operating system.

Operations management is concerned essentially with the utilisation of resources, *i.e.*, obtaining maximum effect from resources or minimising their loss, under utilisation or waste. The extent of the utilisation of the resources' potential might be expressed in terms of the proportion of available time used or occupied, space utilisation, levels of activity, etc.

Each measure indicates the extent to which the potential or capacity of such resources is utilised. This is referred as the objective of resource utilisation.

Operations management is also concerned with the achievement of both satisfactory customer service and resource utilisation. An improvement in one will often give rise to deterioration in the other. Often both cannot be maximised, and hence a satisfactory performance must be achieved on both objectives.

All the activities of operations management must be tackled with these two objectives in mind, and many of the problems will be faced by operations managers because of this conflict. Hence, operations managers must attempt to balance these basic objectives.

MANAGING GLOBAL OPERATIONS

The term 'globalization' describes businesses' deployment of facilities and operations around the world. Globalization can be defined as a process in which geographic distance becomes a factor of diminishing importance in the establishment and maintenance of cross border economic, political and socio-cultural relations.

It can also be defined as worldwide drive towards a globalized economic system dominated by supranational corporate trade and banking institutions that are not accountable to democratic processes or national governments.

There are four developments, which have spurred the trend towards globalization.

These are:

1. Improved transportation and communication technologies;
2. Opened financial systems;
3. Increased demand for imports; and
4. Reduced import quotas and other trade barriers.

When a firm sets up facilities abroad it involve some added complexities in its operation. Global markets impose new standards on quality and time. Managers should not think about domestic markets first and then global markets later, rather it could be think globally and performance locally.

Also, they must have a good understanding of their competitors. Some other important challenges of managing multinational operations include other languages and customs, different management style, unfamiliar laws and regulations, and different costs.

Managing global operations would focus on the following key issues:

- To acquire and properly utilize the following concepts and those related to global operations, supply chain, logistics, etc.
- To associate global historical events to key drivers in global operations from different perspectives.
- To develop criteria for conceptualization and evaluation of different global operations.
- To associate success and failure cases of global operations to political, social, economical and technological environments.

- To envision trends in global operations.
- To develop an understanding of the world vision regardless of their country of origin, residence or studies in a respectful way of perspectives of people from different races, studies, preferences, religion, politic affiliation, place of origin, etc.

SCOPE OF PRODUCTION AND OPERATIONS MANAGEMENT

Production and operations management concern with the conversion of inputs into outputs, using physical resources, so as to provide the desired utilities to the customer while meeting the other organizational objectives of effectiveness, efficiency and adoptability. It distinguishes itself from other functions such as personnel, marketing, finance, etc., by its primary concern for 'conversion by using physical resources.'

Following are the activities which are listed under production and operations management functions:

- Location of facilities
- Plant layouts and material handling
- Product design
- Process design
- Production and planning control
- Quality control
- Materials management
- Maintenance management.

LOCATION OF FACILITIES

Location of facilities for operations is a long-term capacity decision which involves a long term commitment about the geographically static factors that affect a business organization. It is an important strategic level decision-making for an organization. It deals with the questions such as 'where our main operations should be based?'

The selection of location is a key-decision as large investment is made in building plant and machinery. An improper location of plant may lead to waste of all the investments made in plant and machinery equipments. Hence, location of plant should be based on the company's expansion plan and policy, diversification plan for the products, changing sources of raw materials and many other factors. The purpose of the location study is to find the optimal location that will results in the greatest advantage to the organization.

PLANT LAYOUT AND MATERIAL HANDLING

Plant layout refers to the physical arrangement of facilities. It is the configuration of departments, work centres and equipment in the conversion process. The overall objective of the plant layout is to design a physical arrangement that meets the required output quality and quantity most economically. "Plant layout is a plan of an optimum arrangement of facilities including personnel, operating equipment, storage space, material handling equipments and all other supporting services along with the design of best structure to contain all these facilities". 'Material Handling' refers to the 'moving of materials from the store room to the machine and from one machine to the next during the process of manufacture'. It is also defined as the 'art and science of moving, packing and storing of products in any form'.

It is a specialised activity for a modern manufacturing concern, with 50 to 75 per cent of the cost of production. Operation and maintenance of material handling devices.

Material handling devices increases the output, improves quality, speeds up the deliveries and decreases the cost of production. Hence, material handling is a prime consideration in the designing new plant and several existing plants.

PRODUCT DESIGN

Product design deals with conversion of ideas into reality. Every business organization have to design, develop and introduce new products as a survival and growth strategy. Developing the new products and launching them in the market is the biggest challenge faced by the organizations.

The entire process of need identification to physical manufactures of product involves three functions: marketing, product development, manufacturing. Product development translates the needs of customers given by marketing into technical specifications and designing the various features into the product to these specifications.

Manufacturing has the responsibility of selecting the processes by which the product can be manufactured. Product design and development provides link between marketing, customer needs and expectations and the activities required to manufacture the product.

PROCESS DESIGN

Process design is a macroscopic decision-making of an overall process route for converting the raw material into finished goods. These decisions encompass the selection of a process, choice of technology, process flow analysis and layout of the facilities.

Hence, the important decisions in process design are to analyse the workflow for converting raw material into finished product and to select the workstation for each included in the workflow.

PRODUCTION PLANNING AND CONTROL

Production planning and control can be defined as the process of planning the production in advance, setting the exact route of each item, fixing the starting and finishing dates for each item, to give production orders to shops and to follow up the progress of products according to orders.

The principle of production planning and control lies in the statement 'First Plan Your Work and then Work on Your Plan'. Main functions of production planning and control includes planning, routing, scheduling, dispatching and follow-up.

Planning is deciding in advance what to do, how to do it, when to do it and who is to do it. Planning bridges the gap from where we are, to where we want to go. It makes it possible for things to occur which would not otherwise happen.

Routing may be defined as the selection of path which each part of the product will follow, which being transformed from raw material to finished products. Routing determines the most advantageous path to be followed from department to department and machine to machine till raw material gets its final shape.

Scheduling determines the programme for the operations. Scheduling may be defined as 'the fixation of time and date for each operation' as well as it determines the sequence of operations to be followed.

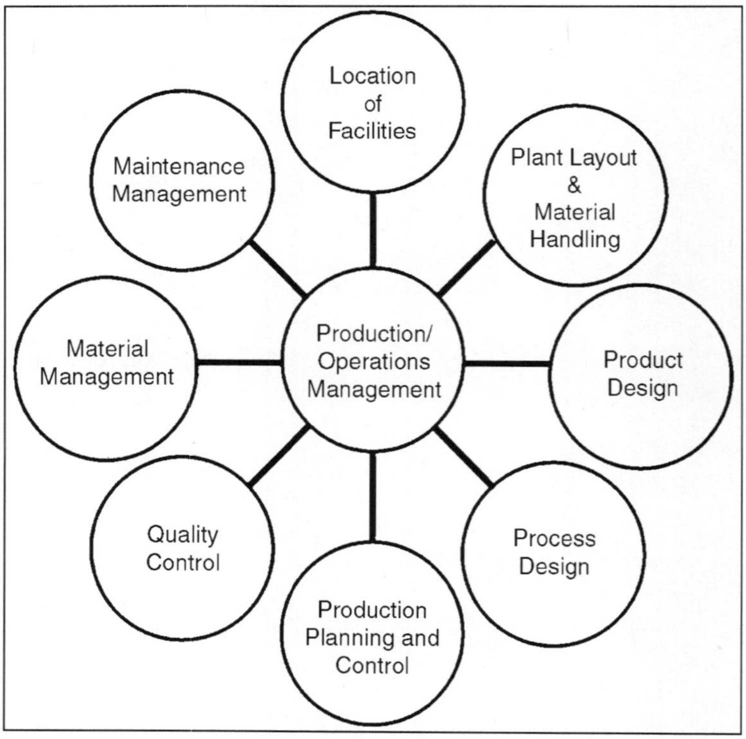

Fig. Scope of Production and Operations Management

Dispatching is concerned with the starting the processes. It gives necessary authority so as to start a particular work, which has already been planned under 'Routing' and 'Scheduling'. Therefore, dispatching is 'release of orders and instruction for the starting of production for any item in acceptance with the route sheet and schedule charts'. The function of follow-up is to report daily the progress of work in each shop in a prescribed proforma and to investigate the causes of deviations from the planned performance.

QUALITY CONTROL

Quality Control may be defined as 'a system that is used to maintain a desired level of quality in a product or service'. It is a systematic control of various factors that affect the quality of the product. Quality control aims at prevention of defects at the source, relies on effective feed back system and corrective action procedure. Quality control can also be defined as 'that industrial management technique by means of which product of uniform acceptable quality is manufactured'. It is the entire collection of activities which ensures that the operation will produce the optimum quality products at minimum cost.

The main objectives of quality control are:

- To improve the companies income by making the production more acceptable to the customers *i.e.*, by providing long life, greater usefulness, maintainability, etc.
- To reduce companies cost through reduction of losses due to defects.
- To achieve interchangeability of manufacture in large scale production.
- To produce optimal quality at reduced price.
- To ensure satisfaction of customers with productions or services or high quality level, to build customer goodwill, confidence and reputation of manufacturer.
- To make inspection prompt to ensure quality control.
- To check the variation during manufacturing.

MATERIALS MANAGEMENT

Materials management is that aspect of management function which is primarily concerned with the acquisition, control and use of materials needed and flow of goods and services connected with the production process having some predetermined objectives in view.

The main objectives of materials management are:

- To minimise material cost.
- To purchase, receive, transport and store materials efficiently and to reduce the related cost.
- To cut down costs through simplification, standard-isation, value analysis, import substitution, etc.
- To trace new sources of supply and to develop cordial relations with them in order to ensure continuous supply at reasonable rates.
- To reduce investment tied in the inventories for use in other productive purposes and to develop high inventory turnover ratios.

MAINTENANCE MANAGEMENT

In modern industry, equipment and machinery are a very important part of the total productive effort. Therefore, their idleness or downtime becomes are very expensive. Hence, it is very important that the plant machinery should be properly maintained.

The main objectives of maintenance management are:

- To achieve minimum breakdown and to keep the plant in good working condition at the lowest possible cost.
- To keep the machines and other facilities in such a condition that permits them to be used at their optimal capacity without interruption.
- To ensure the availability of the machines, buildings and services required by other sections of the factory for the performance of their functions at optimal return on investment.

ORGANIZATIONAL AND OPERATIONAL CONTROL

The concept of organizational control is implicit in the bureaucratic theory of Max Weber. Associated with this theory are such concepts as "span of control", "closeness of supervision", and "hierarchical authority". Weber's view tends to include all levels or types of organizational control as being the same. More recently, writers have tended to differentiate the control process between that which emphasizes the nature of the organizational or systems design and that which deals with daily operations.

To illustrate the difference, we "evaluate" the performance of a system to see how effective and efficient the design proved to be or to discover why it failed. In contrast, we operate and "control" the system with respect to the daily inputs of material, information, and energy. In both instances, the elements of feedback are present, but organizational control tends to review and evaluate the nature and arrangement of components in the system, whereas operational control tends to adjust the daily inputs. The direction for organizational control comes from the goals and strategic plans of the organization. General plans are translated into specific performance measures such as share of the market, earnings, return on investment, and budgets.

The process of organizational control is to review and evaluate the performance of the system against these established norms. Rewards for meeting or exceeding standards may range from special recognition to salary increases or promotions. On the other hand, a failure to meet expectations may signal the need to reorganize or redesign. In organizational control, the approach used in the programme of review and evaluation depends on the reason for the evaluation — that is, is it because the system is not effective (accomplishing its objectives)? Is the system failing to achieve an expected standard of efficiency? Is the evaluation being conducted because of a breakdown or failure in operations? Is it merely a periodic audit-and-review process?

When a system has failed or is in great difficulty, special diagnostic techniques may be required to isolate the trouble areas and to identify the causes of the difficulty. It is appropriate to investigate areas that have been troublesome before or areas where some measure of performance can be quickly identified. For example, if an organization's output backlog builds rapidly, it is logical to check first to see if the problem is due to such readily obtainable measures as increased demand or to a drop in available man hours. When a more detailed analysis is necessary, a systematic procedure should be followed.

In contrast to organizational control, operational control serves to regulate the day-to-day output relative to schedules, specifications, and costs. Is the output of product or service the proper quality and is it available as scheduled? Are inventories of raw materials, goods-in-process, and finished products being purchased and produced in the desired quantities? Are the costs associated with the transformation process in line with cost estimates? Is the information needed in the transformation process available in the right form and at the right time? Is the energy resource being utilized efficiently?

The most difficult task of management concerns monitoring the behaviour of individuals, comparing performance to some standard, and providing rewards or punishment as indicated. Sometimes this control over people relates entirely to their output. For example, a manager might not be concerned with the behaviour of a salesman as long as sales were as high as expected. In other instances, close supervision of the salesman might be appropriate if achieving customer satisfaction were one of the sales organization's main objectives.

The larger the unit, the more likely that the control characteristic will be related to some output goal. It also follows that if it is difficult or impossible to identify the actual output of individuals, it is better to measure the performance of the entire group. This means that individuals' levels of motivation and the measurement of their performance become subjective judgements made by the supervisor. Controlling output also suggests the difficulty of controlling individuals' performance and relating this to the total system's objectives.

Problems of Control

The perfect plan could be outlined if every possible variation of input could be anticipated and if the system would operate as predicted. This kind of planning is neither realistic, economical, nor feasible for most business systems. If it were feasible, planning requirements would be so complex that the system would be out of date before it could be operated. Therefore, we design control into systems.

This requires more thought in the systems design but allows more flexibility of operations and makes it possible to operate a system using unpredictable components and undetermined input. Still, the design and effective operation of control are not without problems. The objective of the system is to perform some specified function. The purpose of organizational control is to see that the specified function is achieved; the objective of operational control is to ensure that variations in daily output are maintained within prescribed limits. It is one thing to design a system that contains all of the elements of control, and quite another to make it operate true to the best objectives of design.

Operating "in control" or "with plan" does not guarantee optimum performance. For example, the plan may not make the best use of the inputs of materials, energy, or information — in other words, the system may not be designed to operate efficiently. Some of the more typical problems relating to control include the difficulty of measurement, the problem of timing information flow, and the setting of proper standards.

Measurement of Output

When objectives are not limited to quantitative output, the measurement of system effectiveness is difficult to make and subsequently perplexing to evaluate. Many of the characteristics pertaining to output do not lend themselves to quantitative measurement. This is true particularly when inputs of human energy cannot be related directly to output. The same situation applies to machines and other equipment associated with human involvement, when output is not in specific units.

In evaluating man-machine or human-oriented systems, psychological and sociological factors obviously do not easily translate into quantifiable terms. For example, how does mental fatigue affect the quality or quantity of output? And, if it does, is mental fatigue a function of the lack of a challenging assignment or the fear of a potential injury? Subjective inputs may be transferred into numerical data, but there is always the danger of an incorrect appraisal and transfer, and the danger that the analyst may assume undue confidence in such data after they have been quantified.

Let us suppose, for example, that the decisions made by an executive are rated from 1 to 10, 10 being the perfect decision. After determining the ranking for each decision, adding these, and dividing by the total number of decisions made, the average ranking would indicate a particular executive's score in his decision-making role. On the basis of this score, judgements — which could be quite erroneous — might be made about his decision-making effectiveness. One executive with a ranking of 6.75 might be considered more effective than another who had a ranking of 6.25, and yet the two managers may have made decisions under different circumstances and conditions. External factors over which neither executive had any control may have influenced the difference in "effectiveness".

Quantifying human behaviour, despite its extreme difficulty, subjectivity, and imprecision in relation to measuring physical characteristics is the most prevalent and important measurement made in large systems. The behaviour of individuals ultimately dictates the success or failure of every man-made system.

Information Flow

Another problem of control relates to the improper timing of information introduced into the feedback channel. Improper timing can occur in both computerized and human control systems, either by mistakes in measurement or in judgement. The more rapid the system's response to an error signal, the more likely it is that the system could overadjust; yet the need for prompt action is important because any delay in providing corrective input could also be crucial. A system generating feedback inconsistent with current need will tend to fluctuate and will not adjust in the desired manner.

The most serious problem in information flow arises when the delay in feedback is exactly one-half cycle, for then the corrective action is superimposed on a variation from norm which, at that moment, is in the same direction as that of the correction. This causes the system to overcorrect, and then if the reverse adjustment is made out of cycle, to correct too much in the other direction, and so on until the system fluctuates out of control. If, at Point A, the trend below standard is recognized and new inputs are added, but not until Point B, the system will overreact and go beyond the allowable limits. Again, if this is recognized at Point C, but inputs are not withdrawn until Point D, it will cause the system to drop below the lower limit of allowable variation.

One solution to this problem rests in anticipation, which involves measuring not only the change but also the rate of change. The correction is outlined as a factor of the type and rate of the error. The difficulty also might be overcome by reducing the time lag between the measurement of the output and the adjustment to input.

If a trend can be indicated, a time lead can be introduced to compensate for the time lag, bringing about consistency between the need for correction and the type and magnitude of the indicated action. It is usually more effective for an organization to maintain continuous measurement of its performance and to make small adjustments in operations constantly. Information feedback, consequently, should be timely and correct to be effective. That is, the information should provide an accurate indication of the status of the system.

Setting Standards

Setting the proper standards or control limits is a problem in many systems. Parents are confronted with this dilemma in expressing what they expect of their children, and business managers face the same issue in establishing standards that will be acceptable to employees. Some theorists have proposed that workers be allowed to set their own standards, on the assumption that when people establish their own goals, they are more apt to accept and achieve them. Standards should be as precise as possible and communicated to all persons concerned. Moreover, communication alone is not sufficient; understanding is necessary.

In human systems, standards tend to be poorly defined and the allowable range of deviation from standard also indefinite. For example, how many hours each day should a professor be expected to be available for student consultation? Or, what kind of behaviour should be expected by students in the classroom? Discretion and personal judgement play a large part in such systems, to determine whether corrective action should be taken. Perhaps the most difficult problem in human systems is the unresponsiveness of individuals to indicated correction. This may take the form of opposition and subversion to control, or it may be related to the lack of defined responsibility or authority to take action. Leadership and positive motivation then become vital ingredients in achieving the proper response to input requirements.

Most control problems relate to design; thus the solution to these problems must start at that point. Automatic control systems, provided that human intervention is possible to handle exceptions, offer the greatest promise. There is a danger, however, that we may measure characteristics that do not represent effective performance or that improper information may be communicated.

RESOURCE ALLOCATION AND OPERATIONAL EFFICIENCY

As stressed earlier, budget preparation is an iterative process between the Ministry of Finance and spending ministries. Therefore, it is a combination of a top-down approach, with the Ministry of Finance giving guidelines or communicating instructions to spending ministries, and a bottom-up approach, with spending ministries presenting requests for budget allocation to the Ministry of Finance.

Either approach followed in isolation would have adverse effects: "A budget created from the bottom-up may lead to excessive spending and instability, if not carefully organized and subject to pre-established limits. By contrast, a highly centralized exercise introduces rigidities and loses the vision of those who are close to the service recipients. The articulation of the top-down and bottom-up approach is crucial since it determines how priorities and fiscal targets will be taken into account over the budget preparation process.

TOP-DOWN APPROACH

As previewed earlier, the starting points for budget preparation are a clear definition of fiscal targets and a strategic framework consisting of a comprehensive set of objectives and priorities. Thereafter, strong coordination of the budget preparation is required to achieve the necessary iteration and to avoid major departures from the initial framework. Giving a hard constraint to line ministries from the start of budget preparation favours a shift from a "needs" mentality to an "availability" mentality.

Moreover, to translate strategic choices and policies into programmes, line ministries require clear indications on available resources. Finally, a hard constraint increases the de facto authority and autonomy of the line ministries, weakening the claim of the Ministry of Finance to a role in determining the internal composition of the line ministries' budget. This calls for notifying spending agencies of the initial budget ceilings and preferably in absolute terms, or at least through the provision of accurate and complete parameters.

These ceilings may be defined either at the very beginning of the dialogue between the Ministry of Finance and the line ministries, or after a first iteration when line ministries communicate their preliminary requests. In practice, two variants are found in countries that have good financial discipline. In some, line ministries are notified of the sectoral ceilings at the very start of the budget preparation process. Other countries, where budget preparation may last more than ten months, establish ceilings in two steps. In the first step, some flexibility is left to line ministries to translate guidelines in terms of budget envelopes.

Then, after a brief review and discussion of the preliminary requests, the Ministry of Finance notifies the line ministries of the binding ceilings. In countries with strong government cohesion and stable and well-organized arrangements for budget preparation, the two variants are equally workable, since financial constraints are more or less taken into account by line ministries when preparing their preliminary request. Moreover, when budget preparation lasts nearly one year it would be very difficult to set definite ceilings at the start of the process. However, in countries where fiscal discipline and government cohesion are not firmly established adopting a gradual approach to building financial constraints into the budget preparation process could mean a simple comeback to a fully open-ended process.

Therefore, the notification of definite budgetary envelopes at the beginning of the budgetary process is highly desirable in these countries. Coordination and consistency of budget policy with overall economic and social policy is a central concern of Cabinet, although the Ministry of Finance must play the key role in analysis and formulating recommendations. Generally, the Ministry of Finance should be responsible for setting the sectoral ceilings, but it should of course coordinate with the center of government, which must also review the ceilings in detail and approve them.

In some countries, the sectoral ceilings are discussed within interministerial committees; in other countries, proposed ceilings and guidelines for budget preparation are submitted to the Cabinet. Where responsibilities for budgeting are split between a Ministry of Finance and a Ministry of Planning, the preparation of sectoral expenditure ceilings must be undertaken by a joint committee including at least the two ministries.

The institution responsible for overall financial management should coordinate the setting of the sectoral ceilings to ensure that they fit the aggregate expenditure consistent with the macroeconomic framework.

BOTTOM-UP APPROACH

Line ministries are responsible for preparing their requests within the spending limits provided. Depending on the severity of the fiscal constraint and the organization of the budget preparation process, additional requests from line ministries could be allowed for new programmes.

However, the principal request should be consistent with the notified ceilings or guidelines, and costs of programmes included in the additional requests should be clear and fully adequate for proper implementation, without any underestimation. Naturally, no request for new programmes should be entertained without a clear demonstration of its purpose and, where appropriate an estimate of the demand for the services to be provided.

Line ministries' budget requests should clearly distinguish:

- The amount necessary to continue current activities and programmes; and
- Proposals and costing for new programmes.

Before deciding to launch any new expenditure programme it is necessary to assess its forward budget impact. This is particularly important for development projects and entitlement programmes, which may generate recurrent costs or increased expenditures in the future.

This assessment is required whether or not a formal exercise of multiyear expenditure programming is carried out. For this purpose, requests must show systematically the forward annual costs of multiyear or entitlement programmes, and the Ministry of Finance should take into account the forward fiscal impact of these programmes when scrutinizing the budgetary requests from line ministries. Estimates of future costs related to multiyear commitments could be annexed to the overall budget document. These estimates would facilitate the preparation of the initial ceilings for the next budget.

In addition to their budget requests, the submission from the line ministries should include:

- A brief policy statement spelling out the sector policies and expected outcomes;
- Where applicable, realistic and relevant performance indicators, including results from the previous period and expected performance for the future;
- A statement of how the objectives will be achieved;
- Proposals for achieving savings and boosting efficiency; and
- Clear measures for implementing the proposals effectively.

Line ministries must coordinate the preparation of the budget of their subordinate agencies and give them appropriate directives. The submission of budget requests from subordinate agencies.

NEGOTIATION

Once it receives the requests of line ministries, the Ministry of Finance reviews their conformity with overall government policy, and compliance with the spending limits; reviews performance issues; and takes into account changes in the macroeconomic environment since the start of budget preparation. Almost always, these reviews lead the Ministry of Finance to suggest modifications in the line ministries' budget requests. Negotiation follows. Formal negotiation between the Ministry of Finance and line ministries can take the form of a budgetary conference. Professional staff from the Ministry of Finance and line ministries should also hold informal meetings to avoid misunderstandings and minimize conflicts. Major differences of opinion will normally be referred to the center of government, depending largely on the relative balance of administrative and political power between the Ministry of Finance and the specific line ministry concerned.

PREPARING EXPENDITURE CEILINGS

In preparing the sectoral expenditure ceilings, the following elements must be taken into account:

- Macroeconomic objectives and fiscal targets;
- The results of the review of ongoing programmes for the sector;
- The impact of ongoing expenditure programmes on the next budget, and their degree of rigidity;
- The strategy of the government concerning possible shifts in the intersectoral distribution of expenditure, and the amount of resources that could be allocated to new policies as well as service demand projections where appropriate.

Preparing these initial ceilings is largely an incremental/decremental exercise. Budgets are never prepared from scratch. Debt servicing, multiyear commitments for investment; pensions and other entitlements; rigidities in civil service regulations; and the simple reality that government cannot stop at once all funding for its schools, health centers or the army, etc, limit possible annual shifts to perhaps 5-10 per cent of total expenditures. In theory, this percentage could be higher in developing countries than in developed countries.

But in practice, because of earlier over commitments the room to maneuver is often even lower in developing countries. If one excludes emergency or crisis situations, when preparing the budget the government should focus on new policies, savings on questionable programmes, and means of increasing the efficiency of other ongoing programmes. It is clear, once again, that any significant policy shift requires a perspective longer than one year and some advance programming, in whatever form that is appropriate and feasible in the specific country.

A Subceiling for Capital Expenditure

As discussed earlier, a separate budget preparation process for capital and current expenditure presents problems, but a separate presentation is desirable. Aside from that question, however, should separate ceilings for capital and current expenditures be set at the start of the budget preparation process? The answer depends on the sector concerned. Obviously, if only a global ceiling is set, line ministries would be able to make tradeoffs between their current spending and their capital spending, and if separate ceilings are set, the distribution between current and capital spending is fixed for each sector. In certain sectors, such as primary education, it is generally preferable to leave the choice between current and capital spending partly to line ministries, since both current and capital expenditures are "developmental," and line ministries presumably know better than the Ministry of Finance what would be the most efficient allocation of resources within their sector.

However, in some cases, the sector budget depends largely on the decision of whether or not to launch a large investment project. For example, the budget of a Ministry of Higher Education would largely depend on the decision whether to construct a new university.

Because such large investment projects are a government policy issue, not only a sectoral policy issue, separate ceilings would be appropriate in these cases. Depending on circumstances and fiscal policy issues, separate subceilings may also be needed for other expenditure items, such as personnel expenditures and subsidies.

Efficiency "Dividends"

In recent years, Australia demanded from each spending unit, efficiency dividends, *i.e.*, required savings in their ongoing activities. On the surface, this practice may look like the typical across-the-board cuts made by the Ministry of Finance when finalizing the budget.

However, there are two major differences:

- Efficiency dividends are notified early in the process and within a coherent multiyear expenditure framework; and
- The allocation of savings among activities and expenditure items is entirely the responsibility of the spending agencies, which alleviates the arbitrary nature of the approach.

Savings "measures are much more likely to be implemented within the ministry when the line ministry itself is arguing for them rather than when they are set by the central agencies", with the knowledge and skills of the programme agency being devoted to criticism and obfuscation". This approach appears to have achieved effective results in Australia during 1985-90. Sweden has adopted a similar approach. In developed countries, the potential for fiscal savings and efficiency improvements exists.

Before considering introducing efficiency dividends in developing countries, the country context must be carefully reviewed. Efficiency dividends differ from acrossthe-board cuts only if there are adequate technical capacities in line ministries and a willingness to make their own hard choices. In those developing countries where the current budget is too inadequate to allow departments even to function normally, the real question is not how to generate a gradual increase in efficiency, but how to restructure the public expenditure programme by eliminating questionable programmes altogether. Certainly, in the long run, the savings from the efficiency dividends system may be expected to weaken.

And, where evaluation capacity is weak, the risk that the efficiency dividends are achieved by diminishing service or programme quality are very real. However, this practice may be an invaluable aid to introducing greater performance orientation in a complacent administrative system, and triggering more structural improvements.

THE ROLE OF MULTIYEAR ESTIMATES IN BUDGET PREPARATION

When fully integrated into the budget process, rolling multiyear expenditure programming can contribute to enhancing the preparation of the annual budget. In some developed countries multiyear expenditure estimates prepared the previous year are the starting point of the budget preparation process. Budgetary negotiations focus on new policies, with costs of ongoing programmes being updated only on technical grounds based on the multiyear estimates prepared the previous year. In the U.S., the Office of Management and Budget and the Congressional Budget Office prepare five-year projections.

When launching budget preparation, the multiyear estimates prepared the previous year are used to assess constraints related to existing policy commitments. This assessment and estimate of the financial constraints give the basis for estimating initial expenditure ceilings that frame the preparation of sector requests. Then, the multiyear expenditure programme is updated and rolled over when preparing the budget.

This process ensures both that the initial ceilings are prepared appropriately and that forward costs of programmes are taken into account when preparing the budget. Unfortunately, a "rolling" programme is often only cosmetic, with attention really focused only on the first budget year. For a rolling approach to be genuine and thus effective, the key steps would be the following: The Ministry of Finance updates the costs of the MYEs prepared the previous year, taking into account expected developments in economic parameters, budget execution and expenditure reviews.

In carrying out this task, it consults line ministries to get appropriate information, including on changes in the level of demand for services but the exercise is made on a technical basis, without interference or "bargaining" for additional resources. Taking into account policies, implementation problems, and possible improvements in efficiency, the Ministry of Finance identifies savings that can be made on ongoing programmes over the planned period. Once the global envelope for the annual tranches of the MYE is established, the annual envelopes for new programmes are set.

The sectoral distribution of the annual envelopes for new programmes is determined, in conformity with government priorities, by the Ministry of Finance or by an interministerial committee, consulting the line ministries when necessary. For the planned period, annual sectoral ceilings are communicated to line ministries, distinguishing ongoing programmes and envelopes for new programmes. Depending on the context, they may also include other elements, such as estimated costs of large investment projects, funds to be reserved to finance the counterpart costs of ongoing projects, and caps on personnel expenditures. Line ministries are free to identify realistic new savings on ongoing programmes, and to recapture the corresponding resources within the limits of the ceilings. Requests from line ministries are reviewed by the Ministry of Finance, then in joint committee.

This approach requires the preparation of sound cost estimates and discipline in budgeting and decision making. Even if a full-fledged MTEF covering all expenditures is not feasible, linkages between a rolling investment programme and annual budgeting can be established. A multiyear approach permits reconciling the reality that budgeting is inevitably incremental in large part, with the need for significant shifts in the composition of public expenditure.

2

Risk Management

Banks' credit relationship (originating, holding and monitoring loans until their ultimate recuperation) is changing. Loans and their risk elements are increasingly tradable. This trend has helped to enhance the liquidity of financial markets-with one adverse consequence: potentially higher volatility. Financial crises or turmoils have heightened the interest of financial firms in risk management, especially with respect to:

- Improving risk diversification.
- Optimising the funding or the liquidity of the firm.
- Holding selected risks that the firm is capable of managing profitably (involving a positive risk-reward analysis) and transferring the other risks.
- Setting equity capital at a level that maximises the firm's market value.

RISK DYNAMICS

In a dynamic world characterised by unending and unexpected change, the management of risk is a continuous process. It starts with the identification and measurement of risk elements, and with ascertaining their linkages. Accurate measurement is crucial to the appropriate pricing of risk elements. Other functions of risk management include forecasting the behaviour of risk factors over a given time horizon, speedy reporting and monitoring, internal control and audit, internal and external rating of exposure positions, independent evaluation and eventual adjustments for risk mitigation.

Since the risk profile of a financial firm changes rapidly, the risk manager has to be forward looking when assessing the impact of past and current decisions and practices, and when giving advice on the potential risks/rewards of future strategies and decisions.

This responsibility entails continuous vigilance: in identifying areas of risk, and in improving measurement tools under the supervision of top management. The latter's primary concern is to choose those risks it can manage profitably and to transfer the others.

The array of risks encountered by the management of a financial firm is varied. Five major categories of risk-credit risks (debtors or counterparties), portfolio concentrations, market volatility and liquidity risks, legal risks and operational risks-and extraneous problems, including governmental mismanagement. A firm's chief risk officer has to grapple with various risk elements using a holistic approach. This enterprise-wide risk management acknowledges

- The fact that risks are interconnected, and
- The need to gauge risk exposures more accurately in order to quantify the economic capital needed.

Some risk elements are very difficult to measure, for example those linked to payment systems and reputation. The important elements in the pricing of a financial product to a single loan transaction. Banks use different debt rating models, which vary with respect to methodology and the choice of key qualitative and quantitative factors to assess the probability of default by a borrower and to estimate the average loss on a homogeneous portfolio of borrowers. Statistical techniques are applied to historical data to identify, measure and price the risk factors.

These techniques are also used to assess the risk impact (reduction, increase or neutral) of adding another product, for example a new loan to a particular credit portfolio. Credit scoring is one method of estimating the relative creditworthiness of a customer within a given category of borrowers. Such a method is, however, retrospective in that it focuses on how parties have handled their loans in the past, while current loans are extended against future income. Therefore credit scoring has to be supplemented by other, forward-looking evaluations.

Helped by their long experience, diverse exposure and sophisticated expertise, large global banks are developing reliable analytical and predictive tools to assess the riskiness of customers, counterparties, products and facilities

RISK MITIGATION

Banks and other firms use various risk-management techniques. The techniques used to mitigate credit risk include:

- The syndication of large loans or exposures among several financial firms.
- The sale by a firm of a given category of loans (such as accounts receivable or promissory notes) to a specialised financial institution known as a 'factor'; the latter usually buys the financial assets in question on a non-recourse basis and at a discount that reflects the interest charge and the risk of default by the debtors.
- Asset-backed securitisation, that is, the sale of a given portfolio of a firm's standardised loan assets to specially created, separate legal

entity or special-purpose vehicle whose securities are issued for placement with private or institutional investors.

The total or partial transfer of credit risk to underwriters or insurers.

The use of flexible interest rates on loans to allow for repricing or the transfer of changes to a bank's funding costs (for example interest on deposits) to the loans, thereby maintaining stable interest margins for the bank concerned.

Hedging market and credit risks through the use of derivative instruments such as futures and options traded on regulated exchanges, and OTC swaps, options and forwards;

Selective approval at origination of credits and other exposures to optimise concentrations.

An increasingly greater number of the risks encountered by a financial firm or its clients can now be mitigated. This can be done inter alia for computer breakdown and for political risks. The former can be transferred for a fee to an IT services vendor, who assumes responsibility for computer maintenance and back-up. Political risk insurance is provided by private underwriters (for example Lloyd's and Zurich-American), national agencies (in the case of the richer trading nations of the OECD) and multilateral agencies.

Multilateral political insurance agencies are affiliated to intergovernmental development institutions such as the World Bank, the Inter-American Development Bank and other regional development banks. The function of the Multilateral Investment Guarantee Agency (MIGA) of the World Bank is to encourage the flow of funds for productive purposes to its 127 developing member countries, mainly through the issuance of investment guarantees against political risk. This international insurance market has grown considerably in coverage capacity, with increased cooperation among insurers to share risks (by reinsurance or coinsurance) and to draw on each other's special capabilities.

VALUE-AT-RISK

Several models have been developed to measure and control risk. None, however, has proven foolproof. Notable among these models is the value-at-risk (VaR) model, which purports to show the maximum loss (say x) a financial firm might incur on an asset or a portfolio of exposures.

It assumes:

- Immediate liquidation of the portfolio,
- A given probability or confidence level (for example 99 per cent),
- A given time horizon or holding period (for example 10 working days);
- Sufficient data on the firm's recent experience.

This means that, on average, in 99 holding periods out of 100 the loss on the portfolio under consideration will not exceed x. Put differently, in one 10-day spell out of 100, the portfolio will, on average, sustain a loss greater than x.

However the VaR does not provide information on the timing or the size of the loss in excess of x.

For financial firms, in principle it is possible to design market-risk VaR models for the trading book (trading portfolio) and credit-risk VaR models for the banking book (loan portfolios). The existence of a large volume of empirical data on securities prices and the availability of this data on a daily basis have enabled financial firms to develop VaR trading-book models and to evaluate their reliability. Similar information is not readily available for VaR banking-book models, so researchers use bond data as a substitute for loan performance. Although most VaR models integrate the effects of diversification and hedging, the prudent manager should not overlook a detailed risk analysis of significant individual positions within the portfolio under scrutiny. The limitations of these models arise, inter alia, from the following:

- Price changes are distributed normally, thereby understating the probability of large price declines (and consequently the probability of large losses).
- Too small a number of correlations between price changes are used.
- The historical data used may understate risk, especially illiquidity risk during periods of crisis.
- The composition of the portfolio is assumed to be fixed during any one day.
- The probabilities of price changes used as certainties are in fact statistical estimates.

The future will not, however, replicate the past, upon which the VaR models are based, so risk analysts complement their evaluation with the scenario approach, which predicts how the firm might be affected by a complex chain of events, including a worst case scenario. However few analysts are able to imagine the full range of nightmare scenarios. This was the case with the UBS, whose post-tax loss reached CHF 659 million in 1997 and CHF 987 million in 1998 (over $1. 1 billion in these two years). The loss in 1997 was attributed to problems with its global equity derivatives business, the main elements of which were risks resulting from the use of an inappropriate model on its 'worst of dual asset call spread options' (CHF 120 million), loss on its Japanese convertible bonds (CHF 275 million), an 'adverse' change in the UK's fiscal legislation (CHF 80 million) and high volatility in the international shares market (CHF 150 million). The UBS's loss in 1998 resulted from participation in a large hedge fund, the Long Term Capital Management (LTCM), and a non-hedged credit to the LTCM.

The LTCM, founded in 1994, had on 31 August 1998 $125 billion in assets on a capital of $4. 8 billion at the beginning of that year-that is, a 25:1 leverage ratio. Fourteen of the large banks and securities firms who were creditors of the LTCM in 1998 failed to enforce their own credit risk management standards.

Although large and sophisticated, the UBS did not have documentation on the execution and supervision of its transactions with the LTCM, and failed to identify or properly to evaluate major risks. The lax behaviour of senior bankers can be partly explained by the following factors:

- The 'halo' bestowed on the LTCM by virtue of the fact that three of its principals had outstanding credentials: a former vice chairman of the Federal Reserve Board and two Nobel laureates.
- The attractive past performance of the LTCM and other hedge funds created an infatuation with these funds, even on the part of sophisticated financial firms, and there was a degree of herd-like behaviour.
- The generally favourable economic conditions in 1995-97 prompted over optimism by bankers

It was established that the analytical tools used by banks and by securities and futures firms to assess the LTCM's risks were flawed: they did not question the fact that the LTCM's strategy across markets was uniform, that is, it lacked appropriate differentiation. Furthermore they underestimated the size of potential shocks in world markets, and the constraints on the rapid liquidation of the LTCM's positions.

THE ROLE OF JUDGEMENT

Risk models, no matter how sophisticated, cannot encompass all risks and their linkages. Furthermore, they are subject to human error. Hence they should be looked upon as aids to-not substitutes to-the making of judgements. Independent expert control of risks should exist within the firm on a continuous basis to assist top management to assess the risks taken by its managerial staff, including traders. Chief financial market traders can receive bonuses of 10-15 per cent of their group's profits, and consequently are motivated to scout around for financial firms that are willing to take risks in order to make outsize gains.

One such trader personally earned some $15 million over four months while operating in the investment banking unit of the Credit Suisse Group. Other financial firms have chosen to reduce the level of risk their trading officers can take. The remuneration package of the latter does not incite them to focus solely on short-term gains, thereby neglecting longer-term positive results for the bank. The Swiss Federal Banking Commission has found that bonuses can reach several times the annual salary of a trader, and that these are linked to short-term gains, even though they are only partially realised. Usually banks bear the losses alone, some of which arise in the medium or longer term.

For banks that have invested heavily in information technology, data on exposure can be obtained in real time. In the management of risks, better informed senior executives can thus make their decisions on sounder bases and exercise control without costly delay. Several private rating agencies are in the business of judging the capacity of companies or countries to honour their financial obligations. Their ratings are usually made at the demand of borrowers, who pay the agencies for their services.

In recent years, major rating agencies have started to publish 'unsolicited ratings', reportedly to counter the tendency of debt issuers to shop around for the lowest fees among the agencies and/or for better ratings. Credit-rating agencies have occasionally failed to identify looming risks and to warn investors about the increased vulnerability of borrowers, for example in the case of the Asian crisis in 1997-8. Certain risks cannot be reasonably measured or anticipated, particularly systemic risk (the risk of failure of the financial system). This refers to the domino-like transmission of disruption of default risk (of a firm, a market segment, a payment and settlement system, and so on) to other institutions and/or countries.

Contagion spreads to institutions or countries that are perceived by investors or creditors to have similar problems or to be economically vulnerable to the collapse of the first victim. The impact of the Asian crisis, which broke out in Thailand in the second half of 1997, was estimated by the IMF to have halved world economic growth in 1998 and 1999 from a projected 4 per cent to 2 per cent.

The management of systemic risk and other macroeconomic risks is the responsibility of the public authorities, and individual banks need not hold capital against the possibility of an overall financial breakdown. Nevertheless the more capital a bank has, the higher the losses it can absorb, including those that arise from systemic risk. The central bank, in its responsibility as lender of last resort, normally protects sound and solvent banks against a liquidity crisis in the event of massive transfers or cash withdrawals by panicky depositors. Otherwise a forced liquidation of assets could lead banks-hitherto sound and safe-into insolvency and default. Such default can also affect debtors, whose credit lines are cut, and cascade-like breakdowns can become systemic, with a chain reaction of financing problems affecting many economic agents and disrupting payments, savings and credit distribution channels.

WHAT IS RISK MANAGEMENT?

Risk is a reality for all of us. Each day, in the normal course of our lives, we risk:

- Injury to ourselves or others
- Loss or damage to our and others property
- Having legal action taken against us for things we do or fail to do

These risks can be managed in many ways. Think about what most of us do when we enter an unfamiliar setting. We tend to look around where we are to see what, if any, risks we are facing. If we identify a risk, we will generally assess its probability and likely impact. Most of us are prepared to accept risks that have a low probability and only minimal consequences. As the likelihood or seriousness of effects increases, we become increasingly concerned. Those risks that concern us most are those that are likely to happen and which would have quite serious effects.

Once we have identified a risk and have an idea of its probability and likely impact, we need to work out our response to the risk. One strategy we use to respond to some risks is to simply avoid them. For example, one good way of reducing or eliminating the risks associated with smoking tobacco is to simply stop smoking.

A second way of dealing with a risk is to transfer it to someone else. For instance, while it might be possible—and cheaper—for most of us to install a television antenna on our own roofs, some of us perceive the risk of falling to be sufficiently great that generally we will get a trades person to do it.

Another approach is to control things like the frequency or extent of loss arising from a risk. Loss control measures include seat belts in cars, fire alarms and sprinklers in buildings, and keeping copies of important documents.

Insurance is another common way in which we respond to risk. Life insurance, property insurance and public liability insurance are all ways that we insure ourselves against the risks that we face.

Finally, people may choose to retain risks, eg, there is a risk that you might catch a cold if you get wet from the rain. People whose health is otherwise fine might be prepared to accept that risk, while those whose health is not so fine, or who otherwise wish to avoid catching a cold, will take measures to avoid catching a cold. Risk retention is an acceptable strategy particularly for those risks, which are both unlikely to occur, and of only minimal severity.

In ideal risk management, a prioritization process is followed whereby the risks with the greatest loss (or impact) and the greatest probability of occurring are handled first, and risks with lower probability of occurrence and lower loss are handled in descending order. In practice the process of assessing overall risk can be difficult, and balancing resources used to mitigate between risks with a high probability of occurrence but lower loss versus a risk with high loss but lower probability of occurrence can often be mishandled.

Intangible risk management identifies a new type of a risk that has a 100 per cent probability of occurring but is ignored by the organization due to a lack of identification ability. For example, when deficient knowledge is applied to a situation, a knowledge risk materializes. Relationship risk appears when ineffective collaboration occurs. Process-engagement risk may be an issue when ineffective operational procedures are applied. These risks directly reduce the productivity of knowledge workers, decrease cost effectiveness, profitability, service, quality, reputation, brand value, and earnings quality. Intangible risk management allows risk management to create immediate value from the identification and reduction of risks that reduce productivity.

Risk management also faces difficulties in allocating resources. This is the idea of opportunity cost. Resources spent on risk management could have been spent on more profitable activities. Again, ideal risk management minimizes spending (or manpower or other resources) and also minimizes the negative effects of risks.

INTRODUCING RISK MANAGEMENT IN YOUR ORGANISATION

The types of strategies outlined above are ways that we manage risks in our own life. They can also be used for managing risks in your organisation. This material will show you how to develop and implement a risk management plan through:

- Identifying the risks your organisation faces
- Assessing the probability and likely severity of those risks
- Developing strategies for managing those risks
- Implementing and monitoring your risk management plan

The ideas provided here will assist your organisation in managing its risks across a range of areas. A risk management plan can be applied to areas such as human resource management, control of your organisation's stock and property or choice of insurance policies. In fact, risk management principles can be applied anywhere that a risk exists. Your risk management plan will need to be regularly reviewed and updated. Risks, and the strategies available to manage them, change over time. For example, the mass marketing of low cost fire alarms has provided an affordable addition to the range of strategies available to manage the risk of fire in the home. Likewise, new ventures, changed legislation, altered work practices, a change in staffing, and so on, can all affect the range of opportunities and risks you face. Your risk management plan needs to be kept up to date to reflect such changes.

Getting Started

Risk management is a management committee responsibility. The management committee has the ethical, and in most cases, the legal responsibility for what happens within the organisation they govern. As a first step, the management committee can form a small working group to develop a risk management plan. To ensure that the broad ranges of interests within the organisation are considered, the working group should include at least one staff member and one member of the management committee. While the working group will be responsible for developing the risk management plan, the management committee should oversee the process and make the final decisions required to implement the plan.

Identifying the Risk

The types of risks your organisation could be exposed to include: Loss, theft or damage to property Loss of life or damage to health Breaches of corporate duties by an organisation or its officers Breaches of other laws Professional negligence Loss of your organisation's good name

Inspecting the Site

Look around your work place. What potential risks can you find? Look at the workplace from the perspective of the different people who use it. Are there hazards for children, older people or people with impaired sight? What are the fire hazards? Are there loose electrical connections, or damaged furniture? How hot is your hot water, and how accessible is it to children? Take some photos, perhaps even a video if you can, and study it closely. It is a good idea to have a couple of people do the site inspection, so that you can compare notes.

Reviewing your Organisation's Work Practices

The activities carried out in your organisation will have varying degrees of risk. Do staff members work with potentially dangerous clients? Is staff required to perform physical activity which may result in injury (for example, lifting clients)? Is your organisation's work particularly stressful? Is staff required to do a lot of driving, and if so, are they using their own cars, your organisation's cars or both?

Review your work practices from the perspective of other people who use your service. Are clients exposed to risks from other clients, people off the street, or from other sources? What about volunteers and management committee members?

Explore your Legal Exposures

Your organisation may be exposed to a number of legal risks associated with issues such as workplace health and safety, liability to clients, judiciary duty or anti-discrimination legislation. Remember, many laws require strict compliance and their prescriptions must be met as there is no option to just „accept the risk of being detected by regulators. You must comply with the law.

Do A "What If" Analysis

For example, what if:

- Your organisation's coordinator or manager had a serious accident tomorrow?
- Your organisation's files were burnt or stolen?
- You discovered someone had embezzled several thousand dollars?
- There was a major industrial accident?
- Industrial action was taken?
- Your organisation was sued?

Talk to Staff

The people who do the work often have the best idea of the risks the organisation faces. Talking to staff and volunteers can be done through individual interviews, raising the issue of risk at a staff meeting, or having specially structured sessions.

Brainstorm

Get as many staff, volunteers, and management committee members along for a brainstorming session. Write up every suggested risk.

ASSESSING RISK

Assuming the working group has done its job, you will have generated a long list of risks covering everything from someone stealing the petty cash, through to what would happen if your organisation were sued by one of its clients. The task now is to assess those risks according to how likely they are to occur, and how severe the consequences would be if they did occur. A useful approach is to use four categories of severity and four categories of likelihood. The four categories of severity are:

- Disastrous risks
- Very serious risks
- Serious risks Minor risks

The four categories of likelihood are:

- Almost certain
- Very likely
- Likely
- Unlikely

Remember, legal prescriptions must be complied with, no matter what the cost or inconvenience. The following section explains in some detail what each of the categories of risk severity entails.

Disastrous Risks

The most serious risks include those that would result in death or serious physical injury. For example, while the likelihood of a staff member being killed by a client is low, it could happen and it is a risk which organisations should take into account.

Other very serious risks are those that would put your organisation's future survival in jeopardy. Organisations which rely heavily on public donations or volunteers would probably suffer a serious financial setback if their reputation were harmed for some reason. Similarly, poor financial controls can lead to situations where an organisation goes into liquidation.

Finally, people within your organisation face a range of personal liabilities by virtue of their involvement in the organisation. Staff providing professional advice, and board or management committee members, can potentially be sued for negligence if they are derelict in their duties.

Very Serious Risks

Next we have those risks that would result in a major reduction in the level of service your organisation can provide, or which would require a very significant use of your organisation's resources to recover from. Loss of premises, destruction or theft of essential files or vital equipment might all be included under this heading. For organisations which have responsibility for the care of at-risk groups of people, very serious risks might include the risk of repetitive abuse of clients by one or more staff members.

Serious Risks

Serious risks include those that would result in a noticeable impact on your organisation, and which would require a significant use of your organisation's resources to recover from. Examples of serious risks include theft or damage to non-essential equipment, or the unanticipated long term absence of a senior member of staff.

(For a small organisation, such an absence might even be an example of a very serious or disastrous risk.) Another serious risk could be the risk of staff or others breaching the confidentiality of a client.

Minor Risks

These are risks which are easily covered in the day-to-day running of the organisation. Examples include minor theft of petty cash, accidental breakage of cheap office equipment, and so forth.

RESPONDING TO RISKS

The final step in preparing your risk management plan is to develop a response for each of the risks you have identified. This section explains how this can be done. Starting with category A risks, go through the Risk List and develop responses to each of the risks that you have identified. (Note: each risk in categories A, B, and C should have at least one response, but may have more!)

In working out your responses, think about the following approaches to dealing with risk:

- Avoiding The Risk
- Transferring The Risk
- Controlling The Risk
- Insuring Against The Risk
- Accepting the Risk

These five approaches are discussed in more detail below.

Avoiding the Risk

One way to reduce risk is to stop doing whatever it is that creates the risk. For example, many organisations use cheques or direct deposits to avoid risks associated with having large amounts of cash on the premises. Some organisations have informal practices where blank cheques are signed by one co-signatory, with the other co-signatory filling out the details at a later stage. Sensible organisations, and people who countersign cheques, invariably avoid this practice.

Transferring the Risk

Risk transfer occurs when you get someone else to bear the risk for a particular activity. For example, a child care centre might seek to transfer the risks associated with an outing by having parents sign a form waiving their rights to sue if their child is injured. Similarly, if you are purchasing a new computer, you will probably want a warranty.

Warranties are a means of spreading risks from one party (the person buying the equipment) to another party (the organisation selling the equipment). Remember however that there is often a cost in transferring risks to another party. For example, extended warranties can be purchased for office equipment, vehicles, and so forth. These warranties transfer certain risks to another party, but clearly at a price.

Controlling the Risk

Work though each of the risks you have identified and see if there are ways that you can reduce the likelihood of the risk occurring or of lessening the consequences of the risk. Some common strategies which can be used both to decrease the likelihood of risk, and lessen the consequences, include:

- Make sure that there are clear procedures in place for areas with identified high risks. These procedures might include what to do in the event of fire, procedures for dealing with hostile clients or financial management procedures.
- Provide adequate supervision for high risk areas. For example, where inexperienced staff is dealing with potentially hostile clients, it is important that adequate supervision be provided.
- *Provide information*—people need to know what to do if they are exposed to a risk. Consider "fire exit" signs, "warning" signs near hazardous materials and so forth. Information on how to use equipment and what to do in the event of accidents should be readily available.
- *Keep things in order*—prompt repairs, removal of rubbish, and generally maintaining a clean and tidy work environment does a lot to lessen the frequency and impact of risks. An added benefit of

keeping things in order is that it makes for a more pleasant environment.

- *Provide training*—the likelihood of risk will be greatly reduced when staff and volunteers have received proper training, for example in managing difficult clients. Look for technological solutions—many risks can be reduced this way. Fire alarms and extinguishers, personal alarms, and burglar alarms each serve to lessen risks. Technical solutions should be used on a case by case basis, and should generally be used where the cost of the risk being covered exceeds the cost of technology. Make backups—the impact of the loss, theft or damage of files can be reduced if paper and computer copies or backups of important files are kept. It is good practice to store copies in a separate place to the original documents, and to back up files regularly on the computer.
- Assign responsibilities and be clear about who can represent your organisation in different settings, sign cheques, enter into contracts, make media releases or represent your organisation's policy position at public events.

PUBLIC INTERVENTION

MOTIVATION

Protection of the banking system is of particular concern to the public authorities in modern economies in view of the fact that the banking system is at the centre of the payment and settlement system, the mobilisation of savings, the allocation of credit and the creation of money. Indeed banks provide most of an economy's stock of money through the extension of loans to households and companies. The payment and settlement system is a fundamental infrastructure in a modern economy in that every economic transaction necessitates a payment. Besides the legal tender-that is the banknotes and coins produced by the monetary authorities-bank deposits lodged by individuals and institutions are a major source of payment funds. Since bank deposits are a leading liquid asset for individual and institutional depositors, banks offer payment services linked to these deposits, and hence they have assumed a central role in the payment system.

The failure of banks-in view of their central role in the payment and financial intermediation systems-thus has a stronger adverse effect on the real economy than the failure of other firms. An efficient financial sector is essential to the growth and stability of modern economies at the national, regional or international levels. Public intervention in the financial sector is therefore prompted by the objective of

- Setting the requisite conditions for the safe and efficient operation of the banking/financial system,

- Forestalling payments crises. Such crises produce considerable ill effects, such as recession, disruption of production, social conflict and loss of property or life. This is readily illustrated by the many crises that hit several countries in various parts of the world during the

1990s. The vulnerability of financial intermediaries-and notably banks-derives largely from five inter-related factors:

- Banks prefer to rely on third-party funding (or debt) in lieu of owner's funding (or equity) because of the lower financial cost of debt financing compared with equity; debt charges are furthermore treated as expenses before the assessment of corporate taxation, which is not the case with dividends. Consequently banks tend to minimise the cushion of equity or risk capital.
- Banks depend for a significant portion of their third-party resources on depositors' funds, which have to be repaid at their face value and on demand (or at very short notice).
- Banks transform liquid or short-term resources into illiquid or longer-term assets in the expectation of reaping higher interest margins. Furthermore they tend to keep a small fraction of their callable deposits in liquid assets, since these assets produce only modest or no income.
- Banks are highly interdependent owing to their intertwined business relations (interbank lending, syndicated loans, joint clearing and settlement mechanisms, counterparty operations, agency relations, joint ventures and so on). The losses of a defaulting bank spread through the payment and settlement system, and are thus bound to affect other banks.
- Depositors are likely to panic if adverse rumours spread, in view of the maturity mismatch between banks' liabilities and assets and in view of the opacity of information on risks that banks disclose to the public. Depositors are therefore prone to rush to withdraw their funds, not only from unsound or unsafe institutions, but also from solvent institutions.

The principal aim of legislation on and regulation of the financial sector is to protect general welfare and improve market efficiency, notably with respect to consumer protection, transparency, systemic risk and moral hazard. First, consumer protection is needed against the possible abuse of market power by dominant financial intermediaries. Intermediaries have sought to increase their size for multiple reasons, notably to achieve greater efficiency and higher returns through economies of scale (since the initial cost of setting up a financial activity is relatively very large and the cost of an additional unit of product or service is very low or nil), and economies of scope (through the synergy created by offering multiple products to satisfy various complementary needs of customers). Regulators have to ensure that the abovemen-tioned economies benefit consumers.

Second, the financial sector is characterised by information asymmetry, indicating that the parties to a transaction do not have the same information. Indeed depositors have incomplete information on their depository bank. Regulators can require the latter to disclose the information needed to enable depositors and other users of financial services to make sound decisions. Small depositors often lack the willingness, time, skills or resources to identify and analyse the risk of financial intermediaries, delegating that function to the public authorities, which are in a better position to obtain the required information and to impose appropriate penalties on intermediaries that transgress the rules.

Third, regulation can eliminate or moderate systemic risk. The latter results from the potential chain effect of the failure of one intermediary in a given country triggering-through the payment system-liquidity and solvency crises for other intermediaries in the same country, as well as in other countries. The rapid transmission of risk can be explained by the fact that banks are closely interconnected. Solvent intermediaries can be faced by a massive, irrational run by panicking depositors subject to herd-like behaviour and can-in the absence of adequate funding-be obliged to effect a 'fire sale' of financial assets. This will set in train a series of price declines and insolvencies unless the regulators and monetary authorities intervene appropriately and in the early stage of the problem. Fourth, safety nets are put in place to prevent or quell runs on banks that might spread rapidly from weak banks to strong ones. They are normally available through three standby arrangements:

- A lender-of-last-resort service for solvent banks;
- Deposit guarantees-and in some situations an explicit (or implicit) bail-out promise-to individual institu-tions (notably big ones); and
- Intra-day credit from the clearing authorities (*viz.* the central bank) to participating banks, normally against collateral.

Safety nets carry with them the seed of 'moral hazard'. The latter means that financial institutions and their customers expect central banks, deposit insurance institutions, other governmental agencies and multilateral international organisations to intervene to prevent the failure of a financial intermediary in the event of a financial crisis-a situation which fosters mismanagement.

PUBLIC PROTECTION AND MARKET DISCIPLINE

Financial crises and their costly aftermath have prompted public authorities to improve their regulatory framework and provide safety nets. The results of this are distorted competition and weakened market discipline. In particular safety nets.

- Reduce the incentive of depositors and other creditors to monitor their bank and to charge that bank in accordance with its risk profile;

- Induce depositors to entrust their funds to banks at lower interest rates than would be acceptable in the absence of deposit insurance;
- Reduce bankers' prudence by enticing them to take greater risks (in the expectation of higher returns) in the knowledge that the funds provided by creditors are secured by deposit guarantees; and
- Enable banks to finance customers at interest costs that are not commensurate with the risk posed by these customers, thereby leading to a suboptimal misalloca-tion of economic resources.

The propensity of management to neglect professional rigour can be counteracted by the effective enforcement of prudential regulations (such as rules focusing on adequate liquidity, exposure limits and risk-adjusted capital), and by imposing appropriate penalties on banks and their managers for irresponsible behaviour. Bank management would accordingly be required continuously to enforce the observance of various laws and regulations, including prudential rules.

This could be verified by efficient control and audit systems within the firm, under the supervision of designated public agencies and accredited independent external auditors. Deviant or fraudulent actions by top management should be subject to appropriate punishment. This could start with a reprimand and ultimately lead to the temporary or permanent withdrawal of operating permits, or jail sentences for executives if warranted.

The involvement of public authorities in regulatory and supervisory functions and safety nets does not mean that market participants can assume risks without bearing the consequences of their actions. In protecting the public interest, bank regulators act as agents for two principals: the taxpayer, who is shielded against the eventuality of being called upon to share the cost of a bank failure; and the customer (whether debtor or creditor), who is safeguarded against exploitation and the misuse of his or her financial resources by unscrupulous parties within or without the bank.

Regulators, as the agent for the taxpayer, do not invariably act in the best interests of the latter as they are supposed to do. Indeed they may be tempted to delay addressing the problems of troubled banks under their jurisdiction in order to cover up past mistakes or oversights in the hope of an improvement in the circumstances of the banks. They are comforted by the fact that insured depositors are protected and that an insolvent bank can continue to operate for a long period. The delay in closing an insolvent bank, with operational losses still accruing, will increase the cumulative losses sustained by the bank. This will in turn increase the cost to the taxpayer, who will be called upon to absorb the losses suffered by insured depositors.

A bank's risks can change rapidly and thus render existing information obsolete. For troubled banks it is recommended that thorough on-site examinations be conducted more frequently than is the case for sound banks.

This type of inspection would, however, be costly in terms of the labour of qualified persons assigned to that function, as well as burdensome for the banks being examined as their day-to-day operations would probably be disrupted. Low-risk banks should therefore be subject to a less intensive supervisory programme.

Off-site surveillance complements on-site examination by offering an appreciation of the bank's circumstances on an ongoing basis. This can take the form of

- A series of ratios, known as 'supervisory screens', calculated from the financial accounts of a bank-problems can be detected when the ratios diverge from the standard values established on the basis of past experience; or
- Econometric models based on selected ratios that produce a single number that reflects the degree of solidity of a bank. Econometric models are considered to be more useful than supervisory screens in detecting problems with safety and soundness. Judgement remains, nevertheless, an important element in detecting problem situations. In view of
- The delays in reporting mishaps by the management of troubled banks to the regulatory authorities,
- The inadequate or imprecise measures currently available for assessing bank risks, and
- The lags in corrective measures or sanctions by the regulatory authorities, it is advisable to resort to market signals to trigger managerial rigour, and thus contain or moderate moral hazard.

Governmental entities (such as the Federal Deposit Insurance Corporation, FDIC, in the US) cannot readily recognise changes in the risk profiles of deposit-taking banks. Indeed deposit insurance cannot involve actuarial methods similar to those used, for instance, by the life insurance business.

The latter offers a reliable statistical calculation of the risks and premia needed to build a fund capable of absorbing predictable future losses. However bank failures cannot be accurately forecast: they occur irregularly and very occasionally in large numbers. If the governmental deposit insurance-which substitutes the credit standing of a private bank for that of the central government-undercharges for risk, the bank will in effect be benefitting from a concealed subsidy. Bearing in mind the above considerations, it is essential for the soundness and efficiency of the banking system to price as fairly as possible the risk exposure of each bank.

Towards that objective, transparency of information on a bank's operations enables rational market participants with money at stake to produce a collective judgement on the riskiness of the said bank, and the premia they will require for channelling their savings to it. Markets can evaluate the risk of widely traded financial instruments belonging to entities whose operations are sufficiently transparent.

Market discipline will have been exercised when lending charges (including premia on risks) increase and credit availability decreases in parallel with the increase in the borrower's risk profile. If a bank assumes excessive risks, depositors have the possibility of withdrawing their funds if they doubt the bank's solvency.

In the case of default, management and the shareholders should fully bear the brunt of the losses, followed by subordinate creditors. The orderly liquidation of an insolvent bank benefits the economy in the long term as it prompts the management of other banks to exercise prudence.

This principle should apply to all institutions, regardless of the size and scope of their activities. In the absence of an international framework for handling insolvencies, a professional association of operators and regulators from the financial sector has offered recommendations for the speedy handling of the insolvency of global financial institutions. Market signals could be built into the safety nets to ensure that participants in the financial system have a strong incentive to behave prudently.

Such signals are premised on the existence of transparency (that is, the dissemination of reliable, detailed and up-to-date data on risk exposures), on the efficient functioning of a competitive market place, on rational behaviour by market participants on both the supply and the demand side for funds, and on prompt reaction by all parties concerned. Various measures for the promotion of market signals have been proposed, including the following:

- Regulations could require all banks to issue, besides their share capital, subordinated debt for public subscription. Investors are normally sensitive to a bank's 'prudence and performance' record. The lower the prudence, the higher the cost of placing subordinated debt with potential investors. More generally, the disclosure of a bank's risk-based capital (including information on innovative, complex and hybrid capital instruments) will enable market participants to judge the bank's capacity to absorb financial losses.

This information needs to be complemented, for the benefit of investors, with disclosure on various risk exposures.

A governmental deposit insurance safety net should carry a coinsurance element (for example 20 per cent), whereby each depositor shares in the risk by accepting an element of self-insurance and bearing a tranche of the eventual loss on her/his deposit. This coinsurance would encourage depositors, especially large ones, to demand greater transparency from their deposit-taking bank so that they could assess their bank's safety and soundness: they would discipline risky institutions by withdrawing their funds or demanding higher interest rates on their deposits. Should a bank deny its depositors the requisite information, it would be shunned or obliged to pay a risk premium for its opacity. Partial private insurance or reinsurance of a proportion (say 5 per cent) of a bank's deposits could also be used. Risk-assessed premia on deposits charged by the private sector would then act as a supplementary market signal. A rise in such premia should trigger regulatory action, in the same way as would an increase in the spread required by investors on the subordinated debt of a bank, over and above a risk-free rate (for example that of a governmental security).

A governmental deposit insurance entity-besides using market signals to price its protection of bank deposits-would need the authority to inspect banks and the means to make banks comply. These means could include:

- Penal insurance rates.
- The dismissal and replacement of inefficient or miscreant executives.
- Denying deposit insurance to a delinquent bank.
- Ultimately, the closure of a bank.

The Central Role of Equity

The solidity of a bank in the long term is based on three main pillars: earning capacity, prudence and equity. Prudence calls on management to maintain appropriate liquid reserves to meet unexpected withdrawals of funds, and to avoid excessively risky operations. The survival of a firm in periods of difficulty is dependent on the relative size of equity or owners' capital at risk. Owner's capital demonstrates three characteristics: permanency, a residual status in the distribution of income or assets, and initial responsibility for absorbing eventual losses. Capital's functions are primarily fourfold:

- To cover unexpected losses (expected losses can be integrated into the charges levied on individual products and services, or can be absorbed by specifically constituted loss provisions).
- To finance-in an environment of uncertainty-the start-up costs of a bank's activities (including those relating to physical infrastructure or the acquisition of know-how and talents), and the expansion of these activities over time.
- To secure depositors by increasing the owner's stake in the bank; this serves to moderate the interest paid on deposits and third parties' funds,
- To ensure that the level of capital requirement moves in tandem with the overall risk of a bank's activities.

In view of the fact that equity capital generally costs more than borrowed funds, the firm's top management endeavours to constitute adequate equity base capable of maximising the value of their enterprise. By comparison, public regulators of banks, in prescribing minimum capital requirements, are primarily concerned with protecting the public interest-notably that of ensuring a safe and sound banking system capable of serving all concerned parties efficiently. The first attempt by central bankers and regulators to institutionalise their cooperation in the field of prudential standards was the creation of the Basle Committee on Banking Supervision at the end of 1974. The membership of this committee currently comprises senior representatives of the monetary-supervisory authorities of the major financial centres. The committee has no supranational supervisory authority: its task is to recommend best practice standards and guidelines.

The committee was established in the wake of the foreign exchange turbulences in 1974 that culminated in the collapse of Bankhaus I. D. Herstatt, which defaulted on more than $600 million in claims. More than 12 US-based banks that had paid out Deutschmarks to Herstatt were unable to get US dollars in settlement at the opening of the clearing system in New York at 10. 30 am as Herstatt's had been closed before its dollars could be credited to its foreign counterparties, which suffered considerable losses. The ensuing unsettlement in the interbank trading market hurt other banks, which were charged onerous risk premiums of 2 per cent for six weeks. This type of cross-currency settlement risk is a time-zone-induced credit risk in spot forex transactions and has come to be referred to as the 'Herstatt risk'.

Prompted by the objective of ensuring both prudent behaviour and the convergence of regulatory standards among banks, over the years the Basle Committee has formulated a series of guidelines for national bank regulators. With the approval of the G10 central bank governors, the committee proposed the application of a framework for minimum regulatory capital, beginning in 1988. Banks operating transnationally were asked to cover four categories of bank loan exposure with minimum capital charges, rising in accordance with their estimated riskiness.

These charges were set at 0 per cent (OECD governments), 1. 6 per cent (banks in OECD countries), 4. 0 per cent (residential mortages) and 8. 0 per cent (all other loans) of the face value of the respective claims. Capital was defined as consisting of two tiers: tier 1 or core capital, comprising common shares and retained earnings; and tier 2 capital, comprising mostly medium- to long-term subordinated debt instruments. In 1997 the committee enlarged the minimum capital requirement for banks to cover market risks, notably with respect to banks' trading portfolios. Equity standards were adopted in 1988 after a negotiated compromise among the committee members.

These standards have proved too simplistic, and often arbitrary or inconsistent. For example, in the case of bank credit the rules assign to the best-rated corporations (AAA) the same minimum regulatory capital coefficient as that for lower-rated corporations, that is, 8 per cent of the face value of such loans. Such rules encourage banks to operate perversely by reducing assets whose risks and capital charges are overestimated by the regulators, and increasing assets whose risks and capital charges are underestimated by the regulators. Use of the static, 'one-size-fits-all' approach also fails to address differences in the nature of banks' businesses. The standardised uniform weights have not been confined to credit risk, but have also been used in the case of market risks. Indeed in 1997 the committee introduced a regulatory capital charge on the trading account of banks, set at a fixed minimum multiplier of three for value-at-risk (VaR), plus an 'add-on' of one to make a total of four VaR, when the banks' internal models and their stress testing prove to be inaccurate. Stress testing estimates the potential loss resulting from the large changes in key risk factors that can occur in periods of extreme difficulty. During 1999-2001 the Basle Committee embarked on a revision aimed at fine-tuning its regulatory capital framework, guided by four objectives:

- Safety and soundness in the financial system.
- Competitive equality among banks.
- A comprehensive approach to addressing risks.
- Generalised coverage for all banks (the 1988 recommendations were intended solely for internationally active banks) in view of the liberalisation of domestic financial markets.

The committee's 2001 proposals also underline three major requirements:

- Expanding capital requirements to cover additional risks (such as operational and interest-rate risks);
- Giving regulators additional power to raise (above the general minimum of 8 per cent) a bank's capital adequacy if warranted by the risk encountered by that bank; and
- The disclosure of more details to the general public in order to encourage market participants to differentiate among banks by reference to safe and sound banking practices. The committee has also recommended greater reliance on independent credit rating agencies and on banks' own risk-management models and internal ratings (instead of the preassigned standard ratios imposed by the regulators). The latter recommendation is premised on the assumption that management has full and ready knowledge of the risks of its operations on a continuous basis, and that its models are capable of identifying risk variables and of accurately calculating their weights and behaviour. One can argue that the committee's approach poses several challenges, notably the following:
- The validation of internal models by the regulatory authorities requires a coherent approach to assessing these models, not only within a single country but also across several countries that might use different accounting methods.
- It is possible that certain current or prospective credit rating agencies could supply, in response to demand by or pressure from rated entities, better ratings than would be warranted by strictly objective criteria.

- Credit rating agencies are not likely to have full and immediate knowledge of a bank's rapidly changing risk circumstances.
- The proposed weights for risk exposure, though an improvement over those of 1988, are still rough and static estimates and are often the product of negotiated compromises reached at a given point in time by representatives of the bank supervisory authorities.
- Banks may continue to practice 'regulatory arbitrage' by favouring activities whose regulatory capital requirement underestimates their effective risk.
- The committee has yet to address each individual bank's risk diversification by reference to its full range of portfolios, both on and off balance sheet. Such enterprise-wide calculations for a financial institution can produce an overall risk profile, which can be higher or lower depending on the correlations for defaults and/or credit losses within and across different credit risk concentrations.

Researchers are exploring new avenues for assigning capital charges to assets held by financial intermediaries. They include:

- Precommitment of capital (PCA) to the trading portfolio of a bank. The management of the latter would be asked to choose a level of capital to back the said portfolio over a given period of time. Should the cumulative losses exceed the capital cover at any time during that period the regulators would fine the bank ex-post. The PCA approach could well prompt most banks to develop accurate models and to communicate the results truthfully to the regulators. The task of the regulators would be to choose an appropriate structure of penalties to induce bank managements to moderate their risk levels or provide an additional capital cushion. The stiffer the penalty, the greater the prudence of management in terms of risk taking. PCA would have the advantage of reducing regulators' involvement in the setting of capital requirements by putting the onus on individual bank managements.
- Rewarding banks that avoid losses with a reduction in the standard capital charges. Banks could moderate their risk profile by various means, such as acquiring safe assets, resorting to hedging, disposing of assets (sell-downs or securitization) or enhancing internal controls. Introducing contingent liability for bank stockholders upon the default of their institution. 'Double liability' was applied to national banks in the US from 1863 to 1933. Contingent liability could also be imposed on the managers of failed banks.

Expanding the Reach of Regulation

The gradual dismantling of barriers in financial intermediation and markets has led to greater interdependence at the global level, thereby presenting both opportunities and challenges for competition and risk control. National regulators and supervisors are reluctant to surrender their prerogatives. In the absence of a supranational global regulatory and supervisory entity, which is unrealistic in light of the current and prospective state of world affairs, it is imperative that the various parties in the international financial community enhance their cooperation in order to avoid systemic risk and preserve a sound and resilient global financial market.

International regulatory cooperation has increasingly focused on:

- The observation of uniform principles for healthy risk management and harmonised safe capital requirements;
- Common accounting plans that allow for accuracy and transparency in the reporting of the economic circumstances of financial institutions, and for comparability of reporting techniques across time and space;
- The auditing of the consolidated activities of an enterprise; and
- The appointment of an accredited regulatory agency to act as primary supervisor or principal coordinator of all national regulatory agencies concerned with the world-wide supervision of diversified, transnational financial groups.

Governments interested in boosting their economies have deliberately exonerated from regulation all or selected activities of financial firms. These exonerations vary considerably among jurisdictions. Moreover, regulatory and informational gaps exist even in advanced market economies that are deemed to be well regulated. This is the case, for example, in the US, where the Securities and Exchange Commission does not have the authority to monitor and regulate unregistered affiliates of broker/dealers and futures commission merchants. These companies have large positions in OTC derivatives and are major contributors to hedge funds.

Information gaps exist when risks are not identified and assessed industrywide for the benefit of regulators and operators. Such gaps can well be the source of financial troubles. Indeed this has been the case with the US regulatory system, which does not have a mechanism for pooling information on the risks assumed by financial firms in relation to a specific customer. Industry-wide aggregation of the risks per customer might have alerted the regulators to the excessive leverage of the LTCM, which in 1998 managed to distribute its liabilities among 14 large financial firms. The exposure to the LTCM assumed by each financial firm was not among its largest, and this is the reason why US regulators did not recognise the potential threat posed by the LTCM.

Several European countries have well-established agencies for centralising risk assessment. Their functions are to aggregate the exposures assumed by financial providers vis-à-vis individual customers, be they business enterprises or consumers, and to share the aggregated information with the financial firms concerned. In order to protect their indepen-dence and neutrality, these agencies are not affiliated to any particular private financial firm and usually operate under the aegis of the central bank. The supervisory authorities and the financial firms are therefore able to obtain aggregated information on the size of exposure of an individual customer. With such information, each firm is then able to ascertain the comprehensive exposure its customer has assumed vis-à-vis the financial services industry, and is in a position continuously to monitor its own exposure and judiciously manage its relationship with that customer.

Aggregated information on customers' exposure, which is increasingly available on-line to financial firms, can be of great help in averting the excessive concentration of risks on individual customers within the financial services industry, and in taking timely corrective action. Moreover, under the aegis of the European Central Bank, transnational cooperation among several European risk assessment agencies is expanding the reach of the agencies concerned.

Within the financial sector, the hedge-fund branch is generally under no obligation to disclose risks in its portfolios. The majority of these funds are highly leveraged investment pools (also known as highly leveraged institutions, HLI). Their participants are a few financial institutions or wealthy individuals-no more than 100. They are often organised as limited partnerships and so far have no disclosure requirements. The general partners risk their own money and are responsible for day-to-day management. The limited partners provide their funds for investment by the general partners and do not become involved in management. The latter follow aggressive investment strategies, and take long and short positions with full use of market derivatives.

Recent failings in sophisticated financial firms' models and risk management make vigilance by the supervisory authorities all the more necessary if crises are to be averted or forestalled. In late September 1998 the US Federal Reserve regulators, fearing that a systemic risk might result from the near-collapse of the LTCM, urged that additional financing be provided to this fund by its creditor-investor financial firms. The abrupt and disorderly unwinding of large positions and the liquidation of collaterals held by counterparties would have further strained the financial markets and compounded the difficulties of all participants in the globally interconnected markets.

To limit the ability of financial firms to evade prudential regulation and to close the gap between international supervisory practices, cooperation among the regulators and supervisors of different countries is necessary. For financial firms operating internationally, it appears reasonable to have as main supervisor the agency from the country where the firm has its central headquarters. It is legitimate for a country to bar the entry of a financial firm if its home country does not have an adequate regulatory-supervisory framework. The Basel

Committe called on lender banks to seek both quantitative and qualitative disclosure from borrowing HLIs on their investment risks.

Some transparency is needed if market participants are to anticipate excessively risky situations and avoid aggressive financial strategies that could lead to the collapse of large HLIs, disrupting national and international financial systems. The US authorities favour such a policy for HLIs with capital in excess of $1 billion (less than 20 out of about 2500 funds in the US). The possible failure of any of these large HLIs is deemed to be a source of systemic risk.

It was proposed that they report to the US Federal Reserve their total assets, leverage ratios and market risks, for release in due course to the public. Such legislative disclosure is also espoused by the Financial Stability Forum (FSF), which was created in 1999 by the G7 to forestall crises similar to the Asian and Russian ones of 1997-98. The disclosure requirements could generate market discipline on the part of hedge funds and their counterparties, eventually leading to safer conduct. Should this fail, further legislative action may be needed. The impact of national legislation, even in a major financial centre such as the US, will be limited unless it is emulated by other financial centres. Otherwise fund managers could move offshore in order to maintain secrecy about investment strategies that they consider 'proprietary'. If a large player discloses its strategy, it could be taken advantage of by counterparties or other players, especially when it needs to liquidate its positions.

The Basel Committee on Banking Supervision and its sister bodies the Committee on the Global Financial Systems and the Committee on Payment and Settlement Systems, which operate within the BIS, focus on sound, safe and efficient practices for banks, financial markets and payments systems, respectively. The regulatory aims are shared by other global rule-setting bodies, such as the International Organisation of Securities Commissions (IOSCO) and the International Association of Insurance Supervisors (IAIS). All are concerned with contributing to global financial prudence, and therefore stability.

FINANCIAL STABILISATION

Sources of Instability

Greed, irrational exuberance and negligence are generally deemed to be at the root of financial crises. According to this interpretation, herd-like euphoria causes decision makers to underestimate risk and/or overestimate returns. A sudden shift in market expectations and loss of confidence-triggered by a particular adverse event-can lead to the opposite process of overestimation ending in a paroxysm of gloom, investor panic and financial contagion.

Crises can also be provoked or exacerbated by unsound or incoherent macroeconomic policies. Alternatively they can be averted, moderated or mastered by judicious policies. To illustrate, a crisis in an open economy can be provoked by an excessive fiscal deficit. The latter will generate a vicious circle of rising domestic demand and prices, followed by the further swelling of public indebtedness.

To stabilise domestic demand, the government may inappropriately resort to monetary measures such as raising interest rates. This will in turn attract foreign hot money, or cause domestic firms to engage in less expensive foreign borrowing: capital inflows will then create additional upward pressure on domestic prices, and lead to an overvalued exchange rate. Deterioration of the country's current account and an increase in its foreign debt will follow. To maintain the exchange rate and the flow of foreign capital, interest rates are raised further, forcing more and more domestic borrowers into liquidity and solvency problems and eventually leading to a cascade of collapses in various sectors and a recession in the domestic economy. This will be accompanied by capital flight and the collapse of the exchange rate. The end result is likely to be a banking crisis.

The globalisation phenomenon, while increasing diversification opportunities, has led to a higher degree of uncertainty, deriving inter alia from the enormous financial resources that can be used for cross-country speculation, potentially leading to destabilisation. The rising interdependence between financial firms and markets has also contributed to an increase in the transmission of risks across institutions and markets. All crises have particular elements of their own.

Fundamental to the Asian financial crisis, which hit Thailand, South Korea, Indonesia and Malaysia in 1997-98, was the conjunction of certain international events with domestic policy and structural distortions, including, notably, the following interrelated factors:

- Banks and corporations in these four countries had resorted to excessive short-term borrowing in US dollars for their local-currency, long-term loans. In the absence of hedging, these banks became vulnerable to the depreciation of national currencies, and to liquidity crises because of their inability to roll over their foreign short-term debts. (The current Basle Capital Adequacy rules appear to have induced banks to favour short-term interbank loans to emerging economies, instead of more appropriate longer-term maturity loans.)
- Given the limited absorptive capacity the Asian national economies faced in the mid 1990s, with a massive influx of foreign capital in search of more attractive opportunities (compared with the yields then obtaining in capital exporting countries) the prices of domestic shares and real assets in the capital-importing countries were allowed to rise considerably, thereby presaging a bust after the boom.

Domestic banks imprudently channelled their lending to certain business sectors of dubious productivity and profitability, including sectors suffering from excess capacity. Furthermore loan reimbursements were not rigorously enforced by bank management, thanks to rampant self-dealing, nepotism, cronyism and corruption. Private projects of high risk or poor profitability benefited from subsidies, cheap credit, authorised monopolistic practices (for example under the aegis of conglomerates) and explicit or implicit government guarantees. State-owned companies (including banks) were extensively used as sources of political patronage.

With rising domestic prices and national currencies effectively pegged to an appreciating dollar, the four economies suffered a reduction in export cost-competitiveness, which in turn reduced their capacity to earn sufficient foreign exchange to meet their foreign-currency-denominated financial obligations on time. Their export earnings suffered further from the stagnation of the Japanese economy, and from competing exports by China, partly boosted by the 50 per cent devaluation of the Chinese currency in January 1994.

Regulatory frameworks and enforcement of the prudential rules governing domestic financial intermediaries proved inadequate. Indeed, regulators condoned and covered up flagrant violations of laws or standards by influential or politically linked executives who had falsified accounts to conceal abuses and losses. In an environment of corruption and bribery, law enforcement officials thus allowed domestic banks to operate with negative capital ratios and flout various other rules.

Early diagnosis of a financial crisis would enable those responsible for its management to produce an appropriate remedy. Some authors have called on the IMF to base its diagnosis on a purely logical, mathematically formalised and econometrically tested model. Such a model would include the interconnections between the factors responsible for the crisis, and the instruments capable of restoring both the soundness of the financial system and economic growth. One should nevertheless be cautious about relying solely on mathematical models based on past experiences to predict future crises and/ or prevent their outbreak. Some judgemental discretion may well be needed to reach an innovative or creative approach to interpreting novel situations.

The current supervisory standards in developing and emerging economies need to be improved, guided by proper prudential principles. Financial supervision should be carried out by competent independent examiners whose authority and judgement rests to a significant degree on the integrity of the financial sector. Both external examiners and risk managers of financial firms will need to be provided with appropriate financial and occupational incentives (such as attractive pay and adequate job security) if they are to carry out their functions efficiently. Moreover bankruptcy procedures should be diligently enforced on insolvent institutions.

The developed, richer economies of North America, Europe and Japan have an important role to play in global financial stability. They are the world's major creditor and capital exporting countries, financing inter alia the heavily indebted developing economies. If foreign currency debts and related economic data are fully disclosed without delay by creditor and debtor countries, market forces will be able to alert investors/creditors in time, as well as the supervisory agencies, thereby enabling them to reach sounder decisions.

This will help to forestall crises or at least moderate their impact. The opacity or scarcity of up-to-date reliable information on changing economic conditions in individual countries (and notably emerging economies) have prevented financial markets from functioning efficiently and providing optimal solutions before crises strike. Creditor countries therefore need to improve the supervision of their financial intermediaries' exposure to emerging or developing economies. Facilitating access by the products of poor, heavily indebted developing countries to the markets of developed economies (by waiving duty and quota restrictions) should enhance the ability of these debtor countries to honour their financial commitments and attenuate the intensity of debt crises. In this respect, a proposal was made by the World Bank and the IMF for government ministers to meet within the Development Committee in April 2000 under the joint auspices of the two institutions. The US trade representative would not, however, countenance this approach.

MUTATIONS IN FINANCIAL MARKETS

Over the past few decades, large business enterprises in developed market economies, led by US firms, have been successfully tapping the securities markets for lower-cost funding than that obtainable from banks. Begining in the 1980s various firms, including banks, started to unload selected portfolios of standardised credits through securitisation. The latter enables the bank to shift the credit risk and the funding of these portfolios to investors, enticed by the attractive terms of asset-backed securities. Banks that securitise portfolios of loans seek to generate fee income upon performing certain functions: originating and distributing credit, risk assessment, monitoring borrowers, collecting interest and capital reimbursements, and various accounting and administrative services.

In more recent years, smaller enterprises have been able to turn to financial markets to satisfy some of their funding needs. Even development capital and start-up equity can be partially raised through various specialised stock exchanges or trading platforms. The opportunity to issue stocks and other securities has been enhanced by the willingness of individual and institutional savers to channel a significant portion of their wealth into tradable financial instruments.

EXCHANGES

Exchanges are organised markets that have traditionally focused on the trading of equity shares and commodities. In more recent years derivatives and fixed-income securities (such as corporate bonds and commercial papers) have become tradable on exchanges, mostly electronically: in early 2000 the Swiss Exchange, for example, traded some 40 per cent of the Eurobond retail volume, valued at euro 541. 12 billion (the wholesale market was over 10 times larger). In 2000 the largest electronic trading system for European government bonds, Euro MTS, accounted for over 30 per cent of all trading volumes (14 billion euros worth of transactions a day) in these securities.

Venture capitalists and high-growth companies are increasingly able to raise capital through exchanges geared to their needs, at conditions more favourable than bank financing. With the globalisation of financial markets gathering momentum, competition has been building up among exchanges at the national and international levels to raise fresh capital for all kinds of business enterprises and for trading in various financial instruments. Exchanges have been competing for the custom of users by enhancing the utility of their services through a variety of novel approaches.

NASDAQ is one example of an exchange based on an electronic communication system, whereby market makers display the prices at which they are willing to buy or sell stocks for their own account or for their customers. It has pioneered the provision of capital access to budding high-technology and/ or high-growth companies, such as those in information technology. In contrast the New York Stock Exchange (NYSE) is based on the traditional auction system.

It has stricter listing requirements for firms with respect to size, equity, shareholding and performance, including those seeking an initial public offering (IPO). Furthermore it has erected protective barriers, for example it denies other exchanges the right to trade in the stocks it lists. A few exchanges have also limited the flow of data and routing orders, thereby constraining the growth of electronic systems.

Under the aegis of governmental regulatory entities, most exchanges are authorised by the jurisdictions in which they operate to be self-regulated. This covers the control of market manipulations and the supervision of broker/dealer conduct. Besides operational efficiency, the challenge for interconnected exchanges and the Internet is to agree generally accepted regulatory rules to protect the markets from false information.

The opening of new exchanges in competition with established ones has yielded significant advantages in terms of improved service and lower charges. Emulating NASDAQ, several new exchanges have helped young start-up and high-growth companies (mostly in the high-tech field) to raise finance by overcoming the stringent listing of traditional exchanges. For IPOs the latter normally require an operating history, and set minimum conditions in respect of profitability or sales over recent periods, as well as minimum levels of capital and assets, and a minimum number of founding shareholders with lock-up periods (that is, with the obligation of keeping their shares over pre-agreed minimum periods). In 2000 the European exchanges for innovative companies comprised the Brussels-based Easdaq, the Alternative Investment Market (AIM) in London and the Euro NM alliance of five continental European exchanges. The latter enables investors in these five exchanges to transact shares listed in any of the partner exchanges, using the same trading and settlement system.

The proliferation of independent exchanges has, however, the potential to fragment liquidity pools. Such fragmentation could be overcome by alliances or mergers of exchanges aimed at creating common platforms with shared rules for the cross-border listing, margining, transaction, clearing and settlement of trade. Alliances or mergers might be prompted by a number of expected benefits: extension of the distribution network and client base, improved division of labour, economies of size (for example through joint research or shared investment in new technologies), cross-trading arrangements and an improved competitive position for the cooperating parties vis-à-vis rivals.

In the field of derivatives, one example of a successful international alliance is Eurex, a common electronic trading system set up by the Frankfurt and Zurich exchanges. Eurex has also entered into an alliance with the Chicago Board of Trade, the Helsinki Exchange and others with the objective of connecting international derivatives markets. Its major competitor in the derivatives sector is the Globex Alliance, which links the Paris Bourse, the Chicago Mercantile Exchange and the Singapore International Monetary Exchange, joined later by the Montreal and Brazilian exchanges.

Other examples include the merger (with their respective ownerships) of the French (60 per cent), Dutch (32 per cent) and Belgium (8 per cent) stock exchanges in early 2000, driven by pressure to reduce costs. The Paris, Amsterdam and Brussels exchanges thus became a single exchange called Euronext, with one membership, one rule book (including listing) and one clearing-netting and settlement system. Euronext handles equities, options, derivatives and commodities. The London Stock Exchange and the Deutsche Börse followed suit in May 2000 to form the biggest European co-owned exchange. The latter intended to become a global trading platform through alliances-notably with NASDAQ to be effected through cross-shareholding. However, the deal collapsed later that year.

Technological advances can be illustrated by reference to electronic trading systems, which are replacing the floor-based, open outcry method. The latter (also known as pit trading) consists of a public auction at a centralised exchange, where financial instruments are traded by authorised floor participants who make bids and offers to each other verbally or through hand signals. In contrast electronic trading systems, commonly referred to as electronic communications networks (ECNs), are screen-based: they allow authorised investors (institutions and persons) to use computer terminals-regardless of geographical location-anonymously to enter bids and offers into a host computer, which matches orders and executes operations. These operations cover order-routing, clearing and settlement, and allow investors to trade after hours at the major traditional exchanges.

ECNs have several advantages: they reduce the market impact of transactions; they eliminate bid/offer spreads or dealer-broker commission; and they are neutral. Some ECNs, such as Island, anonymously display all limit orders (those in which investors specify the purchase or sale price at which they are willing to transact) in a format available on the Internet at no charge. ECNs are also important to NASDAQ's trade, accounting for about 30 per cent. By trading on ECNs, institutional and private traders reduce their reliance on market makers.

Some stock exchanges have also combined their equity and fixed income operations with ECNs (Market XT and Archipelago respectively). Investors and traders thus receive multiple benefits: extended trading hours, access to information and stocks from several exchanges, regulator oversight, high-speed electronic trading and access to more opportunities. Other exchanges have announced similar plans. Greater market transparency can be achieved by requiring the full range of investor limit orders received by competing exchanges, electronic systems and stand-alone dealers to be displayed. This would permit all market participants to ascertain the extent of supply and demand for any stock, and it would enhance the liquidity of financial markets.

E-TRADING

On-line business via the Internet-by means of personal computers and mobile devices-has proliferated and enjoyed spectacular growth. By easing access to markets, cutting trading costs and broadening the range of investment opportunities, on-line brokers have attracted millions of investors. Some brokers are independent while others are affiliated to diversified financial firms. A few on-line brokers may not be guided by professional practices and ethics, notably the rules of 'suitability' and 'know your customer' observed by traditional firms that offer judicious advice aimed at protecting investors from inappropriate financial risks. Beyond distributional advantages, investment bankers-thanks to their research capabilities-can offer large institutional investors quality advice.

Electronic commerce (often referred to as e-commerce) is bound to expand with customer adaptation to change, ready access to technology, transparency of costs and prices, and assurances about the protection of privacy. Relationship-based financial transactions are increasingly being replaced by automated operations. 'Over the counter' instruments (equity, debt, derivatives, indices and so on)-hitherto with prices quoted privately-will thus become increasingly available on-line, not only for institutions but also for savvy individuals. Investors all over the world can now directly access actively traded instruments in the secondary market and newly launched securities such as IPOs in the primary market at negligible marginal cost. Investors are likely to reap certain advantages by trading with electronic brokers via the Internet, rather than with traditional dealer/broker firms. The following advantages can be realised, subject to the judicious choice of an efficient and neutral broker (that is, without its own portfolio to compete with its customers):

- Lower cost structure and lower fees and commissions (for transaction, clearing, settlement and so on).
- Direct electronic access to major stock exchanges, and global reach.
- Instantaneous trade execution, with speedy settlement and clearance.
- Extended trading hours (24-hour access to brokers).
- Greater transparency through real-time prices, up-to-date news, performance measurement and charting.
- Better prices (except after normal trading hours, when the bid-ask spreads are larger, the choice of stocks is smaller, the information is less complete, volumes are smaller and prices are more volatile).

The trading-hour constraint is rapidly disappearing with the creation of alliances among stock exchanges in different time zones, notably the exchanges in America, Asia and Europe. Investors thus have 24-hour platforms of active trading. Furthermore competition has prompted on-line stockbrokers to expand their range of activities.

One rapid means of expansion is by takeover, as was done in early 2000 by E Trade (buying Telebank Financial, the Internet banking group) and Charles Schwab (buying US Trust, a financial firm in investment management, private banking, estate planning and fiduciary services). One of the world's largest electronic brokerages-Reuters' Instinet-caters for institutional investors and equity brokers.

In 2000 it expanded its offering to include fixed-income securities and retail business. Through a single brokerage vehicle, Instinet offers its customers access to the major market-economy exchanges, thereby providing them with a large pool of liquidity, global opportunities and lower transaction costs. In addition to its brokerage business, it offers trading research and analytics to its institutional customers.

Its participation interests span over other independent electronic trading platforms, such as Tradepoint in the UK and Archipelago in the US.

A continuous stream of current data and the ability to trade on a real-time basis are increasingly available not only to financial firms and their traders, but also to private investors.

Sophisticated, high-speed order routing and execution systems enable investors and traders to be linked directly (that is, without an intermediate firm being involved in routing orders) to other traders and to market makers in various stock markets. Transactions are executed within seconds of traders placing their orders, against the payment of fees for computer and electronic services. On-line traders and investors do not, however, have the benefit of the advice normally provided by a full-service broker/dealer on the suitability of a particular trade.

BANKING AND IT DEVELOPMENTS

Notwithsanding the spectacular growth in financial markets instruments, bank credit remains important for two categories of borrower: individuals and small enterprises that are unable to access the financial markets, and institutions that need custom-made advice and financing, for example for major projects such as energy generation or mining.

Standard bank products (such as consumer lending and mortgages) with transparent terms can increasingly be purchased via e-channels. The latter are cost efficient for commoditised credit products and for simple high-frequency bank services such as bill payments, fund transfers, information provision, stock and mutual fund trading, personal planning modules and so on.

Compared with individual investors in corporate bonds, banks have four major comparative advantages in handling credit risks. First, banks have the means and the expertise to monitor and assess the wealth, income, spending behaviour and debt servicing of their customers. Second, they enjoy economies of scale in their credit operations because of the large number of transactions. Third, they are capable of achieving a higher degree of diversification among borrowing customers.

Fourth they can obtain on a continuing basis from their borrowing customers specific information that is not readily available to investors since the borrowers know that their bank, for competitive reasons, will protect proprietary information from public disclosure.

Banks are increasingly at the forefront of using state-of-the-art information technology to protect their market share in the financial services industry against encroachment by new players. Their jump into cyberspace has been spectacular: from dispensing cash and accepting deposits through automatic teller machines from the late 1960s, to the current provision of Internet banking to corporate and individual customers.

Financial firms' considerable investments in IT are aimed at tapping a very large potential market for a wide array of standardisable products or services, such as credit cards, debit cards, stored-value cards, consumer or mortgage loans, fund transfers, foreign exchange, cash and/ or asset management, trading in mutual funds and financial instruments, insurance policies, bills payment, corporate research, portfolio evaluation and advice.

Modern banks' activities are based fundamentally on processing information. In this respect their methods of servicing their customers have generally progressed through five stages, beginning in about 1960:

- The automation of the 'back office' and the reduction of paper-based, manually processed operations.
- The provision of self-service banking via ATMs inside or outside the bank premises.
- The provision of banking services via the telephone to customers in offices, shops or at home.
- The provision of Internet banking, further easing customers' access to banking services and allowing new financial service providers to enter the market.
- The delocalisation of the traditional bank-customer relationship with the arrival of mobile devices that enable customers to interface with their banks and other financial market participants whenever and wherever.

The use of the Internet for transactional purposes has increased considerably for the following reasons: ease of entry by service providers and customers; cost effectiveness (about one tenth of the cost of a transaction in a traditional bank office); and improved transparency in the terms of the products and services offered by banks, including prices.

The Internet has also allowed the rise of independent 'information providers', who search for and aggregate the terms of products and services offered by financial firms. Independent distributors have also sprung up on the Internet, thus widening customers' choice in respect of various products and services, such as mutual funds, deposits, mortgages, consumer credit, life insurance, stockbrokerage, credit cards and so on.

Banks are adding to their traditional function of financial intermediation the novel function of facilitator of e-commerce. In the latter capacity they are currently developing a variety of services, notably:

- Internet portals: these 'supersites' are open to many providers of products or services. They provide potential buyers with an opportunity to view, compare and choose. Offerings need not be limited to financial products or services.
- Certification of identity: each bank certifies the identity of its own account holders, and acts as a channel for its customers to verify the identity of account holders at other banks.
- Assisting small businesses: banks court the custom of small enterprises by offering to set up Web sites for them. These Web sites have interactive transactional capabilities.

Electronic billing: within the framework of their cash management services, banks can offer to companies that send large volumes of bills to their customers an electronic billing and remittance-processing service through the interbank payment system.

Facilitating e-commerce: banks have an interest in offering technology for electronic business-to-business commerce in order to automate the flow of transactions relating to procurement, the distribution of goods and related services. Besides generating fee income from that activity, they expect a positive fallout for other activities, such as cash management.

Electronic money: with the availability of computers equipped with smart card readers, banks are able to provide electronic money that can be stored on these cards for use on the Internet. In addition, electronic cheques are being designed for use by businesses or individuals.

The ongoing cybernetic revolution implies heavy investment by financial firms to strengthen their relationship with existing customers, create new opportunities and fend off competition from other financial and non-financial firms, including technology companies. Yet, potentially profitable IT developments are difficult to identify with certainty, and there is a danger of committing resources to an IT channel that turns out to be economically unviable. In this case the firms concerned could loose substantially in non-amortisable investments and reduced market share or turnover.

SECURITY CONCERNS

E-commerce is particularly vulnerable to technological problems (for example the breakdown of individual computers or networks), and imposters or other parties seeking to harm users or providers. Attacks could include:

- Stealing important information, such as credit card numbers and other personal data.
- Damaging or destroying computer files and contaminating computer systems by planting viruses.
- Illicit operations, such as unauthorised transfers of funds.
- Denying service by maliciously congesting targeted Web sites.

Unless computer security and law enforcement are improved, e-brokerage business-which was estimated to account for about 16 per cent of all stock trade in the US in 2000-and other e-commerce could be hurt. Various users of the Web, including the operators of interbank transfer systems, could be equally hurt by cyber-terrorism. This calls for identification of the Internet's weak links, and for continuous upgrading of security systems in areas such as encryption, digital signatures, finger-print scanning and coding, traffic filters to ascertain legitimate users, and the rerouting of traffic from logged computer servers to others. For the unfettered growth of Internet operations, official security certification at the international level and the prosecution of offenders are essential.

Besides raiders illegally cracking into ostensibly heavily protected computer systems, individual Internet users can be vulnerable to those seeking to embezzle unsuspecting and credulous persons through the use of such claims as 'Get rich quick', 'Free stock' and 'Exceptional high returns', as well as pyramidal schemes and other scams.

Internet fraudsters are being pursued at the international level, and national agencies in 28 countries are monitoring suspect Web sites. The US Federal Trade Commission is spearheading the global sweep, with the help of international agencies. A permanent data base is being established to store information on fraud site operators, their physical locations and the victims of their misdeeds. Fraudulent operators on the Internet are thus increasingly being tracked down.

STATE SUPPORT AND MEGA-INSTITUTIONS

It is reckoned that a few governments of developed market economies that profess to espouse a policy of free and competitive markets in fact follow contrary approaches, offering favourable treatment to certain categories of financial institutions. Recently the debate in Europe has centred on Germany, where the 12 state-owned Landesbanken have been capitalised by regional governments at favourable conditions not available to their competitors and continue to benefit from explicit or implicit state guarantees. This has given these banks higher credit ratings and the possibility of raising funds more cheaply, thereby undercutting their privately owned rivals and allowing them to expand their activities. Such privileges create an uneven playing field at the expense of competitors in national and international markets.

As a result of this governmental support some of the Landesbanken have become very sizeable, including the Westdeutsche Landesbank. The latter is backed by the regional government of North-Rhine Westphalia through unlimited state guarantees and subsidies in the form of property transfer. The European Commission has estimated that the government subsidy amounts to 1. 6 billion Deutschmarks and is asking for its return to the authorities, along with 0. 6 billion Deutschmarks of accrued interest. Governmental support has enabled the Westdeutsche Landesbank to outgrow its regional bank status and become a major commercial bank with offices in 37 countries. It has taken risky exposures, notably in investment banking and lending to emerging markets, such as those in Asia.

Governments in other major market economies have equally failed to maintain a level playing field in their financial markets. In the US, two of the biggest government sponsored financial institutions, the Federal National Mortgage Association and the Federal Home Loan Mortgage Association, were set up by the federal government in 1938 and 1970 respectively and were later transformed into privately owned, profit-making enterprises. Both enjoy certain privileges not available to other private lenders, large or small. In particular they are exempt from state and local corporate income tax, banks can invest in the securities of the two institutions without limitation (that is, the risk concentration rules have been waived), their capital requirements are about one third of those applying to large banks, they benefit from the patronage of the US president who appoints five members of their boards, and the US Treasury provides them with an emergency credit line of $8. 5 billion.

Their quasi-public status enables them to obtain lower-cost funding in financial markets, estimated in 1996 at $6 billion a year on their $1 trillion debt. It is thought that one third of the subsidy is not passed to mortgages but handsomely benefits shareholders, top executives and employees.

The implicit government guarantee is a source of moral hazard, and the borrowing costs of these two institutions do not reflect their risk profile. Without such a guarantee it is likely that they would refrain from extending lower-quality loans: in 2000 some of their borrowers paid a meagre down payment of 3 per cent and allocated 50 per cent of their income to servicing their mortgages (at a time when the standard percentage was a maximum of 36 per cent for housing and other credit expenses). Loans with low down payments are, by statutory requirement, subject to private mortgage insurance. The two institutions were nevertheless held responsible for stifling competition from other private lenders, and for aggravating the credit bubble through their aggressive expansion, thereby putting the US taxpayer at risk if post-bubble difficulties had called for rescue by the government. It is pertinent to note that large national banks finance mortgages with consumer deposits insured by the government-owned FDIC.

Unlike Fannie Mae and Freddie Mac, these banks are not constrained by federal charters to finance domestic housing solely; banks can diversify their activities by offering financial products and services in various markets and countries.

The ongoing consolidation of the financial industry in various parts of the world is producing several large and complex financial firms that engage in a variety of activities. They seek to satisfy the needs and serve the convenience of their customers by offering a broad range of products and services, so-called 'one-stop shopping'. Yet these institutions pose challenges to public policy with respect to (1) their dominant position in selected products and markets and the antitrust implications of this, and (2) governments' reluctance to close institutions whose soundness and safety are in doubt lest their action provokes a systemic risk. The existence of 'too big to fail' (TBTF) institutions has often resulted in public authorities giving implicit guarantees to non-insured depositors and other creditors of these institutions. This policy is bound to deflect from market discipline in the management of mega-institutions.

Large financial institutions have, furthermore, risk exposures in multiple products and sectors, and in extensive geographical areas. Characterised by increasing complexity and diversity, these institutions are accordingly not amenable to standardised rules of risk control. Each needs to construct specifically designed risk models to assess its risks and capital requirements. In view of their potential impact on national or international systemic risks, their operations have to be scrutinised on a continuous basis by a team of highly qualified inspectors. Financial conglomerates now have a greater opportunity to develop in the US market, thanks to the Gramm-Leach-Bliley Act of 1999. The Act effectively dismantled the functional barriers previously imposed on financial providers by the Glass-Steagall Act of 1933. The latter had segregated the ownership and operation of investment banks (securities firms or merchant banks) on the one hand, and deposit-taking institutions (notably commercial banks) on the other. Furthermore the replacement of the Pepper-McFadden Act of 1927 by the Riegle-Neal Interstate Banking and Branching Efficiency Act of 1997 has eliminated geographical barriers to bank extension within the US.

Financial regulatory agencies in certain countries continue to focus on risks and sound practices in their assigned areas in the financial sector: banks, mutual funds, securities and derivatives markets, and insurance. In the US they include the Federal Deposit Insurance Corporation, the Federal Reserve System, the Office of the Comptroller of the Currency, the Office of Thrift Supervision, the Securities and Exchange Commission, the state banking authorities, and insurance regulatory agencies. US bank regulators have joined in the Shared National Credit Programme to assess the risk posed by large syndicated loans to participating banks. The programme does not evaluate other risks. US regulators have not yet properly addressed risks interrelationships across the various segments of the financial sector.

Integrated financial regulation and supervision recognises that the formal separation between financial intermediaries and their products and services is becoming increasingly blurred, especially in view of the growth of financial conglomerates and the increasing substitutability of financial products and services. A single, comprehensive regulatory agency can identify and assess industrywide risks more easily than a fragmented system of multiple agencies, each focusing on different categories of financial services companies. Moreover the centralisation of regulatory functions in one institution yields economies of size and efficiency, and facilitates the recruitment and retention of qualified personnel.

From the standpoint of enterprises, large firms with diverse activities are better off under a single regulatory agency as they avoid having to deal with a multiplicity of agencies. Small firms, however, fear being faced by an overbearing and bureaucratic mammoth to which they have to submit regardless.

The regulation of financial conglomerates poses important challenges with respect not only to setting appropriate prudential rules, but also to avoiding possible conflicts of interest between the different units of conglomerates and their customers, who are entitled to fair and impartial treatment. Greater transparency and timely disclosure of information enables experienced financial customers and analysts to evaluate the terms of the products and services offered, and to assess the risks and results of firms, including their constituent units. Market participants are then able to value shares, subordinated debts and other financial instruments more realistically, thereby prompting management to focus continuously on sustaining productivity and earnings. However at the moment market participants are not fully informed, and some investors may set more store on short-term than on longer-term performance.

Beyond the supervision of risks, public authorities have to concern themselves with the protection of customers of financial conglomerates in two principal areas: consumer privacy and oligopolistic power. With regard to the former, consumers may be concerned about financial firms' legal right to pass on or sell their personal data without prior consent to affiliated or associated companies. The latter include unaffiliated enterprises that perform services for or function on behalf of a financial firm, and joint mechanisms between two or more financial firms for the marketing of financial products and services. The information disclosed can cover, inter alia, the customer's assets, liabilities, sources of income, spending patterns, insurance coverage, retirement plans and even health matters.

The dominance by a small number of financial firms in selected products or markets has been strengthening. The effect of such a concentration could well be to drive up the margins, commissions or premiums that financial conglomerates impose on their services. Moreover such oligopolist control could eventually lead to a reduction in the choices offered to consumers, and increase the opacity of the information available to market participants.

The foregoing calls for constant vigilance on the part of the regulatory authorities which is not always the case. In the UK, for example, the authorities have reportedly tolerated the bending of free market rules. In particular, regulators have allowed the big four UK banks-which control the payment system and about 70 per cent of the personal market-to inhibit competition. These banks' practices included

- Locking in customers by means of high barriers against defection;
- Interbank agreements aimed at discouraging potential entrants;
- Imposing excessive charges that are unrelated to the costs, for example when customers use other banks' cash dispensing machines;
- Charging excessive fees to retailers that accept credit and debit cards; and
- Charging excessive fees for bundled products and services. These practices have produced excessive profits compared with those made by other enterprises. Furthermore the chairman of the banking review, Don Cruickshank, deemed that the 'over-cosy relationship' between

the UK big banks, the government and the regulators was unwarranted for systemic reasons, such as possible bank runs.

TOWARDS GLOBAL STABILITY

Intergovernmental institutions such as the International Monetary Fund (IMF), the World Bank and the Bank for International Settlements (BIS) play an important role in promoting global financial stability. The leading governmental members of these institutions represent the world's major financial markets. Crises have prodded these governments to cooperate more closely in respect of

- The exchange, pooling and dissemination of information pertinent to the efficient functioning of world financial markets,
- Greater coordination between national and interna-tional regulatory bodies, and
- The implementation of international best standards and practices.

The foremost multilateral institution in terms of monetary financial cooperation is the IMF. Established in 1945, it works towards various goals: collaboration on international monetary problems, balanced expansion of international trade, exchange stability and the elimination of foreign exchange restrictions. It also provides temporary support to correct maladjustments in members' balance of payments.

Synergetically with the IMF's objectives, the Financial Stability Forum (FSF), established by the G7 in 1999, functions as a coordinator for various institutions with the aim of reducing the risk of global financial instability. It focuses on financial intermediaries, financial markets and payment infrastructures. The FSF does not have an operational mandate and seeks a concerted approach by international organisations and standard-setting entities (for example the BIS, the IMF, the World Bank and the OECD), along with national regulatory agencies, finance ministries and the central banks of the G7 and non-G7 countries with major financial centres.

In view of its status as the global intergovernmental monetary institution (183 countries), the IMF has been entrusted with the major responsibility of promoting global financial stability. Its main role is to help member countries to shore up their balance of payments by providing stand-by facilities, subject to certain rules. Notable among the latter are first, a ceiling of borrowing based on the relative economic weight of the member country) and second, strict enforcement (monitored by the IMF) of an agreed-upon economic programme. These policies aim to promote macroeconomic stability over the long term within the framework of an open market economy.

Governments that experience financial distress often call on the IMF after the fact instead of asking for assistance at the inception of the problem, when the help provided can be more effective and can moderate some of the high economic and social costs of adjustment. In administering its limited resources the IMF has not invariably abided by its own rules.

Moreover it has been directly influenced by its major funders, notably the US, which is the largest contributor to the IMF's resources (17. 35 per cent of the total subscription). One example concerns the 1994-95 financial debacle in Mexico, which led to the exchange rate of the peso plummeting by some 50 per cent on 21 December 1994. At the urging of the US government, the IMF agreed to a stand-by arrangement for Mexico of up to $17. 8 billion immediately after President Clinton announced that the US would provide financial assistance of $20 billion. The total assistance package was raised to $47. 8 billion when Canada and the BIS offered additional aid, beefed-up by a supplementary funding commitment of $2. 8 billion by the World Bank. Several of the member countries complained that the IMF executive Board had not been adequately consulted on the Mexican rescue operation.

Moreover the IMF's financing amounted to 688 per cent of Mexico's subscription quota. The statutory cumulative limit for financial support is about 300 per cent of the member's quota, and is subject to detailed negotiation and agreement between the IMF and the debtor country. The latter normally makes a commitment to reform its macroeconomic and financial policies (with a timetable for targets) in order to ameliorate or eliminate its external payments problem. The US government was concerned-it is pertinent to note-about the negative externalities of the Mexican financial crisis, notably:

- The threat posed to US trade, employment and immigration interests.
- The threat of contagion posed to other countries.
- Solidarity vis-à-vis a fellow member of the North American Free Trade Agreement.
- Concern that Mexico's move towards a market-oriented economy and political democratisation (to be emulated by other emerging economies) could be thwarted.

Critics within the US administration, the US Congress and other creditor countries (the G10) contested the above and further invoked the moral hazard factor as a possible contributor to Mexico's financial crisis. That factor already existed because of the financial assistance provided by the IMF and various creditor nations during Mexico's foreign debt crisis of August 1982. This financial rescue operation could have encouraged Mexico and other emerging capital importing countries to follow risky macroeconomic and financial policies, and unduly encouraged foreign investors or creditor banks to relax their monitoring of risks. Public funds were thus used during the financial rescues of Mexico, South Korea and Russia to repay short-term debt to private parties, despite the fact that these parties had enjoyed high interest rates when they chose to finance these countries. Foreign banks and investors might, on the basis of past bailouts by the IMF and creditor nations, anticipate similar treatment and therefore take more risks. The IMF's promise to provide financial support to financially distressed member countries therefore entails a moral hazard factor. National deposit insurance mechanisms in creditor counties, which explicitly or implicitly provide banks and their depositors with government guarantees, add to the moral hazard factor. However, no guarantees are cost-free, and several investors and lenders (domestic and foreign) have sustained large losses during past financial crises regardless of the IMF's and creditor nation's support to member governments. To reduce moral hazard and enhance market discipline, lenders and investors should be made to share the cost of crises they have been involved in causing, thus providing them with an incentive to engage in prudent behaviour. Official and private entities have raised several important questions about the optimal future role of the IMF, including the following:

- Should the IMF act more like a central regulatory authority by extending its surveillance function over member countries to cover
- Macroeconomic reforms and stabilisation, and
- Banking and financial market regulation and supervision?
- Should it assist member countries in their endeavour to anticipate, avoid or resolve financial crises, thereby acting as a quasi international lender of last resort for countries hit by creditor panic and currency flight?
- Could the IMF act as an international deposit insurance entity for member countries that borrow on the international financial markets, by levying differentiated premia in accordance with its rating of the creditworthiness of the members concerned? Is it realistic to assume that the IMF has sufficient knowledge and political backing to carry out that function, which would include management of the financial reserves accumulated from such premia?
- Should the IMF be confined to the function of a mediator between creditors (sovereign and private entities) and debtor countries in times of financial distress, and help both parties by facilitating speedy negotiations and workable solutions to settle claims, thereby replacing the ad hoc meetings between public sector creditors (known as the Paris Club) or private sector creditors (the London Club) and the defaulting debtor countries?

Should the IMF continue to address poverty alleviation (mostly through the Poverty Reduction and Growth Facility, and the Heavily Indebted Poor Countries debt relief) or should this be left to its sister organisation, the World Bank, and similar institutions?

Should the IMF maintain its longer-term lending programme (which extends up to 10 years) in order to finance structural reforms in member countries, or should it instead focus on temporary, short-term lending to countries that encounter payment and liquidity problems? A few critics have questioned the IMF's failure-despite its oversight and conditionality prerogatives-to detect irregularities in member countries, leading to a failure to enforce policy changes and to the misuse of the IMF's resources. They also question the ability of the IMF to forewarn governments about looming crises. IMF officials acknow-ledged in 1999 that they had failed to obtain timely information on some countries that had faced financial distress, although, they had managed to alert certain countries of an impending foreign exchange crisis, to no avail as it turned out. In the case of Thailand, the IMF's warning was reportedly not made public in order to avoid precipitating the very crisis it was aiming to prevent. Moreover crises can deepen or become protracted if appropriate solutions are not adopted in time, or if governments renege on their commitments under the IMF support programmes.

Several entities (official and non-official) have called on the IMF to require greater transparency from member countries so that problems can be identified before they turn into crises. Some holders of high office in government or finance have put in doubt the effectiveness of the IMF's oversight and rescue measures: they consider that its advice is more relevant to past crises than to unfolding ones. For doctrinal reasons or reasons of national interest, very few have called for the outright abolition of the IMF. Most critics suggest that the IMF needs to be more focused and should function primarily as lender of last resort in order to contribute effectively to global financial stability. The emphasis on short-term support to member countries is espoused by the current managing director of the IMF, Horst Köhler, and the US Treasury. Both believe that long-term lending should be primarily the concern of the World Bank. Last-resort lending, as a safety net, carries with it a moral hazard risk.

The members in question are eligible for sufficient last-resort lending, subject to policy conditionality on macroeconomic matters and prudent regulation of their financial sector, with rigorous enforcement of rules and standards.

Lending is made at a penalty rate to limit the demand by countries actually or potentially facing a liquidity crisis, or those susceptible to systemic risk, and on condition that these countries are in a position fully to honour their obligations; for poor countries with no prospect of repaying a loan, aid is more appropriate.

The private sector should carry out its own risk analysis, monitoring and self-regulation; thus capital exporters (creditors and investors), along with capital importers, should have to bear the brunt of the consequences of their risky behaviour by sustaining losses or ultimately being forced into bankruptcy.

The application of reliable accounting, monitoring and regulatory standards, namely those set up by the Basle Committee on Banking Supervision, the IMF Special Data Dissemination Standard, and IOSCO. By enhancing the quality of the available information and assuring the transparency of key data, regulators and markets can more efficiently monitor financial players in the global market.

An embryonic, very modest international lender of last resort facility was started up in April 1999 when the IMF launched its Contingent Credit Lines (CCL) facility for a two-year trial period. The CCL provides member countries with short term-financing (up to two years) to protect them against contagion risks.

IMF support of this sort is intended to send a message to the international financial community about its confidence in a member's economic policies. The criteria for approval for such support are stringent, and include the prerequisite that 'the member must be implementing policies that make it unlikely it will need to use the resources [sic] and it must not already be facing balance of payments difficulties as a result of contagion'. The CCL support is capped at 500 per cent of the member's quota in the IMF and is subject to a surcharge of 300 basis points in the first year, plus 50 basis points per six-month extension.

Before the IMF can play a genuine lender of last resort role in the world economy the leading creditor countries (the US, the EU and Japan) have to reach a consensus on the IMF's strategy and structure. In particular they have to agree on whether the IMF can substantially increase its members' quota subscriptions and its official borrowing from capital-exporting countries, notably the major industrial countries (the G10). The IMF has yet to tap private sources in the world financial markets directly.

As a universal, multilateral organisation the IMF is likely to have a greater degree of objectivity or neutrality in evaluating data and recommending appropriate policies and reforms than national institutions (although the abovemen-tioned creditor countries will continue to wield considerable influence).

It is more realistic in a world of sovereign states and great diversity to approach global financial cooperation in a gradualistic manner than to attempt a rapid overhaul of the existing web of institutional relations.

Sequencing Liberalisation

Developing countries can expect higher growth in the long run through the gradual liberalisation of their capital accounts, subject to their having sound macroeconomic policies and a solid and well-regulated financial sector. International capital flows are prompted by diverse aims and motives, ranging from productive investment to short-term speculative gains and money laundering.

Unfettered and erratic short-term capital movements can destabilise an economy, especially when the flows are massive in relation to the absorptive capacity of the domestic economy. Some countries, for example South Korea, liberalised short-term financial flows in the mid 1990s while retaining restrictions on long-term capital movements. Such sequencing is deemed inappropriate. Indeed debt, unlike equity, carries with it the risk of default if debtors fail to pay interest or reimburse capital on time. Moreover debt with a short maturity entails a higher degree of volatility. It is accordingly more rational for governments of developing economies to give priority to the liberalisation of direct investment, followed by equity portfolio investment. Furthermore long-term debt-in contrast to short-term debt-has to be judiciously structured to avoid the bunching of reimbursements.

Charges aimed at discouraging hot capital inflows (that is, short term and speculative) could take the form of fiscal levies or non-interest-earning deposit requirements. These charges would be waived for foreign funds employed over longer periods, thereby providing an incentive for additional productive investment. Capital controls (through fiscal charges or other restrictions) on international financial transactions are prompted by a variety of aims, including:

- Marshalling national savings for domestic use by restricting the outward flow of capital in search of safety or higher returns abroad.
- Enhancing macroeconomic (monetary, exchange rate, growth and so on) stability by moderating the size of foreign pools of capital that can precipitately leave the country.
- Changing the composition of capital inflows, for example by favouring those with longer maturity.
- Reducing the impact of capital inflows on currency appreciation (with its adverse effect on exports) or on monetary expansion (with its inflationary pressures).
- Protecting domestic financial firms until they attain maturity (for example through economies of scale and scope).
- Favouring certain domestic economic activities and/or protecting nationally owned enterprises from foreign acquisition.

Capital controls carry administrative costs, generate corruption, create distortions and institute rigidities in the domestic economy, which then looses the benefits of free trading in assets. These benefits include risk-sharing, diversification, growth, technology transfer and enhanced competitiveness.

Prior to the liberalisation of capital movements, developing countries in an interdependent world economy therefore need to introduce appropriate structural reforms (for example reforms aimed at strengthening the financial sector) and macroeconomic policies that are capable of mobilising domestic savings for productive investment in a market-oriented economy.

As summarised by one well-documented source, 'External financial liberalisation should not be considered an isolated or primary goal, achievement of which automatically raises the sophistication and resilience of the domestic financial system. Rather, it should be part of a concurrent, integrated and comprehensive policy approach to macroeconomic and structural reform with individual elements of this policy package reinforcing each other. ' Even if they have carried out appropriate structural reforms, small and medium-sized economies will continue to fear the adverse effects of massive (measured in proportion to gross domestic product) and speculative cross-border capital flows. They therefore need international organisations to provide some assurance of support in times of trouble if they are fully to liberalise short-term capital movements. The moral hazard such assurance would induce in the behaviour of various economic actors, notably financial firms, has to be weighed against the benefit of preventing the propagation of systemic risk.

3

Methods of Risk Management

Trading on Forex the investor has opportunities to multiply his money, but he also risks losing future profit and, moreover, invested capital. Deviation from expected profit average is what determines the investor's risk on the financial market.

This deviation can bring both high profits and big losses. Financial risk management does not automatically imply successful trading, but influences it to a great extent.

Every currency transaction is subjected to risks, therefore, it is possible to reduce potential losses by applying general methods of risk management:

- Using stop-orders;
- Partial investment;
- Trend-oriented trade;
- Managing emotions.

Risk management methods are applied after positions are opened. The main risk management method is making orders reducing losses. Stop-loss is a point when the trader leaves the market in order to avoid an unfavourable situation. When opening a position it's better to use stop-loss to insure against extra losses.

There are several types of stop-signals:

- *Initial stop*: It determines the percentage of the amount of the deposit that the trader is prepared to lose. With a price moving against position and reaching a level of the position settled by trader, the position is closed with losses.
- *Trailing stop*: With a price moving together with the position, the stop-signal is used right after it in a proportion determined by the trader. In the case of changing of this tendency the price reaches this signal and the trader leaves the market, but maybe even with some profit.
- *Withdrawal profit*: The position is closed after pay-profit is received.
- *Timed stop*: If the market can not provide the expected percentage of profit within a certain period of time, the position is closed.

RISK ASSESSMENT

Within the workplace, owners of a business are legally required to assess the risks of injury and ill health affecting employees. Risk assessment is the careful examination of the diverse factors that can bring about these risks. Risk assessment should also make sure that enough precautions are implemented in order to prevent harm coming to an employee.

Ill health and accidents can have a very serious affect on business. They can ruin lives and damage business output. They can also lead to costly court cases and increased insurance costs. Risk assessment procedures should help to dispense with the above and make the workplace a safer environment for employees.

In risk assessment, the most important factor is to decide what is a hazard in the workplace. If the risk is determined to be significant enough, precautions should be put into place so that the risk is minimized or dispensed with altogether. For example, electricity in the workplace is hazardous, but provided that all proper protection is in place, the risk to employees becomes insignificant.

There are five steps that should be undertaken when conducting a thorough risk assessment. The first step is to look for hazards. Take a tour of the workplace and check for potential dangers. Concentrate on anything with the potential to cause serious harm to employees. Also ask for employee opinions on the subject. Accident and ill-health records are a good way of revealing why and how accidents have occurred in the past.

The second step is to decide who might be harmed and how. Decide who might be particularly at risk. Trainees, young workers or expectant mothers may be high on this list. Members of the public who are not familiar with the workplace or anyone who is not in the workplace full time and may not be familiar with the layout may also be at risk.

With the third step, you must calculate whether there have been enough precautions put into place to counter the hazard. For each risk you find, a decision should be made whether you have established enough precautions to reduce the risk. Has your risk assessment procedure taken into account all the health and safety aspects required by law? Is there anything further you can do to reduce the risk, such as issuing protective clothing or preventing access with guardrails? The next step is to record your findings. Your risk assessment check must show that you have dealt with all the obvious hazard areas. It should also show that you have checked with employees who might be affected and that any hazards that remain have been dealt with and are now reasonably low.

The final step is to review your risk assessment procedures and make revisions if necessary. In the future, new machinery, substances and work procedures could be implemented in the workplace. This is when your revision should take place to ensure that the work environment is risk fee and will continue to be so in the future.

EXPLANATION

Risk assessment consists in an objective evaluation of risk in which assumptions and uncertainties are clearly considered and presented. Part of the difficulty of risk management is that measurement of both of the quantities in which risk assessment is concerned - potential loss and probability of occurrence - can be very difficult to measure.

The chance of error in the measurement of these two concepts is large. A risk with a large potential loss and a low probability of occurring is often treated differently from one with a low potential loss and a high likelihood of occurring. In theory, both are of nearly equal priority in dealing with first, but in practice it can be very difficult to manage when faced with the scarcity of resources, especially time, in which to conduct the risk management process. Expressed mathematically,

$$R_i = L_i p(L_i)$$

Financial decisions, such as insurance, express loss in terms of dollar amounts. When risk assessment is used for public health or environmental decisions, loss can be quantified in a common metric,such as a country's currency, or some numerical measure of a location's quality of life.

For public health and environmental decisions, loss is simply a verbal description of the outcome, such as increased cancer incidence or incidence of birth defects. In that case, the "risk" is expressed as:

If the risk estimate takes into account information on the number of individuals exposed, it is termed a "population risk" and is in units of expected increased cases per a time period.

If the risk estimate does not take into account the number of individuals exposed, it is termed an "individual risk" and is in units of incidence rate per a time period. Population risks are of more use for cost/benefit analysis; individual risks are of more use for evaluating whether risks to individuals are "acceptable"....

RISK ASSESSMENT IN PUBLIC HEALTH

In the context of public health, risk assessment is the process of quantifying the probability of a harmful effect to individuals or populations from certain human activities.

In most countries, the use of specific chemicals, or the operations of specific facilities is not allowed unless it can be shown that they do not increase the risk of death or illness above a specific threshold.

For example, the American Food and Drug Administration regulates food safety through risk assessment. The FDA required in 1973 that cancer-causing compounds must not be present in meat at concentrations that would cause a cancer risk greater than 1 in a million lifetimes.

HOW THE RISK IS DETERMINED?

In the estimation of the risks, three or more steps are involved, requiring the inputs of different disciplines:

1. *Hazard Identification*, aims to determine the qualitative nature of the potential adverse consequences of the contaminant and the strength of the evidence it can have that effect. This is done, for chemical hazards, by drawing from the results of the sciences of toxicology and epidemiology. For other kinds of hazard, engineering or other disciplines are involved.
2. *Dose-Response Analysis*, is determining the relationship between dose and the probability or the incidence of effect. The complexity of this step in many contexts derives mainly from the need to extrapolate results from experimental animals to humans, and/or from high to lower doses. In addition, the differences between individuals due to genetics or other factors mean that the hazard may be higher for particular groups, called susceptible populations. An alternative to dose-response estimation is to determine an effect unlikely to yield observable effects, that is, a no effect concentration. In developing such a dose, to account for the largely unknown effects of animal to human extrapolations, increased variability in humans, or missing data, a prudent approach is often adopted by including safety factors in the estimate of the "safe" dose, typically a factor of 10 for each unknown step.
3. *Exposure Quantification*, aims to determine the amount of a contaminant that individuals and populations will receive. This is done by examining the results of the discipline of exposure assessment. As different location, lifestyles and other factors likely influence the amount of contaminant that is received, a range or distribution of possible values is generated in this step. Particular care is taken to determine the exposure of the susceptible population(s).

Finally, the results of the three steps are then combined to produce an estimate of risk. Because of the different susceptibilities and exposures, this risk will vary within a population.

Small Subpopulations

When risks apply mainly to small subpopulations, there is uncertainty at which point intervention is necessary. What if a risk is very low for everyone but 0.1 per cent of the population? A difference exists whether this 0.1 per cent is represented by *all infants younger than *X* days or *recreational users of a particular product. If the risk is higher for a particular sub-population because of abnormal exposure rather than susceptibility, there is a potential to consider strategies to further reduce the exposure of that subgroup.

If an identifiable sub-population is more susceptible due to inherent genetic or other factors, there is a policy choice whether to set policies for protecting the general population that are protective of such groups or whether if the group is too small, or the costs to high.

Sometimes, a suitable position is to at least limit the risk of the more susceptible to some risk level above which it seems too inequitable to leave them out of the risk.

RISK ASSESSMENT IN AUDITING

In auditing, risk assessment is a very crucial stage before accepting an audit engagement. ISA315 *Understanding the Entity and its Environment and Assessing the Risks of Material Misstatement*, "the auditor should perform risk assessment procedures to obtain an understanding of the entity and its environment, including its internal control.

Then, auditor obtains initial evidence regarding the classes of transactions at the client and the operating effectiveness of the client's internal controls.In auditing, audit risk includes inherent risk, control risk and detection risk.

RISK ASSESSMENT IN INFORMATION SECURITY

There are two methods of risk assessment in information security field, qualitative and quantitative. Purely quantitative risk assessment is a mathematical calculation based on security metrics on the asset.

Qualitative risk assessment is performed when the organization requires a risk assessment be performed in a relatively short time or to meet a small budget, a significant quantity of relevant data is not available, or the persons performing the assessment don't have the sophisticated mathematical, financial, and risk assessment expertise required.

Qualitative risk assessment can be performed in a shorter period of time and with less data. Qualitative risk assessments are typically performed through interviews of a sample of personnel from all relevant groups within an organization charged with the security of the asset being assessed. Qualitative risk assessments are descriptive versus measurable.

Quantitative Risk Assessment

Quantitative risk assessments include a calculation of the single loss expectancy of an asset. The single loss expectancy can be defined as the loss of value to asset based on a single security incident. The team then calculates the annualized rate of occurrence of the threat to the asset.

The ARO is an estimate based on the data of how often a threat would be successful in exploiting a vulnerability. From this information, the annualized loss expectancy can be calculated. The annualized loss expectancy is a calculation of the single loss expectancy multiplied the annual rate of occurrence, or how much an organization could estimate to lose from an asset based on the risks, threats, and vulnerabilities. It then becomes possible from a financial perspective to justify expenditures to implement countermeasures to protect the asset.

CRITICISMS OF QUANTITATIVE RISK ASSESSMENT

Barry Commoner, Brian Wynne and other critics have expressed concerns that risk assessment tends to be overly quantitative and reductive.

For example, they argue that risk assessments ignore qualitative differences among risks. Some charge that assessments may drop out important non-quantifiable or inaccessible information, such as variations among the classes of people exposed to hazards.

Furthermore, Commoner and O'Brien claim that quantitative approaches divert attention from precautionary or preventative measures.

Others, like Nassim Nicholas Taleb consider risk managers little more than "blind users" of statistical tools and methods.

PRINCIPLES OF RISK MANAGEMENT

- *Organisational Context:* There's no 'one-size-fits-all' when it comes to Risk Management. Each organisation will be affected by different Political, Economic, Societal, Technological, Legal and Environmental factors. It's also worth pointing out that each organisation will have different internal cultures, communication channels, levels of agile-adoption and existing risk management processes.
- *Stakeholder Involvement:* Involve your stakeholders wherever possible. Keep them informed and understand the role they can/could play at each stage in the Risk Management process > Identify, Assess, Respond, Review.
- *Organisational Objectives:* When assessing and responding to a risk, be sure to keep the overal organisational objectives in mind. When considering a Task-level risk, look at the role it plays towards delivering a User Story. If you're concerned about a User Story, consider the impact it has on delivering your Sprint Objective or the relevant Epic. If you'reconcerned about a particular Epic, then look at the relevant Theme or the Programme of works. Keep things in perspective and don't lose sight of your end-goal.
- *Management of Risk Approach:* This particular principle is less applicable as it refers specifically to the PMBOK Risk Management processes, however the message basically stresses the importance of following best practice guidelines and learning from the mistakes of others.

- *Reporting:* Keep people informed – ensure transparency and visibility. Communication is key!
- *Roles and Responsibilities*: Make sure that everyone understands the role they play at each stage of the Risk Management Life cycle *i.e.* >Identify, Assess, Respond, Review. Ensure that all bases are covered by someone.
- *Support Structure*: Ensure that everyone understands how risk is managed through the Risk Management Life cycle and who to go to if they have any questions. For example:
  - How are risks identified
  - How and when are risks escalated?
  - Where and in what format are risks documented?
  - How and when are risks reviewed, etc.
- *Early Warning Indicators*: Give yourself the best chance of forecasting/ anticipating the transition of a Risk to an active Issue. Ensure that everyone is communicating and that any potential issues are highlighted in the Daily Scrum. It's also important to know how you should react in the event a risk does or is about to be realised *e.g.* who needs to know and how will you inform them – in the Daily Scrum also? Or, maybe in the Scrum of Scrums? Or, maybe you'll just walk over and tell them.
- *Review Cycle*: Make sure that your Risk Board is visible and that you're regularly reviewing it – you could do this via the Retrospective and as an extension to the Daily Scrum by adding a 4th question:
  - What did you do since the last sprint?
  - What will do you today?
  - Is there anything blocking you at the moment?
  - Any changes to the risk board?
- *Overcoming Barriers to the Management of Risk:* Ensure you're doing everything you can to give you the best chance of successfully assessing the risk andresponding to the risk. Some common barriers include:
  - Established roles, responsibilities, accoun-tability and ownership.
  - An appropriate budget for embedding approach and carrying out activities.
  - Adequate and accessible training, tools and techniques.
  - Risk management orientation, induction and training processes.
  - Irregular assessment of Management of Risk approach.
- *Supportive Culture:* Make sure that everyone on the team feels comfortable raising, discussing and managing risks.
- *Continual Improvement*: Use the Retrospective to review the way you manage risk and to assess ongoing risks. Learn from your mistakes.

REPUTATIONAL RISK MANAGEMENT

To protect banks against business, legal and reputation risk, e-banking services must be delivered on a consistent and timely basis in accordance with high customer expectations for constant and rapid availability and potentially high transaction demand. The bank must have the ability to deliver e-banking services to all end-users and be able to maintain such availability in all circumstances. Effective incident response mechanisms are also critical to minimise operational, legal and reputational risks arising from unexpected events, including internal and external attacks, that may affect the provision of e-banking systems and services. To meet customers' expectations, banks should therefore have effective capacity, business continuity and contingency planning. Banks should also develop appropriate incident response plans, including communication strategies, that ensure business continuity, control reputation risk and limit liability associated with disruptions in their e-banking services.

INSURANCE DOLLAR

Risk Management Insurance can alleviate loss from everything from fire and labour disputes, to product liability, lawsuits and publicity disasters. For many types of risk, insuring against financial loss is the best option. In addition, we will show you ways that you can reduce the cost of your risk management insurance. To reduce your total insurance cost while still protecting against disasters, reduce the likelihood of negative events through proactive programmes that manage information and feature accurate training for all employees at point of risk positions. Again, reducing the probability of loss can reduce your risk management insurance costs.

Risk Control and Risk Management

Another key principle in risk management is Risk Control. Managing and controlling an organization's exposure to risk usually involves the following: risk mitigation, contingency planning and close managerial supervision of the combined risk management effort so that adjustments can be made to continually improve the efficiency of the endeavor over time and guard against untreated exposure. One of the essential processes in risk management is assessing an organization's exposure to risk. That process is aptly named the Risk Management Assessment Identifying an organization's exposure to risk is only the beginning. A true assessment of risk means that each risk must be evaluated for its probability of occurrence and its potential impact. Owners of risk must be identified, and their responsibilities must be determined. The Risk Management Assessment is a fact finding mission in support of the planning and development of a risk management strategy. No meaningful approach to risk management can be achieved without a thorough and painstaking assessment of an organization's exposure to risk.

Risk Management Assessment

Three key processes, cornerstones among the principles of risk management, comprise the risk management assessment. Identify exposure to risk; Analyze the risk, meaning measure the likelihood and severity of impact; Prioritize risk. When exposure to risk has been identified, quantified and prioritized, treatments for the organization's exposure to risk can be devised.

Assessment Benefits

The great benefit of effective risk management assessment can be seen in rapid responses that accurately account for an organization's objectives-made possible through effective risk management assessment. When faced with limited resources, especially time, the risk management process breaks down without a thorough assessment. Business moves quickly-more quickly now than ever before. At decision time, the risk management strategy developed from planning the treatment of risk evaluated during the risk management assessment should be in place to guide and instruct decision makers.

Assessment Challenges

Risk can be defined as uncertainty. Measuring the likelihood and the impact of an adverse event can be difficult-a serious challenge in risk management assessment. Events can represent high probability risk, low probability risk, high potential for loss and low potential for loss. Exact measurements for both probability and potential loss are usually impossible, introducing uncertainty best battled by experience. Treatments for these exposures must be managed based on the information generated by the risk assessment and considered against an organization's objectives and goals.

MANAGEMENT OVERSIGHT AND BOARD

Because the Board of Directors and senior management are responsible for developing the institution's business strategy and establishing an effective management oversight over risks, they are expected to take an explicit, informed and documented strategic decision as to whether and how the bank is to provide e-banking services. The initial decision should include the specific accountabilities, policies and controls to address risks, including those arising in a cross-border context. Effective management oversight is expected to encompass the review and approval of the key aspects of the bank's security control process, such as the development and maintenance of a security control infrastructure that properly safeguards e-banking systems and data from both internal and external threats. It also should include a comprehensive process for managing risks associated with increased complexity of and increasing reliance on outsourcing relationships and third-party dependencies to perform critical e-banking functions.

Security Controls

While the Board of Directors has the responsibility for ensuring that appropriate security control processes are in place for e-banking, the substance of these processes needs special management attention because of the enhanced security challenges posed by e-banking.

This should include establishing appropriate authorisation privileges and authentication measures, logical and physical access controls, adequate infrastructure security to maintain appropriate boundaries and restrictions on both internal and external user activities and data integrity of transactions, records and information. In addition, the existence of clear audit trails for all e-banking transactions should be ensured and measures to preserve confidentiality of key e-banking information should be appropriate with the sensitivity of such information.

Although customer protection and privacy regulations vary from jurisdiction to jurisdiction, banks generally have a clear responsibility to provide their customers with a level of comfort regarding information disclosures, protection of customer data and business availability that approaches the level they can expect when using traditional banking distribution channels. To minimise legal and reputational risk associated with e-banking activities conducted both domestically and cross-border, banks should make adequate disclosure of information on their web sites and take appropriate measures to ensure adherence to customer privacy requirements applicable in the jurisdictions to which the bank is providing e-banking services.

PRINCIPLES OF PROJECT RISK MANAGEMENT

The principles of project risk management can be stated very simply. Any project organisation is subject to risks. One which finds itself in a state of perpetual crisis, is failing to manage risks properly. Failure to manage risks is characterised by inability to decide what to do, when to do it, and whether enough has been done.

Risk Management is a facet of Quality, using basic techniques of analysis and measurement to ensure that risks are properly identified, classified, and managed. Risk management is the systematic process of managing an organization's risk exposures to achieve its objectives in a manner consistent with public interest, human safety, environmental factors, and the law. It consists of the planning, organizing, leading, coordinating, and controlling activities undertaken with the intent of providing an efficient pre-loss plan that minimizes the adverse impact of risk on the organization's resources, earnings, and cash flows. In my view the mosthelpful definition is that given by Larry Krantz, Chief Executive of Euro Log Ltd here in the UK. Larry says that 'A risk is a combination of constraint and uncertainty'. We all face constraints in our projects, and also uncertainty. So we can minimise the risk in the project either by eliminating constraints (a nice conceit) or by finding and reducing uncertainty. The illustration plots uncertainty against constraint. The curved line indicates the 'acceptable level of risk', whatever that may be in the individual case. The risk may be reduced to an acceptable level by reducing either or both of uncertainty and constraint.

In practice, few people have the opportunity to reduce constraint, so most focus on the reduction of uncertainty. It is also worth noting from the diagram that total elimination of risk is rarely achieved. So we have to consider how to manage that remaining risk most effectively. There are two stages in the process of Project Risk Management, Risk Assessment and Risk Control. Risk Assessment can take place at any time during the project, though the sooner the better. However, Risk Control cannot be effective without a previous Risk Assessment. Similarly, most people tend to think that having performed a Risk Assessment, they have done all that is needed. Far too many projects spend a great deal of effort on Risk Assessment and then ignore Risk control completely.

THREE ELEMENTS OF RISK ASSESSMENT

Identify Uncertainties

Explore the entire project plans and look for areas of uncertainty.

Analyse Risks

Specify how those areas of uncertainty can impact the performance of the project, either in duration, cost or meeting the users' requirements.

In the same way, Risk Control has three elements, as follows:

Plan for Emergencies

For all those Risks which are deemed to be significant, have an emergency plan in place before it happens.

Prioritise Risks

Establish which of those Risks should be eliminated completely, because of potential extreme impact, which should have regular management attention, and which are sufficiently minor to avoid detailed management attention.

Measure and Control

Track the effects of the risks identified and manage them to a successful conclusion.

Mitigate Risks

Take whatever actions are possible in advance to reduce the effect of Risk. It is better to spend money on mitigation than to include contingency in the plan.

ELEMENTS OF PROJECT RISK MANAGEMENT

In Project Risk Management Principles we have seen an overview of the principles involved.

This article takes a deeper view of the elements of both Risk Assessment and Risk Control, and proposes some whimsical considerations which we believe are worthy of serious thought.

Identify Uncertainties

Explore the entire project plans and look for areas of uncertainty or constraints.

It is not possible to stress too often that "The project will be late." is not a risk, it is an impact. We need to crawl over the plans to search for things which could make the project late. The risk could be expressed as "We have underestimated the likely duration of task xxx." Some examples of areas of uncertainty are:

- Failure to specify very precisely the end users' requirements
- Failure to understand who the project is for
- Failure to secure commitments from people who are needed to assist with the project
- Failure to estimate costs accurately
- Failure to appoint an executive user responsible for sponsoring the project
- Failure to tie in all the people involved in the project with contracts or Documents of Understanding
- Failure to appoint a fully qualified and supported project manager
- Failure to define the objectives of the project
- Failure to provide a good working environment for the project

Elements of Risk Assessment

We have shown these elements as three separate branches of the same tree. This is correct, but it is important to remember that the process is in fact an iterative one, and the Risk Assessment is only completed when the Assessors and Project Manager are satisfied that any undetected risks are now insignificant.

Prioritise and Analyse of Risks

By now you have really done this. Tigers have to be neutralised *i.e.* the risks must be mitigated early on. Alligators have to be watched, and there must be an action plan in place to stop them from interfering with the project. Puppies similarly have to be watched, but less stringently and with less urgent containment plans. Kittens can be ignored at the peril of the project manager. The probability of occurrence of a risk, which is another way of saying how uncertain the success of the task would be, against the Impact. By Impact we mean the severity of the effect on either the budget, the timeliness of project completion, or the ability of the project to meet the users' requirements. Whether the severity of Impact or the Probability is high or low is a matter for the judgement of the Risk Assessor and the Project Manager-even with rational method involved we are still talking of an art! We have classified the four sectors of the graph, perhaps whimsically, as:

Tigers

High Probability, High Impact. These are dangerous animals and must be neutralised as soon as possible.

Alligators

Low Probability, High Impact. These are dangerous animals which can be avoided with care. However, we all remember the old joke that it is difficult to remember when one is up to the arise in alligators that the original objective was to drain the swamp.

Puppies

High Probability, Low Impact. We all know that delightful pup will grow into an animal which can do damage, but a little training will ensure that not too much trouble ensures.

Kittens

Low Probability, Low Impact. The largest cat is rarely the source of trouble, but on the other hand a lot of effort can be wasted on training it! List each of your identified Risks, decide on the probability occurrence of each, and define the expected impact on schedule, budget, and ability to meet the users' requirements.

RISK MANAGEMENT PROCESS

Risk management is a process which could be best described as being systematic. Riskmanagement must never be taken lightly by any organization. It is designed to deal with risks that may occur in regards to any aspect of a project.

While risk management is crucially important, there are a number of additional things that project teams can do to ensure their projects are completed properly and safely. Riskmanagement can be broken down into a number of different steps, and the first of these steps is to take the time to assess the risks that a project faces. By assessing the risks, you are essentially taking the time to think of the things that could go wrong. Once you have an understanding of all the risks that a project faces, you will next need to prioritize them. By prioritizing the risks, you will essentially take the time to figure out which risks are the most important, in other words, you will rate the risk by how dangerous they are, as well as the probability of the risk actually occurring. Risk priority numbers will generally be used to determine the amount of risk the organization faces.

Once this step has been completed, the next step is to take the time to handle the abatement actions. To do this, you will need to take the time to plan and put in place the actions which are needed to lower the impact or the chance of the risk actually occurring. There are a number of different techniques that can be used within the field of risk management.

The techniques will often differ based on the manner in which the risks have been analysed. For instance, the risk could be evaluated or ranked dependent on the severity, as well as the probability of occurrence. Both effects analysis and failure mode may also be used for the purpose of analyzing and measuring risk.

No matter how you look at it, the fact remains that the risk management process is veryimportant when it comes to managing a project in the proper manner. There are often times when the risk management process must be repeated multiple times throughout the life cycle for a given project. The project team must study the risks and then prioritize them.

HOW TEAMS USE RISK MANAGEMENT?

The team which is working on the project will typically take the time to carry out riskmanagement tasks and record the things that it learned from the project. What this means is that many of the things which have been learned from past projects will need to be used in future projects.

While this takes up an enormous amount of effort, the time and money which is wasted could be saved if a certain process was available which allowed the things learned from any given project to be distributed to other projects. This process is described by a Japanese word called yokoten. In basically translates into "one place to another," meaning that information from one project is immediately transferred to other projects. This transfer of data can prove to be quite valuable. One way in which knowledge can be transferred from one project to another is simply to make use of documents such as FMEA or even the risk sheets. However, these methods can prove to be tedious and they come with a number of problems.

The problem with this method is that it requires an enormous amount of effort, because the new project will need to analyse the risk management document from all the projects which have been completed. There is also the issue of time. Sharing the information with all the concurrent projects can prove to be very challenging. Then there is the location issue. If the projects are being conducted in different locations, sharing information can be quite challenging.

AREAS IN RISK MANAGEMENT

As applied to corporate finance, risk management is the technique for measuring, monitoring and controlling the financial or operational riskon a firm's balance sheet..

- *Area 1: ERM implementation*: Many organisations are starting the implementation of their ERM programme. This will require a complete new thinking. Instead of managing different types of risk such as market risk, credit risk and operational risk as separate silos, financial institutions are bringing them together under a single enterprise-wide framework. It will also require a shift from business line aggregation to risk type aggregation of risks and exposures.
- *Area 2: Data quality*: High-quality master and reference data are central to the success of an enterprise risk- management strategy. Each of the components of enterprise risk requires different levels of data input. Other important areas are workflow management and event reporting.
- *Area 3: Systems*: High-quality master and reference data are central to the success of an enterprise. In order to better manage risk, corporations need to bring together data from systems that in the past operated as silos and have seemingly little or no relation to each other. The main challenge in this area is to bring data from different transactional systems, involving different product lines and from different jurisdictions in such a way that data will remain relevant and consistent without duplication or integrity loss.
- *Area 4: Business processes and organisation*: There will be more discussion about 'risk appetite' and 'risk tolerance', which means a greater understanding that companies need to look at their risk culture. Currently they are not yet well embedded as a management concept. There will be a better appreciation that good communication and a learning culture, with openness, lack of blame and analysis of mistakes, is the key to effective risk management. The idea of risk management being embedded in the culture of organisation is central in this context.
- *Area 5: Move from quantitative to qualitative measurement*: One of the reasons of the current financial crisis was cited as over reliance on quantitative approach. The future measurements should combine efficient expert based judgement, risk governance or proper arrangement of roles and responsibilities, stress testing and holistic view of risks. In sound stress testing, management judgement and imagination are essential to determining the scope, likelihood and severity of stress test scenarios.
- *Area 6: Strengthening of the reporting requirements*. Authorities and

boards require relevant and timely information concerning key risks that is captured by the risk reporting system to oversee the efficiency of the organisation's risk management approach.

- *Area 7: Convergence of Market and Operational risk*. Risk managers from different disciplines, especially from market and operational risk are working together to develop more forward-looking risk management approaches and techniques.

Market risk is by its nature very data-driven and already using the forward-looking tools such as scenario analysis and stress testing. In contrast to credit risk, which is still mainly driven by historical quantitative data, Operational risk did not produce sufficient historical data. Instead, the Operational risk has focused on using business specialists' knowledge and expertise to generate scenarios. These scenarios have been applied together with the existing data to produce risk measurements or projections of risk probability and severity.

LIMITATIONS OF RISK ASSESSMENT

Risk assessment is one method in a much broader field of risk management. Risk assessment is a process that does not result in a fixed final answer. It is impossible to determine the true magnitude and extent of any actual contamination at a site.

Research on the effects of chemicals on microbes, plants, animals and humans is patchy at best and confounded by factors such as:

- Variations in individual and species tolerances to the effects of contaminants;
- Environmental conditions and processes affecting the properties of the contaminant such as partitioning, transformation, degradation, temperature, pH, organic material, etc;
- Uncertainty in extrapolating study data between species and within species; and
- Large information gaps about the effects of contaminant mixtures that might have synergistic, magnifying or other effects.
- Large information gaps about the specific mechanisms and processes affecting functions and organs within the body, how these interact, and how they might be affected by a contaminant.

Our understanding of the interactions between affected individual people, plants and animals within a population, populations within a community, and communities within habitats and ecosystems is extremely limited. As a result, generally the best you can hope for is to determine some basic information about the risks posed by the site.

These include:

- Whether there are contaminants present at a site and which contaminants are present;

- Whether these contaminants are likely to have been contained on-site or might be moving off-site;
- What media the contamination has affected including water, soil, air or vegetation;
- Whether these contaminants might possibly be having an effect on microbes, plants, animals or humans; and
- What type of effect that might be.

However, by making informed, careful, and well-documented decisions through a systematic evaluation process, your ability to gauge the relative impact of a contaminant on receptors can be greatly enhanced, and the possibility of underestimating or overlooking adverse effects can be reduced.

RISK MANAGEMENT AND BUSINESS CONTINUITY

Risk management is simply a practice of systematically selecting cost effective approaches for minimising the effect of threat realization to the organization. All risks can never be fully avoided or mitigated simply because of financial and practical limitations. Therefore all organizations have to accept some level of residual risks.

Whereas risk management tends to be pre-emptive, business continuity planning was invented to deal with the consequences of realised residual risks. The necessity to have BCP in place arises because even very unlikely events will occur if given enough time. Risk management and BCP are often mistakenly seen as rivals or overlapping practices.

In fact these processes are so tightly tied together that such separation seems artificial. For example, the risk management process creates important inputs for the BCP. Risk management also proposes applicable controls for the observed risks. Therefore, risk management covers several areas that are vital for the BCP process. However, the BCP process goes beyond risk management's pre-emptive approach and assumes that the disaster will happen at some point.

RISK COMMUNICATION

Risk communication is an interactive process of exchange of information and opinion on risk among risk assessors, risk managers, and other interested parties.

Risk communication is an integral and ongoing part of the risk analysis exercise, and ideally all stakeholder groups should be involved from the start. Risk communication makes stakeholders aware of the process at each stage of the Risk Assessment.

This helps to ensure that the logic, outcomes, significance, and limitations of the Risk Assessment are clearly understood by all the stakeholders. Information may be available from the stakeholder.

Industry stakeholders may, for example have unpublished data crucial to the risk assessors, which may be an essential part of the data needed for the risk assessment. There is also information that is typically presented to the stakeholders as an integral part of the risk analysis process.

The identification of particular interest groups and their representatives should comprise a part of an overall risk communication strategy. This risk communication strategy should be discussed and agreed upon between risk assessors and managers early in the process to ensure two-way communication. This strategy should also cover who should present information to the public, and the manner in which it will be done.

Decisions on risk communication, including what, whom and how, should be part of an overall risk communication strategy. Risk communication is most effective if undertaken in a systematic way, and generally starts with the gathering of information on the risk issue of concern.

Therefore the risk manager and risk assessor must be able to briefly and clearly summarize what this issue encompasses, at an early stage, in order to elicit interest and stakeholder input Communication must then continue throughout the entire process.

Once available information has been used to fully identify the hazards, and decide on and assess the appropriate risks, then the preparation and dissemination of this information is required. This will be followed by further discussion with stakeholders, leading to corrections, amendments, and additions as appropriate, resulting in the final Risk Assessment and risk analysis reports.

COMMUNICATE YOUR IDEAS EFFECTIVELY

If you are not capable of communicating your ideas in an effective manner, then you run the risk of alienating those you are speaking to. On the opposite side of the coin, people will also become agitated if they think you're patronizing them.

The central point of this issue is that you must always have a profound understanding of your audience. It is best to offer good examples and solid information which can assist you in putting the risk into perspective. You must be capable of dealing with uncertainty, and when you talk to people about risks, the results that you get may not be that definitive. You will want to look at the actual sources of uncertainty.

You will want to explain the ways for which the data was gathered, and you will want to study the ways in which it has been analysed. It is also important to show the ways in which the results have been gathered. This shows that after the uncertainties have been showcased, this could lead to a trust increase, and this may further lead to issues which are related to credibility.

At the same time, when you talk about uncertainty, the communicator must take the time to emphasize their knowledge of the subject. This will allow the leader to handle the situation in a way that could block out concerns or fears. There is also the issue of decisions which are related to risk management.

PRINCIPLES OF RISK MANAGEMENT

Risk management is a logical process or approach that seeks to eliminate or at least minimize the level of risk associated with a business operation. Essentially, the process identifies any type of situation that could result in damage to any resource within the possession of the company, including personnel, then take steps to correct factors that are highly likely to result in that damage.

At the core of effective risk management strategies is the desire to find ways to manage the degree of uncertainty that exists within any business enterprise. The first step in the process has to do with evaluating the utilization of resources as they current stand. This step involves understanding the logical flow of the production process and how it relates to the successful manufacturing of goods and services for sale to consumers. Once there is a solid grasp of how the organization functions, it is then possible to move on to refining that process with an eye towards managing that uncertainty factor.

Once the business model is understood, it is possible to identify specific risks that are present throughout the production process, including the delivery of goods and services to buyers. As those risks are identified, they are analyzed for ways to alter the process so that the end result is still achieved, but the degree of risk is minimized or removed altogether. Risk management may be an extremely complicated process or require nothing more than making a few minor adjustments.

For example, risk management as it relates to the production process may include action items such as reworking the maintenance schedule for machinery to ensure there is less opportunity for a breakdown or malfunction. Employees may be required to wear safety goggles, gloves, or earplugs in order to ensure safety and thus minimize the chances of injury through company negligence.

Risk management not only seeks to minimize the potential for injury to employees, but also reduce the opportunity for money and other forms of finance to be abused or utilized ineffectively. By making sure that all resources are utilized in a manner that is safe, logical, and efficient, the profit margin for the company will increase and everyone associated with the company is motivated to continue production.

The actual process of risk management will vary from company to company. The focus may be on employee safety measures, or machinery maintenance. In other companies, risk management may demand revamping policies and procedures in order to rid the company environment of potential risk situations. Risk management normally requires the support of owners and the management team in order to refine the overall operation and achieve the lowest degree of risk possible. Every project manager and business leader needs to be aware of the practices and principles of effective risk management. Understanding how to identify and treat risks to an organisation, a programme or a project can save unnecessary difficulties later on, and will prepare managers and team members for any unavoidable incidences or issues.

Risk underlies and affects every decision that a business makes, and that risk management is not just risk hedging. This chapter reviews some general principles that should govern risk management.

RISK IS EVERYWHERE

Individuals and businesses have only three choices when it comes to dealing with risk. The first is to denial: do not acknowledge that risk exists and hope it goes away. In this idealized world, actions and consequences are logical and there are no unpleasant surprises. The second is fear, take the opposite tack and allow the existence of risk to determine every aspect of behaviour. Cowering behind the protection of insurance and risk hedges, you hope to be spared of its worst manifestations. Neither of these approaches puts you in any position to take advantage of risk. But there is a third choice: accept the existence of risk, be realistic about both its odds and consequences, and map out the best way to deal with it. This, in our view, is the pathway to making risk an ally rather than an adversary.

One of the reasons the study of risk is fascinating is that the nature of risk has changed and continues to change over time, making old remedies dated and requiring constant reinvention. In the last 20 years, there are three broad trends that have emerged in the shifting landscape of risk.

- *Risk is global*: As businesses, economies and markets have become global, so has risk. To illustrate the interconnectedness of markets and the possible "contagion" effects of risk, consider a small but telling example. On February 27, 2007, investors in the United States woke up to the news that stocks in Shanghai had lost 9 per cent of their value overnight. In response, not only did the Dow drop more than 400 points (about 4.3 per cent), but so did almost every other market in the world.
- *Risk cuts across businesses*: In contrast to earlier times, when risks tended to be sector focused, what happens in one sector increasingly has spillover effects on others. In early 2007, for instance, the laxity with which credit had been offered to customers with poor credit histories opened up that entire market, called the sub-prime loan market to a potential shakeout. Analysts following Yahoo, the internet search company, worried that its revenues and earnings would be hurt because so much of the advertising on web sites comes from lenders in the sub-prime market.

- *The Emergence of Financial Market Risk:* As firms have flocked to financial markets to raise both debt and equity and become increasingly sophisticated in their use of the derivatives markets, they have also made themselves more vulnerable volatility in these markets. A firm with healthy operations can be put on the defensive because of unanticipated turbulence in financial markets. Across the worlds, firms are finding that risk can and often does come from financial rather than product markets.

As risks become more international, spread across sectors and encompass both financial and product markets, it should be no surprise that firms are finder fewer and fewer safe havens. As little as 20 years ago, there were still firms that operated in relatively secure habitats, protected by governments or geography against competition. They could predict their revenues and earnings with a fair degree of certainty and could make their other decisions on how much to borrow or pay in dividends accordingly. In the United States, there were large sections of the economy that were insulated from risk; the regulated phone and power companies may not have had stellar growth but they did have solid earnings. In Europe, protection from foreign competition allowed domestic companies in each country to preserve market share and profits even in the face of more efficient competitors overseas.

There is one final point to be made about the ubiquity of risk. In the last decade especially, it can be argued that the balance of power between businesses and consumers has shifted decisively in the consumer's favour. Armed with better information and more choices, consumers are getting better terms and, in the process, lowering profits and increasing risk for businesses.

RISK IS THREAT AND OPPORTUNITY

Changing customer tastes can lay your entire market to waste or allow you to dominate a market. Business failures and large losses come from exposures to large risks but so do large profits and lasting successes.

The trouble with risk management is that people see one side or the other of risk and respond accordingly. Those who see the bad side of risk, *i.e.* the danger side, either argue that it should be avoided or push for protection (through hedging and insurance) against it. On the other side are those who see risk as upside and argue for more risk taking, not less. Not surprisingly, their very different perspectives on risk will lead these groups to be on opposite sides of almost every debate, with the other side tarred as either "stuck in the mud" or "imprudent".

Risk is a combination of potential upside with significant downside and requires a more nuanced approach. If we accept the proposition that we cannot have one (upside) without the other (downside), we can become more realistic about how we approach and deal with risk. We can also move towards a consensus on which risks we should seek out, because the upside exceeds the downside, and which risks are imprudent, not because we do not like to take risk but because the downside exceeds the upside.

MANAGING RISK IS A HUMAN ENDEAVOUR

In keeping with risk being a combination of danger and opportunity, we, as human beings, have decidedly mixed feelings about its existence. On the one hand we fear it and its consequences while on the other we seek it out, hoping to share in the profits. We see this in the behaviour of both investors and businesses, as they seesaw wildly from taking too much risk in one period to too little in the next.

While the traditional theory on risk has been built on the premise of the "risk averse" rational investor with a well-behaved preference function, studies of actual risk taking behaviour suggest that our attitudes towards risk taking are more complicated. To begin with, it is true that we are generally risk averse, but the degree of risk aversion varies widely across the population. More troublingly, though, risk aversion seems to vary for the same individual, depending upon how choices are framed and the circumstances of the choice. For instance, an individual who is normally risk averse can become risk seeking when given a chance to make back money lost on a prior gamble. In fact, behavioural economics and finance have developed as disciplines largely on the basis of findings such as these that suggest that our behaviour when confronted with risk is not always rational, at least as defined in classical economics, and often predictable.

Principle 3: Managing risk is a human endeavor and a risk management system is only as good as the people manning it.

NOT ALL RISK IS CREATED EQUAL

Risk comes from different sources, takes different forms and has different consequences but not all risk is created equal when it comes to how it affects value and it should be managed. To provide one very concrete example, most conventional risk and return models draw a line between risks that affect one or a few firms and are thus diversifiable and risks that affect many or all firms and are not diversifiable. Only the latter risk is rewarded in these models, on the assumption that investors in firms are diversified and can mitigate their exposure to the former.

In fact, there are a number of other dimensions on which we can categorize risk with implications for risk management.

- *Small versus Large Risks:* Risks can be small or large, depending upon the potential impact that they can have on a firm's value. A small risk can be ignored or passed through to investors with little or no worry, but a large risk may need to be assessed and managed carefully because of its potential to cause the firm's demise. Given that size is relative, it is entirely possible that the same risk can be small to one firm while being large to another.

- *Symmetric versus Asymmetric risks:* While we described risk as a combination of danger and opportunity, the upside and the downside are not necessarily symmetric. Some risks offer a small chance of a "very large" upside with a high probability of a "limited downside" whereas other risks offer the opposite combination. Why would it matter? In addition to feeding into some established quirks in risk aversion (loss aversion and a preference for large positive payoffs, for instance), it has implication for whether the risk will be managed (risks with very large downside are more likely to be insured, even if the probability is small) and how we manage it (whether we use derivatives, futures or insurance).
- *Short term versus Long term:* There are some risks that manifest themselves in the near term whereas other risks take longer to have an effect on firm value. Depending upon what they see as their competitive advantages, firms may try to exploit long term risks and protect themselves against short term risks.
- *Continuous versus Discontinuous:* There is some risk that firms are exposed to continuously and have consequences over even small time periods – exchange rates can changes and interests rates can move up or down over the next minute. Other risks, such as damage from a terrorist incident or a hurricane, occur infrequently but can create significant damage. While different risk hedging tools exist for each, it can be argued that discontinuous risk is both more damaging and more difficult to hedge.

A risk inventory, where we listed all potential risks facing a firm, was a good beginning to the risk management process. Breaking the risks down into its components – firm specific or market, small or large, symmetric or asymmetric (and if so in what way), continuous versus discontinuous and short term or long term – will make the risk inventory a more useful tool in risk management.

The saying that risk is in the eye of the beholder does have a foundation. After all, we can look at the risk in an investment through the eyes of the immediate decision makers (the line managers), their superiors (the top managers) or investors in that firm (who are often mutual funds or pension funds).

As a generalization, risks that seems huge to middle managers may not seem as large to top managers, who bring a portfolio perspective to the process, and be inconsequential to investors in the firm, who have the luxury of having diversification work its wonders for them.

RISK CAN BE MEASURED

There is a widespread belief even among risk managers that some risks are too qualitative to be assessed. This notion that some risks cannot be evaluated, either because the likelihood of occurrence is very small or the consequences too unpredictable can be dangerous, since these are exactly the types of risks that have the potential to create damage. The debate should be about what tools to use to assess risk rather than whether they can be assessed. At the risk of sounding dogmatic, all risks can and should be assessed, though the ease and method of assessment can vary across risks.

There are two keys to good risk assessment. The first is better quality and more timely information about the risks as they evolve, so that the element of surprise is reduced.

The second is tools such as risk-adjusted discount rates, simulations, scenario analysis and VaR to convert the raw data into risk measures. On both, it can be argued that we are better off than we were in earlier generations. There is more information available to decision makers, with a larger portion of it being provided in real time. The tools available have also become more accessible and sophisticated, with technology lending a helping hand. Thus, a Monte Carlo simulation that would have been required the services of a mainframe computer and been prohibitively costly thirty years ago can be run on a personal computer with a very modest outlay.

The advances in risk assessment should not lead to false complacency or to the conclusion that risk management has become easier as a consequence for three reasons. First, the risks being assessed are also becoming more global and complex and it is an interesting question as to whether the improvements in information and assessment are keeping up with the evolution of risk. Second, risk management is still a relative game. In other words, it is not just how well a business or investor assesses risk that matters, but how well it does it relative to the competition. The democratization of information and tools has levelled the playing field and made it possible for small firms to take on much larger and more resource-rich competitors. Third, as both the data and the tools become more plentiful, picking the right tool to assess a risk (and it can be different for different risks) has become a more critical component of success at risk management.

GOOD RISK MEASUREMENT/ASSESSMENT

Superior information and the best tools for risk assessment add up to little, if they do not lead to better decisions when faced with risk. In many businesses, those who assess risk are not necessarily those who make decisions (often based on those risk assessments) and this separation can lead to trouble. In particular, risk assessment tools are often not tailored to the needs of decision makers and are often misread or misused as a consequence.

The problems have their roots in why we assess risk in the first place. There are some who believe that assessing risk is equivalent to eliminating it and thus feel more secure with an analysis that is backed up by a detailed and sophisticated risk assessment. There are others who use risk assessments, not to make better decisions, but as cover, if things do not work out as anticipated. Still others think that risk assessment will make them more comfortable, when they have to make their final judgements. The reality is that risk assessment makes us aware of risk but does not eliminate it, and cannot be used as an excuse for poor decisions. Finally, the irony of good risk assessment is that it may actually make you more uncomfortable as a decision maker rather than less; more information can often lead to more uncertainty rather than less.

For risk assessments to lead to better decisions, there are three things that we need to do better:

(1) If risk is assessed and decisions are made are by different entities, each one has to be aware of the other's requirements and preferences. Thus, risk assessors have to understand what decision makers see as the major issues, and tailor both the tools chosen and the output to these needs and constraints. At the same time, those who make decisions have to recognize the flaws and limitations of the information used by risk assessors and understand at least the broad contours of the tools being used to assess risk.

(2) The risk assessment tools have to be built around the risks that matter rather than all risks. We are faced with dozens of risks, of different types and with different consequences and some of these risks matter far more than others. Keeping risk assessment focused on that which matters will make it more useful to decision makers; a shorter, more focused risk assessment is more useful than one that is comprehensive but rambling.

(3) Risk assessment should not become an exercise in testing out only the downside or the bad side of risk, even though that may be what worries decision makers the most. A good risk assessment will hold true to the complete measure of risk and provide a picture of both upside potential and downside risk.

In short, for risk assessment to work, decision makers need to both understand and be involved in the risk assessment process, and risk assessors should not be shut out of the decision making process. The fact that the former tend to be higher in the management hierarchy can make this a difficult task.

DECIDE WHICH RISKS TO AVOID

Investors and businesses face a myriad of risks and it is easy to be overwhelmed. The underlying fundamentals for making these choices are not complicated. You begin with the judgement on which risk or risks you want to exploit because you believe you have a advantage – better information, speedier response, more flexibility or better resources – over your competition.

Looking at the risks you choose not to exploit, you have to weigh the costs of protecting yourself against a risk against the potential benefits from the protection – tax benefits, lower distress costs and a more rational decision making process.

There are some risks that you may be able to reduce or eliminate through the normal course of your operations and thus are costless to hedge, but there are other risks that are costly to hedge. For these risks, the choice becomes complicated especially for publicly traded companies, since they have to compare the costs that they, as companies, would face to the costs that investors in their companies would face to eliminate the same risks. It is this comparison that would lead us to conclude that publicly traded firms are usually better off passing through a significant portion of their firm-specific risk and even exchange rate risk to their investors, rather than incur costs to hedge them.

There are some risks, though, where the company is in a better position than its investors in assessing and hedging the risks. For instance, Being has much more information about its exchange rate risk exposure on individual contracts with foreign airlines than its investors, and be able to hedge those risks more efficiently.

PAYOFF TO BETTER RISK MANAGEMENT

Risk managers are measured and judged on a number of different dimensions, but the only dimension that matters is how it impacts the value of the business. Good risk management increases value, whereas bad risk management destroys value. Choosing any other measure or objective can only distort the process. Consider a few alternatives.

If the success of risk management is measured by how much risk it eliminates from the process, the logical end product is that too little risk will be exploited and too much hedged. That is why firms that focus on reducing earnings or stock price volatility or the deviation from analyst forecasts will end up mismanaging risk. What about a higher stock price? It is true that in an efficient market, stock price and the value of equity move hand in hand, but there are two problems with a stock-price focus.

The first is that in an inefficient market, where investors may focus on the short term or on the wrong variables (earnings variability, for instance) there may be a positive market response to poor risk management decisions. That response will fade over time, but the managers who made the decisions would have been rewarded and have moved on (or up) by then. The second is that the value of a business includes the value of its equity and other claimholders in the firm (lenders, in particular). Decisions relating to risk often alter the balance between debt and equity, and can sometimes make stockholders better off at the expense of lenders. Hence, the focus should be on the value of the business in its entirety rather than just the equity investors.

So, how do we link risk management to value? To begin with, we need much richer valuation models than the ones in use that tend to put all of the focus (at least when it comes to risk) on the discount rate. All of the inputs in a conventional vauaiton model, from cash flows to growth rates to the length of the growth period should be a function of how well risk is managed in the firm. Only then can we see the full impact on value of increasing exposure to some risks and the consequences of hedging or passing through others. Given that most analysts value firms using earnings multiples and comparables, we need to also consider ways in which we can incorporate the full effects of risk management into these comparisons as well.

RISK MANAGEMENT IS PART OF EVERYONE'S JOB

For decades, risk management was viewed as a finance function, with the CFO playing the role of risk measurer, assessor and punisher (for those who crossed defined risk limits). In keeping with this definition, risk management become focused entirely on risk assessment and risk hedging. The elevation of strategic risk management or enterprise risk management in businesses, with its willingness to consider the upside of risk, has come with one unfortunate side cost. Many firms have a person or group in charge of risk management, given primary responsibility for coordinating and managing risk through the organization. While we applaud the recognition given to risk management, it has also led others in the firm, especially in the other functional areas, to think that the existence of a risk management group has relieved them of the responsibility of having to play a role in managing risk.

While there are some aspects of risk management – risk assessment mechanics and hedging – that may be finance-related and thus logically embedded in treasury departments, there are many aspects of risk management, especially risk taking, that cut across functional areas. Taking advantage of shifts in customer tastes for a retailer requires the skills of the marketing and advertising departments. Exploiting technological change to revamp production facilities is not something that the treasury department can do much about but is more the domain of the operations department. In short, every decision made by a firm in any functional area has a risk management component. While we need a centralized group to aggregate these risks and look at the portfolio, individual decision makers have to be aware of how their decisions play out in the big picture.

GOOD ORGANIZATIONAL STRUCTURE FOR SUCCESS

A lot of moving pieces have to work together consistently for risk management to succeed. The challenge is greater if the success has to be repeated period after period. Not surprisingly, firms that succeed at risk management plan for and are organize to deliver that success.

Some of the ingredients of the consistently successful risk taking organization:

a. *Alignment of interests:* The key challenge in any firm, especially a large publicly traded one, is that decision making is spread through the organization and different decision makers have different interests. Some managers are motivated by rewards, in compensation tied to profits or stock prices, whereas others may be motivated by fear that failure may lead to loss of a job. The decisions that they make may reflect those desires or fears and have little to do with what is good for the overall business. To the extent that the interests of different decision makers within the firm can be aligned with those of the owners of the firm with carrots (equity options, stock grants etc) or sticks (stronger corporate governance), risk management has a much better chance of succeeding.
b. *Good and timely information*: Information is the lubricant for good risk management. If reliable information can be provided in a timely fashion to decision makers who are confronted with risk, they can (though they don't always do) make better decisions.
   The question of how best to design information systems in the last decade has sometimes becomes a debate about information technology but really should be focused on improving the response to risk. The test of a good information system should be how well it works during crises at delivering needed information to analysts and decision makers.
c. *Solid analysis*: Information, even if it is reliable and timely, is still just data. That data has to be analyzed and presented in a way that makes better decisions possible.
   Having access to analytical tools such as decision trees and simulations is part of the process but understanding how the tools work and choosing between them is the more difficult component of success.
d. *Flexibility*: If there is one common theme shared by all successful risk takers, it is that they are flexible in their responses to change. They adapt to changed circumstances faster than their competitors, either because they built in flexibility into their original design or because they have the technological or financial capacity to do so. Having a flat organizational structure, being a smaller organization or having less vested in existing technologies all seem to be factors that add to flexibility.

e. *People*: Ultimately, good risk management is dependent on having the right people in the right places when crisis strikes. Good risk taking organizations seek out people who respond well to risk and retain them with a combination of financial rewards (higher pay, bigger bonuses) and non-financial incentives (culture and team dynamics),

POSITIVE RISK MANAGEMENT

Positive Risk Management is an approach that recognizes the importance of the human factor and of individual differences in propensity for risk taking. It draws from the work of a number of academics and professionals who have expressed concerns about scientific rigour of the wider risk management debate, or who have made a contribution emphasizing the human dimension of risk.

Firstly, it recognizes that any object or situation can be rendered hazardous by the involvement of someone with an inappropriate disposition towards risk; whether too risk taking or too risk averse.

Secondly, it recognizes that risk is an inevitable and ever present element throughout life: from conception through to the point at the end of life when we finally lose our personal battle with life threatening risk.

Thirdly, it recognizes that every individual has a particular orientation towards risk; while at one extreme people may by nature be timid, anxious and fearful, others will be adventurous, impulsive and almost oblivious to danger. These differences are evident in the way we drive our cars, in our diets, in our relationships, in our careers.

Finally, Positive Risk Management recognizes that risk taking is essential to all enterprise, creativity, heroism, education, scientific advance – in fact to any activity and all the initiatives that have contributed to our evolutionary success and civilization. It is worth noting how many enjoyable activities involve fear and willingly embrace risk taking.

Within the entire Risk Management literature you will find little or no reference to the human part of the risk equation other than what might be implied by the term 'compliant'. This illustrates the narrow focus that is a hall mark of much current risk management practice. This situation arises from the basic premises of traditional risk management and the practices associated with health and safety within the working environment. There is a basic logic to the idea that any accident must reflect some kind of oversight or situational predisposition that, if identified, can be rectified. But, largely due to an almost institutionalised neglect of the human factor, this situationally focused paradigm has grown tendrils that reach into every corner of modern life and into situations where the unintended negative consequences threaten to outweigh the benefits.

Positive Risk Management views both risk taking and risk aversion as complementary and of equal value and importance within the appropriate context. As such, it is seen as complementary to the traditional risk management paradigm. It introduces a much needed balance to risk management practices and puts greater onus on management skills and decision making. It is the dynamic approach of the football manager who appreciates the offensive and defensive talents within the available pool of players. Every organisation has roles better suited to risk takers and roles better suited to the risk averse. The task of management is to ensure that the right people are placed in each job. The graveyard of former greats is littered with examples where the balance of risk went seriously awry; the ENRON and RBS stories have become iconic references in the pantheon of corporate governance and corporate mortality. Eastman Kodak might be a nominee for the opposite pole – the corporately risk averse.

Positive Risk Management relies on the ability to identify individual differences in propensity for risk taking. The science in this area has been developing rapidly over the past decade within the domain of personality assessment. Once an area of almost tribal allegiance to different schools of thought, today there is wide spread consensus about the structure of personality assessment and its status within the framework of the cross disciplinary progress being made in our understanding of Human Nature. The Five Factor Model (FFM) of personality has been shown to have relevance across many different cultures, to remain consistent over adult working life and to be significantly heritable. Within this framework there are many strands which have a clear relationship to risk tolerance and risk taking.

RISK MANAGEMENT PROGRAMME

Risk Management is a research programme set up by the Geneva Association, also known as the International Association for the Study of Insurance Economics. The focus of this programme is manifold and address the following issues: fostering the use of the tools of risk assessment and risk management in new fields of application such as policy making; providing a platform between the insurance community, the engineering and academic communities and policy makers to discuss risk issues; promoting the concept of the insurability of risks as the natural borderline between State legislation and the market economy; identifying new opportunities for insurers in the emerging sustainability concept in order to enlarge the field of insurable risks.

SELECTED KEY ISSUES

- What are the vulnerabilities in our industrial and services value-added processes?
- Where are the mechanisms for understanding, managing and mitigating these risks?
- How can insurance cope with a more complex and demanding risk scenario?

- What is the new risk environment that has been created in recent years?
- What about technologies being a new source of vulnerability?

Publications

- *Risk Management*, Geneva Association Information Newsletter, The Geneva Association
- *Etudes et Dossiers*, Working Paper Series, The Geneva Association
- *The Geneva Risk and Insurance Review*, formerly The Geneva Papers on Risk and Insurance Theory (until March 2005), The Geneva Association and Springer
- *Pensions and Life Insurance* and *Risk Management/M.O.R.E*, The Geneva Papers on Risk and Insurance-Issues and Practice, Vol.29-No.3/July 2004, Palgrave Macmillan
- *Special Issue on Risk Management*, The Geneva Papers on Risk and Insurance-Issues and Practice, Vol.27-No.2/April 2002, Palgrave Macmillan
- *Strategic Issues in Risk Management and Insurance*, The Geneva Papers on Risk and Insurance-Issues and Practice, Vol.24-No.3/July 1999, Palgrave Macmillan
- *Issues in Risk Management and Insurance*, The Geneva Papers on Risk and Insurance-Issues and Practice, Vol.24-No.2/April 1999, Palgrave Macmillan.
- *Risk Management Strategies*, The Geneva Papers on Risk and Insurance-Issues and Practice, No.80/July 1996
- *Risk Management Issues*, The Geneva Papers on Risk and Insurance-Issues and Practice, No.76/July 1995
- *1973-1993 Twenty Years of Initiatives and Research on the Economic Role of Insurance and Risk Management in Modern Society*, The Geneva Papers on Risk and Insurance-Issues and Practice, No.68/July 1993
- *Risk Management Studies*, The Geneva Papers on Risk and Insurance-Issues and Practice, No.64/July 1992
- *Hazardous Waste Management*, The Geneva Papers on Risk and Insurance-Issues and Practice, No.51/April 1989
- *Risk and Society*, *The Discount Rate* and *Risk and Insurance Issues*, The Geneva Papers on Risk and Insurance-Issues and Practice, No.48/July 1988
- *Risk and Insurance Issues*, The Geneva Papers on Risk and Insurance-Issues and Practice, No.44/July 1987.

RISK MANAGEMENT TOOLS

Risk Management is a non-intuitive field of study, where the most simple of models consist of a probability multiplied by an impact. Even understanding individual risks is difficult as multiple probabilities can contribute to Risk total probability, and impacts can be "units" of cost, time, events (for example, a catastrophe), market states, etc. This is further complicated by there being no straightforward approach to consider how multiple risks will influence one another or increase the overall risk of the subject of analysis.

Risk management tools allow planners to explicitly address uncertainty by identifying and generating metrics, parameterizing, prioritizing, and developing mitigations, and tracking risk. These capabilities are very difficult to track without some form of documentation or, with the advent of information technology, software application. Simple risk management tools allow documentation. More sophisticated tools provide a visual display of risks, while the most cutting edge, such as those developed by Air Force Research Laboratory Headquarters, are able to aggregate risks into a coherent picture. A few tools have predictive capability, which, through collaboration between partners allow fair partition of risks and improvement of business relations.

The following is a list of risk management tools.

Risk-performs risk analysis using Monte Carlo simulation to show many possible outcomes in Microsoft Excel spreadsheet—and predicts how likely they are to occur.

Active Risk Manager-(ARM), addresses enterprise-wide risk management (ERM) and governance, risk and compliance (GRC) requirements, enabling the identification, communication, analysis and mitigation of risks and opportunities in both quantitative and qualitative formats.

The Aggregate Risk Tool-(ART), generates predictive financial data from any probability-impact model.

Bow tie diagrams-a fault identifying visual tool.

Capital asset pricing model-(CAPM) is used to determine the appropriate required rate of return of an asset, if that asset be added to an already well diversified portfolio, based on non-diversifiable risk.

Control Estratégico de Riesgo (CERO)-Software tool with specific tools for each activity of the risk management process. With clients mostly in Latin America.

Cost/Risk Identification and Management System (CRIMS)-Integrated Probabilistic risk assessment model with cost and other variables.

Crystal Ball-performs risk analysis using Monte Carlo simulation, analyzes time series and creates statistical forecasts, and determines the best values of decision variables based on stochastic optimization, all in a Microsoft Excel spreadsheet.

Cura Enterprise-Cura's GRC platform is a highly configurable solution that meets organizational requirements, and provides a balance between qualified and quantified data, all of which can be normalized and reported on across the entire organization. Cura Quants-Is a quantitative modelling solution designed to integrate with the existing Enterprise GRC Platform. Cura Quants enables customers to quickly and easily quantify the impact of capital and project related risks as well as the effects of accompanying treatment strategies.

Dymonda-Dymonda is a software tool that enables Dynamic Flowgraph Methodology (DFM) modelling and analysis. The model explicitly identifies the cause-and-effect and timing relationships between parameters and states that are best suited to describe a particular system behaviour.

Resolve by RPM"'-Cloud software toolbox to manage, track and audit processes associated with risk and safety areas within corporations.

IBM OpenPages GRC Platform-Integrated enterprise governance, risk and compliance solution that includes modules for operational risk management, policy and compliance management, financial controls management, IT governance, and internal audit management

Methodware-Methodware's ERA is a GRC solution that is a scalable,and flexible tool to automate,identify and track risk across departments, regions, and business units effectively.transparency

Operational risk management-The continual cyclic process which includes risk assessment, risk decision making, and implementation of risk controls, which results in acceptance, mitigation, or avoidance of risk.

PIMS Risk-Is a complete risk framework for identifying, analysing and evaluate threats and opportunities. Created for and used by major companies in oil and energy sector.

Probabilistic risk assessment (PRA), Probability Consequence (P/C) or Probability Impact Model-Simple model where estimates of probability of occurrence are multiplied by the consequence (cost, schedule delay, etc.). This is the most common tool, examples are RiskNav and RiskMatrix.

Reference class forecasting – Predicts the outcome of a planned, risky action based on actual outcomes in a reference class of similar actions to that being forecast.

RiskAid products-collaborative web/intranet-based risk management software environments for projects, operations and Enterprise Risk Management (ERM), developed by Risk Reasoning.

RiskAoA – A predictive tool used to discriminate between proposals, choices or alternatives, by expressing risk for each as a single number, so a proposal's trade-space between cost, scheduled time and risk from its desired characteristics can be compared instantly.

RiskAoA and variations of PRA are the only approved tools for United States Department of Defence Military Acquisition.

RiskComplete-Tracks project risk from planning approached to measuring tasks, from concept to manufacture. RiskIssue.com-An online risk management tool for business, projects, teams and processes.

RiskLike'Con-A free probabilistic risk assessment tool. Displays risks in the industry-standard matrix; Probability vs. Consequence.

Risk register-A project planning and organizational risk assessment tool. It is often referred to as a Risk Log.

RiskPath-An improvement of RiskAoA, available to the public, where forecasts are quantified for each alternative.

Safety case-An assessment of the potential risks in a project and of the measures to be taken to minimize them.

SAPHIRE-A probabilistic risk and reliability assessment software tool. SAPHIRE stands for Systems Analysis Programmes for Hands-on Integrated Reliability Evaluations.

SCHRAM-The Schedule Risk Assessment Manager; allows the generation of risk-adjusted schedules; the time of least risk, consequence of rushed/broken schedules.

Allows realistic planning based on operational realities.

TRIMS-Provides insight as a knowledge-based tool that measures technical risk management rather than cost and schedule.

Unified Risk Assessment and Regulatory Compliance-A standards based end-to-end comprehensive cloud service from Unisys that performs model based risk assessment and also provides a real time dashboard for Regulatory and Policy Compliance traceability and transparency.

Xero Risk-Web based enterprise risk governance tool to identify, track and balance risks across an organization using user definable assessment and impact criteria.

RISK REGISTER

A risk register is a tool commonly used in project planning and organisational risk assessments. It is often referred to as a Risk Log (for eg in PRINCE2).

This tool is widely used within Risk Management for identifying, analysing and managing risks. In this context a project risk is essentially an uncertain event that, should it occur, will have an impact on the project (this could be positive or negative).

It contains the information on the identified and collected project risks that the project team identifies when estimating and adjusting the activity durations for risks.

The project team considers the extent to which the effects of risks are included in the baseline duration estimate for each schedule activity, particularly the risks with high impact.

Example Contents

A wide range of contents for a risk register exist and recommendations are made by the Project Management Institute Body of Knowledge (PMBOK) and PRINCE2 among others. In addition many companies provide software tools that act as risk registers. Typically a risk register contains:

- A description of the risk
- The impact should this event actually occur
- The probability of its occurrence
- Risk score is multiplication of Probability and Impact
- A summary of the planned response should the event occur
- A summary of the mitigation (the actions taken in advance to reduce the probability and/or impact of the event)
- The risks are often given a ranking with the highest priority risks clearly identified to all involved.

RISK MANAGEMENT PLANNING

At the heart of Risk Management Planning is information. Planning in risk management is not possible without understanding where and how your entity is exposed to risk, how those exposures relate to your organization's goals and objectives and the expected effect of all possible methods of treatment - acceptance, avoidance, mitigation and transfer - on both the specific risk and on organizational objectives.

Effective risk management planning requires an accurate description of the risk and its causes, the impact should an adverse event occur and the identities of the risk owners and their assigned responsibilities. Documentation can be critical. Owners of risk must understand the treatment of each risk and the actions necessary to implement those treatments.

Most of the information so vital to effective risk management planning is generated during the risk assessment. A risk assessment identifies risk, measures its potential impact - including any impact on an organization's objectives. Risk assessment is a cornerstone among the principles of risk management.

RISK MANAGEMENT SERVICES

From simple lost sales to a major disaster, exposure to risk is a business reality. Your risk management measures should be as real as the issues they are meant to address. Our experts are here to help.

What level of support do you need? Our risk management consultants are seasoned professionals who provide excellent service and the most up to date risk management training. We can even embed our experts directly into your business.

Risk Management: Risk Assessment

Our experienced risk management consultants will work with you to identify and quantify your exposure to risk. We provide detailed summaries that define your risk and effective risk management strategies to help you control events that could result in loss. Our special focus partners are niche experts that can furnish reviews and recommendations in areas such as credit, finance and information technology at risk.

Loss happens. But, it can be managed, mitigated, reduced, and in some cases avoided altogether. Our team of risk management experts can help you reduce potential losses.

We can help you establish proactive mitigation in the form of risk management programmes that can reduce the frequency and severity of events such as workplace accidents, loss of property and more. We can also help you to establish a business continuity plan that will help you get back in business in the event of a major disaster.

Our risk management services include evaluating your business objectives and current conditions to prioritize your efforts and minimize your risk management insurance cost.

The effective use of deductibles, retentions and appropriate policy limits can ensure that your earnings are protected at the lowest cost. We will review financial alternatives with you to be certain that your risk management strategy firmly safeguards your earnings.

RISK MANAGEMENT SOLUTIONS

The right Risk Management Solution for your business is the one tailored to your services, practices, objectives, risk profile and risk appetite. Our approach to risk management is an in depth procedural method to assist you in selecting from a broad range of services to be sure that you get exactly what you need based on your specific circumstances.

Risk Management Strategy

Through discussions with executive management and stakeholders, we can help you define your risk management strategy. That strategy becomes the guiding force in the decisions made by managers at all organizational levels, from parents to subsidiaries to partners.

Effective risk management solutions identify your at risk areas, quantify potential loss and establish plans for control and migation. Our solutions include establishing controls and safeguards for all of your areas at risk. We'll help you to ensure the stability of your business.

Our risk management consultants methodically identify potential losses, evaluate risk control and risk financing alternatives and assist you in the implementation of corrective actions. We will develop a customized programme that ensures you are getting the most value from your account team and from your risk management dollars.

RISK MANAGEMENT STRATEGY

Developing a complete Risk Management Strategy means generating an organized approach for treatment of all exposures to risk from the organizational perspective. Following a risk management assessment, following the planning of specific treatments for specific risks, an organization must develop a comprehensive risk management strategy for treating risk that best serves the objectives and goals of the organization as a whole.

Risk Management Strategy: Challenges

Through the assessment, analysis and planning stages, such treatments as avoidance, retention, reduction and transfer will have been evaluated for specific risks. Evaluating the effect of these treatments on organizational objectives, in light of organizational priorities, can be a difficult and time consuming endeavor. Getting it right is one of the most difficult challenges when developing a risk management strategy.

Tailored Risk Management Solutions

Our experienced risk management professionals have served as consultants for a number of Fortune 1000 clients, many multi-national, and can be invaluable in helping you shape your risk management strategy to best serve organizational goals and objectives. Your risk management strategy should be and - with our risk management expertise - can be tailored to your exact needs.

RISK MANAGEMENT TRAINING

Risk Management Training can provide decision makers and managers the skills needed to perform their risk related duties effectively. When your managers and decision makers lack specific risk management expertise, invest in them. Provide them with risk management training.

In most organizations, those pressed into the role of risk managers have backgrounds in everything other than risk management. Many owners of risk are decision makers in their own departments who have little if any experience with risk management concepts, methods and goals. Risk management training can help you keep your key people in key positions while expanding their capabilities.

Simple: Anyone charged with identifying, reporting, evaluating or managing an exposure to risk needs risk management training. Your executives, managers, project managers, decision makers and systems specialists are typically responsible for some aspect of your organization's overall risk management effort. You can best protect your organization from risk by providing them the skills necessary to perform their risk management related tasks. Risk management is intended to minimize the cost associated with certain types of risk and provide prudent protection. The maintenance of appropriate leve ls of necessary insurance coverage is a key aspect in the risk management process. It deals with pure risks that are characterized by chance occurrence and may only result in a financial loss, as opposed to a speculative risk which affords the opportunity for financial gain or loss. Such pure risks are separated into three major exposure categories: liability, property, and personnel. There are three stages in the risk management process: risk identification and analysis, risk control, and risk treatment.

Identification and analysis requires a review of all aspects of the bank's present and prospective operations to determine where the bank is exposed to loss, including consultation with a reliable insurance professional. Risk control is primarily dependent upon the strength of the bank's internal controls, policies and procedures. Risk treatment refers to choosing the appropriate steps or methods to deal with a particular risk. The objective of this process is to minimize the probability of losses and costs associated with them, such as direct costs of loss prevention measures, insurance premiums, losses sustained, and related administrative expenses. A bank has several options in treating a particular risk. It can implement additional controls to minimize yet retain the risk (*i.e.* become a self insurer), transfer the risk to another party through insurance or contractual transfer, or utilize a combination of both of these approaches. A basic tenet of risk management is that those risks which carry the potential for catastrophic or significant loss should not be retained, if avoidable. Conversely, it is not cost justified to insure losses which are relatively predictable and not severe.

The board of directors must determine the maximum loss the bank is willing and able to assume, and should perform an annual review of the bank's risk and insurance management programme. The real value of insurance lies in the protection it affords against catastrophic losses. To the extent a bank does not have adequate coverage, losses deplete capital and impair the position of depositors and the FDIC. Examiner review and analysis of the adequacy of the bank's insurance programme is clearly necessary. The various types of insurance coverage serve only as a guide and a reference of available insurance protection. The specific needs of a bank must be determined on an individual basis, and only by reviewing each policy in force, can the actual degree of coverage and protection be determined. Any material inadequacies of insurance coverage should be directed to management's attention. Lack of any significant coverage, board of director approval and review, or deficiencies in a bank's loss prevention programme should be appropriately commented upon in the Report of Examination.

FIDELITY INSURANCE PROTECTION

Fidelity insurance protection is appropriate for all banks because it insures against certain risks that contain the potential for significant loss. Section 18(e) of the Federal Deposit Insurance Act (FDI Act) provides that the FDIC may require such coverage, and if it is not obtained, may contract for such protection and add the cost to the bank's deposit insurance assessment.

However, such action would only be taken in rare instances, such as when a bank is able to obtain protection but refuses to do so.

If the bank is without coverage, a thorough investigation should be made to determine the reasons insurance protection is lacking. Such banks must continue diligent, good faith efforts to obtain reasonably priced coverage. Their efforts should be monitored periodically to confirm the actions being taken to obtain coverage, including steps necessary to satisfy any conditions that may have been imposed by an insurer as a prerequisite for coverage. In some cases, a bank may offer alternate arrangements in lieu of the usual insurance bond.

While it is difficult to generalize, these arrangements (i. e. having directors or owners sign personal guarantees or increasing the bank's capital) do not protect the bank against the same risks in essentially the same manner or to the same extent, and therefore, are generally not acceptable as substitutes for insurance coverage.

However, each such offer should be appraised on its merits for whatever additional protection it might provide in the interim. While a periodic review of internal and external security measures and controls is warranted in every bank, it is especially appropriate in a bank that is operating without fidelity insurance coverage.

Ideally, this effort should be undertaken as a special project with responsibility fixed in a particular executive officer. Further, it should include a comprehensive review of the bank's existing programmes, the design and implementation of additional security procedures and controls, and a formal report to the board of directors, with any actions taken by the board based on the report findings noted in the minutes of the meeting. Management should also consider using outside experts, as necessary, to assist in strengthening internal programmes or possibly to help the bank qualify for fidelity protection where a carrier has previously cited specific deficiencies that require correction.

Insurance Carrier

Occasionally, a bank may ask to release all or part of an examination report to an insurance carrier. These enquiries should be discouraged. A bank should be able to demonstrate its insurability to prospective insurers without having to release confidential information from an FDIC examination report. Adequate information is available from the bank's records and from non-confidential sources to enable an insurer to accurately assess its underwriting risk.

INTERNAL HAZARDS

External hazard includes the possibility of dishonest, fraudulent, or criminal acts committed against the bank and its employees by the general public. Robbery, burglary, and forgery are the predominate acts. Banks endeavor to guard against losses from these sources by maintaining vaults and safes, reliable alarm systems, and other security devices which should, at a minimum, meet the requirements set forth in Part 326 of the FDIC's Rules and Regulations. Banks should also attempt to limit the size of such losses by keeping exposed cash and negotiable securities at a minimum. Internal hazard, which poses a far greater risk, deals with the possibility of defalcations by the bank's own personnel. Banks should try to protect themselves against this hazard by maintaining clear records and effective systems of internal routine and controls. The maintenance of an appropriate level of insurance coverage helps to further limit the institution's level of risk related to employee defalcations and other types of internal fraud.

BOND INSURANCE

The most common form of blanket bond used by commercial and savings banks is the Financial Institution Bond, Standard Form No. 24. Other forms may be encountered and should be thoroughly analyzed to determine the extent of coverage. Standard Form No. 24 has two different limits of liability a single loss limit of liability and an aggregate limit of liability. The single loss limit applies to individual claims, whereas the aggregate limit applies to the total of all loss recoverable under the bond. For example, if there is a $500,000 single loss limit and a $1,000,000 aggregate limit, payment of the single loss reduces available coverage for further losses during the bond period to $500,000. When the aggregate limit of liability is exhausted, the bond automatically terminates regardless of the remaining term and without any refund of premium. In order to determine the remaining insurance coverage, the amounts of all prior and pending claims against the bond should be deducted from the stated aggregate limit.

4

Advances in Purchasing Risk Management

INTRODUCTION

Purchasing management directs the flow of goods and services in a company and handles all data relating to contact with suppliers. Effective purchasing management requires knowledge of the supply chain, business and tax laws, invoice and inventory procedures, and transportation and logistics issues. Although a strong knowledge of the products and services to be purchased is essential, purchasing management professionals must also be able to plan, execute, and oversee purchasing strategies that are conducive to company profitability. Sourcing reliable suppliers is a crucial part of purchasing management. Purchasing managers, agents, and buyers usually learn about new products and services from Internet searches, trade shows, and conferences. They meet with potential suppliers in their plants whenever possible. Skills in foreign languages may be helpful for sourcing suppliers in other countries. Purchasing management professionals must always assess potential suppliers in terms of the supplier's ability to deliver quality merchandise at a suitable price on time.

Purchasing management professionals must be good negotiators, understand technical product information, have good mathematical ability, understand spreadsheet software, understand marketing methodology, and be outstanding decision makers. Increased responsibilities in purchasing management require good leadership skills, and higher positions often require a master's degree in a business related subject. Entry level purchasing management positions such as junior buyers, assistant buyers, and purchasing clerks, often require a college degree and some product knowledge.

Larger distributors may require a bachelor's degree for entry level purchasing management positions. Training and learning typically start in sales, then supervision, and invoice and stock monitoring. Professional purchasing management designations include Certified Purchasing Professional in the United States, and Certified Professional Purchaser in Canada. Purchasing managers, buyers, and materials managers control budgets, manage staff, and may analyse procurement methods as well as negotiate supplier contracts. Purchasing management professionals must understand tax laws, purchasing trends, ethics, and global outsourcing issues. Buyers and purchasing agents usually deal specifically with purchasing tasks, while purchasing managers usually supervise others, including purchasing agents. However, titles and duties vary greatly between industries and employers. Buyers often have assistants to place orders and keep track of delivery details.Buyers need the ability to select products that consumers will want to buy, so they need to understand trends as well as economic conditions that affect consumer buying decisions.

Buyers employed in small stores may be responsible for purchasing the store's entire inventory, while buyers working for larger operations may focus on a few product lines. Merchandise managers may work with an advertising team to create a campaign for the goods they purchase. Follow up is an important part of purchasing management as responsibility does not end in purchasing goods. For example, merchandise managers need to check to be sure the products they buy are being displayed well to attract consumers. Buyers must keep track of customer demands for new products as well as determine how well goods are selling.

OBJECTIVES

To maintain uninterrupted flow of materials to support the development schedules:

- To procure materials economically at a cost consistent with the quality and service required. However, generally all purchases may be attempted at the lowest cost.
- To provide the necessary expertise, advice, inform-ation to the Curators and Education Officers with regard to the best quality of material available in the market, supplier's capability and performance etc.
- To develop and maintain good buyer-seller relation-ship.
- To promote source development.
- To maintain NCSM's reputation and credibility in the market by fair dealings and prompt payments.

FUNCTIONS

The main functions of the Purchase Department are defined as follows:

- Procurement of stores through indigenous and foreign sources as required in accordance with the rules in force.
- Checking of requisitions/purchase indents.
- Selection of suppliers for issue of enquiries.
- Issuing enquiries/tenders and obtaining quotations.

- Analysing quotations and bids etc., and preparation of comparative statement.
- Consultation with the Indentor for selection and approval of quotations and with Accounts Officer for pre-audit.
- Negotiating contracts.
- Checking legal conditions of contracts. Consulting Administrative Officer or Secretary, NCSM – where necessary.
- Issue of Purchase Orders.
- Follow-up of purchase orders for delivery in due time
- Verification and passing of suppliers' bills to see that payments are made promptly.
- Correspondence and dealing with suppliers, carriers etc., regarding shortages, rejections etc., reported by the Stores Department.
- Maintenance of purchase records.
- Maintenance of progressive expenditure statement, sub-head wise.
- Maintenance of vendor performance records/data.
- Arrangement for Insurance Surveys, as and when necessary.
- Clearance of foreign consignments.
- Keeping various Departments/Divisions informed of the progress of their indents in case of delay in obtaining supplies.
- Serving as an information centre on the materials' knowledge *i.e.* their prices, source of supply, specification and other allied matters.
- Development of reliable and alternate sources of supply.
  - It shall be particularly ensured:
  - That all purchase are made against properly authorized requisitions, and valid sanctions, showing the correct and detailed end-use.
  - That all the materials requisitioned are duly ordered from the right source after full enquiries on most competitive price taking into account the trade discounts and tax benefits etc.
  - That the right quantity of the goods consistent with the quality and the specification required is bought.
  - That the deliveries of all goods are received within the stipulated period.
  - That claims due to shortages or any other discrepancies are settled promptly.
  - That cordial and harmonious relations with all parts/divisions are maintained for becoming an efficient service unit in the museum/ centre.
- While receiving the planned requirement of the indentors, it should be prevailed upon the Indentors to certify clearly that the quantities indicated are definitely required for the project and specify the period

within which the quantities indented will be consumed. It is the duty of the purchase part to check purchase indents against needs and suggest modification of quantities wherever necessary.

DEFINITION OF PURCHASING

Purchasing refers to a business or organization attempting to acquire goods or services to accomplish the goals of the enterprise. Though there are several organizations that attempt to set standards in the purchasing process, processes can vary greatly between organizations. Typically the word "purchasing" is not used interchangeably with the word "procurement", since procurement typically includes Expediting, Supplier Quality, and Traffic and Logistics in addition to Purchasing.

Purchasing managers/directors, and procurement managers/directors guide the organization's acquisition procedures and standards. Most organizations use a three-way check as the foundation of their purchasing programmes. This involves three departments in the organization completing separate parts of the acquisition process.

The three departments do not all report to the same senior manager to prevent unethical practices and lend credibility to the process. These departments can be purchasing, receiving; and accounts payable or engineering, purchasing and accounts payable; or a plant manager, purchasing and accounts payable. Combinations can vary significantly, but a purchasing department and accounts payable are usually two of the three departments involved.

When the receiving department is not involved, it's typically called a two-way check or two-way purchase order. In this situation, the purchasing department issues the purchase order receipt not required. When an invoice arrives against the order, the accounts payable department will then go directly to the requestor of the purchase order to verify that the goods or services were received. This is typically what is done for goods and services that will bypass the receiving department. A few examples are software delivered electronically, NRE work consulting hours, etc...

Historically, the purchasing department issued Purchase Orders for supplies, services, equipment, and raw materials. Then, in an effort to decrease the administrative costs associated with the repetitive ordering of basic consumable items, "Blanket" or "Master" Agreements were put into place. These types of agreements typically have a longer duration and increased scope to maximize the Quantities of Scale concept. When additional supplies are required, a simple release would be issued to the supplier to provide the goods or services.

Another method of decreasing administrative costs associated with repetitive contracts for common material, is the use of company credit cards, also known as "Purchasing Cards" or simply "P-Cards". P-card programmes vary, but all of them have internal checks and audits to ensure appropriate use. Purchasing managers realised once contracts for the low dollar value consumables are in place, procurement can take a smaller role in the operation and use of the contracts. There is still oversight in the forms of audits and monthly statement reviews, but most of their time is now available to negotiate major purchases and setting up of other long term contracts. These contracts are typically renewable annually.

This trend away from the daily procurement function resulted in several changes in the industry. The first was the reduction of personnel. Purchasing departments were now smaller. There was no need for the army of clerks processing orders for individual parts as in the past. Another change was the focus on negotiating contracts and procurement of large capital equipment. Both of these functions permitted purchasing departments to make the biggest financial contribution to the organization. A new terms and job title emerged – Strategic sourcing and Sourcing Managers. These professionals not only focused on the bidding process and negotiating with suppliers, but the entire supply function. In these roles they were able to add value and maximize savings for organizations. This value was manifested in lower inventories, less personnel, and getting the end product to the organization's consumer quicker. Purchasing manager's success in these roles resulted in new assignments outside to the traditional purchasing function – logistics, materials management, distribution, and warehousing. More and more purchasing managers were becoming Supply Chain Managers handling additional functions of their organizations operation. Purchasing managers were not the only ones to become Supply Chain Managers. Logistic managers, material managers, distribution managers, etc all rose the broader function and some had responsibility for the purchasing functions now.

In accounting, purchases is the amount of goods a company bought throughout this year. They are added to inventory. Purchases are offset by Purchase Discounts and Purchase Returns and Allowances. When it should be added depends on the Free On Board policy of the trade. For the purchaser, this new inventory is added on shipment if the policy was FOB shipping point, and the seller remove this item from its inventory. On the other hand, the purchaser added this inventory on receipt if the policy was FOB destination, and the seller remove this item from its inventory when it was delivered.

Goods bought for the purpose other than direct selling, such as for Research and Development, are added to inventory and allocated to Research and Development expense as they are used. On a side note, equipments bought for Research and Development are not added to inventory, but are capitalized as assets...

ACQUISITION PROCESS

The revised acquisition process for major systems in industry and defence is shown in figure. The process is defined by a series of phases during which technology is defined and matured into viable concepts, which are subsequently developed and readied for production, after which the systems produced are supported in the field.

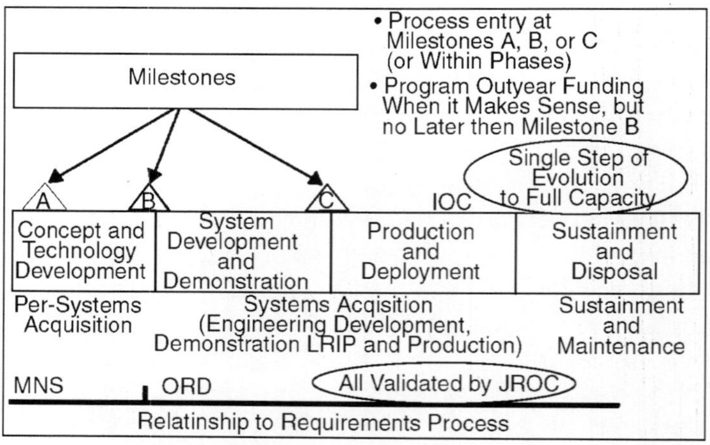

Fig. Model of the Acquisition Process.

The process allows for a given system to enter the process at any of the development phases.

For example, a system using unproven technology would enter at the beginning stages of the process and would proceed through a lengthy period of technology maturation, while a system based on mature and proven technologies might enter directly into engineering development or, conceivably, even production.

The process itself includes four phases of development:

1. Concept and Technology Development: is intended to explore alternative concepts based on assessments of operational needs, technology readiness, risk, and affordability.
2. Concept and Technology Development phase begins with concept exploration. During this stage, concept studies are undertaken to define alternative concepts and to provide information about capability and risk that would permit an objective comparison of competing concepts.
3. System Development and Demonstration phase. This phase could be entered directly as a result of a techno-logical opportunity and urgent user need, as well as having come through concept and technology development.
4. The last, and longest, phase is the Sustainment and Disposal phase of the programme. During this phase all necessary activities are accomplished to maintain and sustain the system in the field in the most cost-effective manner possible.

SELECTION OF BIDDERS

This is the process where the organization identifies potential suppliers for specified supplies, services or equipment. These suppliers' credentials and history are analysed, together with the products or services they offer. The bidder selection process varies from organization to organization, but can include running credit reports, interviewing management, testing products, and touring facilities. This process is not always done in order of importance, but rather in order of expense. Often purchasing managers research potential bidders obtaining information on the organizations and products from media sources and their own industry contacts. Additionally, purchasing might send Request for Information to potential suppliers to help gather information.

Engineering would also inspect sample products to determine if the company can produce products they need. If the bidder passes both of these stages engineering may decide to do some testing on the materials to further verify quality standards. These tests can be expensive and involve significant time of multiple technicians and engineers. Engineering management must make this decision based on the cost of the products they are likely to procure, the importance of the bidders' product to production, and other factors. Credit checks, interviewing management, touring plants as well as other steps could all be utilized if engineering, manufacturing, and supply chain managers decide they could help their decision and the cost is justifiable. Other organizations might have minority procurement goals to consider in selection of bidders. Organizations identify goals in the use of companies owned and operated by certain ethnicities or women owned business enterprises. Significant utilizing of minority suppliers may qualify the firm as a potential bidder for a contract with a company or governmental entity looking to increase their minority supplier programmes.

This selection process can include or exclude international suppliers depending on organizational goals and criteria. Companies looking to increase their pacific rim supplier base may exclude suppliers from the Americas, Europe, and Australia. Other organizations may be looking to purchase domestically to ensure a quicker response to orders as well as easier collaboration on design and production.

Organizational goals will dictate the criteria for the selection process of bidders. It is also possible that the product or service being procured is so specialized that the number of bidders are limited and the criteria must be very wide to permit competition. If only one firm can meet the specifications for the product then the purchasing managers must consider utilizing a "Sole Source" option or work with engineering to broaden the specifications if the project will permit alteration in the specifications. The sole source option is the part of the selection of bidders that acknowledges there is sometimes only one reasonable supplier for some services or products. This can be because of the limited applications for the product cannot support more than one manufacturer, proximity of the service provided, or the products are newly designed or invented and competition is not yet available.

BIDDING PROCESS

This is the process an organization utilizes to procure goods, services or equipment. Processes vary significantly from the stringent to the very informal. Large corporations and governmental entities are most likely to have stringent and formal processes. These processes can utilize specialized bid forms that require specific procedures and detail. The very stringent procedures require bids to be open by several staff from various departments to ensure fairness and impartiality. Responses are usually very detailed. Bidders not responding exactly as specified and following the published procedures can be disqualified. Smaller private businesses are more likely to have less formal procedures. Bids can be in the form of an e-mail to all of the bidders specifying products or services. Responses by bidders can be detailed or just the proposed dollar amount.

Most bid processes are multi-tiered. Acquisitions under a specified dollar amount can be "user discretion" permitting the requestor to choose who ever they want. This level can be as low as $100 or as high as $10,000 depending on the organization. The rationale is the savings realised by processing these request the same as expensive items is minimal and does not justify the time and expense. Purchasing departments watch for abuses of the user discretion privilege. Acquisitions in a mid range can be processed with a slightly more formal process. This process may involve the user providing quotes from three separate suppliers.

Purchasing may be asked or required to obtain the quotes. The formal bid process starts as low as $10,000 or as high as $100,000 depending on the organization. The bid usually involves a specific form the bidder fills out and must be returned by a specified deadline. Depending of the commodity being purchased and the organization the bid may specify a weighted evaluation criterion. Other bids would be evaluated at the discretion of purchasing or the end users. Some bids could be evaluated by a cross-functional committee. Other bids may be evaluated by the end user or the buyer in Purchasing. Especially in small, private firms the bidders could be evaluated on criteria or factors that have little if anything to do with the actual bid. Examples of these factors are history of the bidder with the company, history of the bidder with the company's senior management at other firms, and bidder's breadth of products.

TECHNICAL EVALUATION

Technical evaluations, evaluations of the technical suitability of the quoted goods or services, if required, are normally performed prior to the commercial evaluation. During this phase of the procurement process, a technical representative of the company will review the proposal and designate each bidder as either technically acceptable or technically unacceptable.

COMMERCIAL EVALUATION

Cost of Money is calculated by multiplying the applicable currency interest rate multiplied by the amount of money paid prior to the receipt of GOODS. If the money were to have remained in the buyer's account, interest would be drawn. That interest is essentially an additional cost associated with such Progress or Milestone payments.

The manufacturing location is taken into consideration during the evaluation stage primarily to calculate freight costs and regional issues which may be considered. For instance, in Europe it is common for factories to close during the month of August for Summer holiday. Labour agreements may also be taken into consideration and may be drawn into the evaluation if the particular region is known to frequent labour unions.The manufacturing lead-time is the time from the placement of the order until the goods are manufactured and prepared for delivery. Lead-times vary by commodity and can range from several days to years. Transportation time is evaluated while comparing the delivery of goods to the Buyer's required use-date. If Goods are shipped from a remote port, with infrequent vessel transportation, the transportation time could exceed the schedule and adjustments would need to be made.Delivery Charges - the charge for the Goods to be delivered to a stated point. Bid Validity Packing Bid Adjustments Terms and Conditions Seller's Services Standards Organizations Financial Review Payment Currency Risk Analysis - market volatility, financial stress within the bidders Testing

NEGOTIATING

Negotiating is a key skillset in the Purchasing field. One of the goals of Purchasing Agents is to acquire goods per the most advantageous terms of the buying entity. Purchasing Agents typically attempt to decrease costs while meeting the Buyer's other requirements such as an on-time delivery, compliance to the commercial terms and conditions.

Good negotiators, those with high levels of documented "cost savings", receive a premium within the industry relative to their compensation. Depending on the employment agreement between the Purchasing Agent and the employer, Buyer's cost savings can result in the creation of value to the business, and may result in a flat-rate bonus, or a percentage payout to the Purchasing Agent of the documented cost savings.

Purchasing Departments, while they can be considered as a support function of the key business, are actually revenue generating departments. For example, if the company needs to buy \$30 million USD of widgets and the

Purchasing Department secures the widgets for $25M USD, the Purchasing Department would have saved the company $5M USD. That savings could exceed the annual budget of the department, which in effect would pay the department's overhead - the employee's salaries, computers, office space, etc.

POST-AWARD ADMINISTRATION

Post-award administration typically consists of making minor changes, additions or subtractions, that in some way change the terms of the agreement or the Seller's Scope of Supply. Such changes are often minor, but for auditing purposes must be documented into the existing agreement. Examples include increasing the quantity of a Line Item or changing the metallurgy of a particular component.

METHODS OF PURCHASING MANAGEMENT

The purchase method of accounting in current standards is similar to the "acquisition accounting" method used in previous accounting standards. Its use provides some useful safeguards.

Previous accounting standards allowed two methods of accounting for mergers and acquisitions; merger accounting and acquisition accounting. The former was generally a more favourable treatment in its impact on the P and L. The purchase method of accounting is now compulsory in the US, the EU and wherever IFRSs have been adopted.

The purchase method of accounting must identify the acquirer. Under IFRSs the acquisition must be valued at fair value. The difference between the purchase price and the fair value should be recognised as goodwill.

A company cannot create a restructuring provision to provide for future losses or restructuring costs as a result of an acquisition. Such costs must be treated as post acquisition costs. This makes the impact of restructuring costs on profits more visible, and prevents the abuse of provisions to take an exaggerated hit to profits on acquisition and thereafter boost reported profits in subsequent years.

The use of the purchase method improves accounts, but investors are likely to disregard the impact of goodwill, which is the largest change.

The elimination of provisions is more useful because of the extra visibility and the prevention of abuses:

- *Full*: The purchase of a receivable in its entirety.
- *Partial*: The purchase of immediate installments, with the seller retaining remaining installments and/or the balloon payment.
- *Reverse Partial*: The purchase of future installments, allowing the seller to continue receiving immediate installments for a specified period of time.
- *Split Disbursement Partial*: The purchase of a portion of each

installment for a specified time and amount. Seller receives the remainder of each installment.

- *Multiple Stage Payout*: The full purchase of a receivable by means of a guaranteed staged payout of proceeds equaling or exceeding the principal balance. Seller receives stated payout regardless of the purchased receivable's performance.
- *Multiple Cash Flow*: The purchase of up to 50 per cent of the cash flow created by multiple receivables held by a single seller.
- *Short Life Yield*: A method of calculating a higher buy price on a long term, Grade A receivable, by calculating the purchase price of the receivable as if there were a 10 year balloon payment.

We realise that you may desire an option other than the quote we provide. Please contact us with any questions you may have for an explanation of how these purchase options can be tailored to meet your needs, now or in the future. We look forward to working with you and providing the best service possible!

FUNCTION ANALYSIS SYSTEM TECHNIQUE

Function Analysis System Technique is an evolution of the value analysis process created by Charles Bytheway. FAST permits people with different technical backgrounds to effectively communicate and resolve issues that require multi-disciplined considerations. FAST builds upon VA by linking the simply expressed, verb-noun functions to describe complex systems.

FAST is not an end product or result, but rather a beginning. It describes the item or system under study and causes the team to think through the functions that the item or system performs, forming the basis for a wide variety of subsequent approaches and analysis techniques. FAST contributes significantly to perhaps the most important phase of value engineering: function analysis. FAST is a creative stimulus to explore innovative avenues for performing functions.

The FAST diagram or model is an excellent communications vehicle. Using the verb-noun rules in function analysis creates a common language, crossing all disciplines and technologies. It allows multi-disciplined team members to contribute equally and communicate with one another while addressing the problem objectively without bias or preconceived conclusions. With FAST, there are no right or wrong model or result.

The problem should be structured until the product development team members are satisfied that the real problem is identified. After agreeing on the problem statement, the single most important output of the multi-disciplined team engaged in developing a FAST model is consensus. Since the team has been charged with the responsibility of resolving the assigned problem, it is their interpretation of the FAST model that reflects the problem statement that's important. The team members must discuss and reconfigure the FAST model until consensus is reached and all participating team members are satisfied that their concerns are expressed in the model. Once consensus has been achieved, the FAST model is complete and the team can move on to the next creative phase.

FAST differs from value analysis in the use of intuitive logic to determine and test function dependencies and the graphical display of the system in a function dependency diagram or model. Another major difference is in analyzing a system as a complete unit, rather than analyzing the components of a system. When studying systems it becomes apparent that functions do not operate in a random or independent fashion. A system exists because functions form dependency links with other functions, just as components form a dependency link with other components to make the system work. The importance of the FAST approach is that it graphically displays function dependencies and creates a process to study function links while exploring options to develop improved systems.

There are normally two types of FAST diagrams, the technical FAST diagram and the customer FAST diagram. A technical FAST diagram is used to understand the technical aspects of a specific portion of a total product. A customer FAST diagram focuses on the aspects of a product that the customer cares about and does not delve into the technicalities, mechanics or physics of the product. A customer FAST diagram is usually applied to a total product.

CREATING A FAST MODEL

The FAST model has a horizontal directional orientation described as the HOW-WHY dimension. This dimension is described in this manner because HOW and WHY questions are asked to structure the logic of the system's functions. Starting with a function, we ask HOW that function is performed to develop a more specific approach. This line of questioning and thinking is read from left to right. To abstract the problem to a higher level, we ask WHY is that function performed. This line of logic is read from right to left.

There is essential logic associated with the FAST HOW-WHY directional orientation. First, when undertaking any task it is best to start with the goals of the task, then explore methods to achieve the goals. When addressing any function on the FAST model with the question WHY, the function to its left expresses the goal of that function. The question HOW, is answered by the function on the right, and is a method to perform that function being addressed. A systems diagram starts at the beginning of the system and ends with its goal. A FAST model, reading from left to right, starts with the goal, and ends at the beginning of the "system" that will achieve that goal.

Second, changing a function on the HOW-WHY path affects all of the functions to the right of that function. This is a domino effect that only goes one way, from left to right. Starting with any place on the FAST model, if a function is changed the goals are still valid but the method to accomplish that function, and all other functions on the right, are affected.

Finally, building the model in the HOW direction, or function justification, will focus the team's attention on each function element of the model. Whereas, reversing the FAST model and building it in its system orientation will cause the team to leap over individual functions and focus on the system, leaving function "gaps" in the system. A good rule to remember in constructing a FAST Model is to build in the HOW direction and test the logic in the WHY direction. The vertical orientation of the FAST model is described as the WHEN direction. This is not part of the intuitive logic process, but it supplements intuitive thinking. WHEN is not a time orientation, but indicates cause and effect.

Scope lines represent the boundaries of the study and are shown as two vertical lines on the FAST model. The scope lines bound the "scope of the study", or that aspect of the problem with which the study team is concerned. The left scope line determines the basic function(s) of the study. The basic functions will always be the first function(s) to the immediate right of the left scope line. The right scope line identifies the beginning of the study and separates the input function(s) from the scope of the study.

The objective or goal of the study is called the "Highest Order Function", located to the left of the basic functions and outside of the left scope line. Any function to the left of another function is a "higher order function". Functions to the right and outside of the right scope line represent the input side that "turn on" or initiate the subject under study and are known as lowest order functions. Any function to the right of another function is a "lower order" function and represents a method selected to carry out the function being addressed.

Those functions to the immediate right of the left scope line represent the purpose or mission of the product or process under study and are called Basic Function(s). Once determined, the basic function will not change. If the basic function fails, the product or process will lose its market value. All functions to the right of the basic function(s) portray the conceptual approach selected to satisfy the basic function. The concept describes the method being considered, or elected, to achieve the basic functions. The concept can represent either the current conditions (as is) or proposed approach (to be). As a general rule, it is best to create a "to be" rather than an "as is" FAST Model, even if the assignment is to improve an existing product.

This approach will give the product development team members an opportunity to compare the "ideal" to the "current" and help resolve how to implement the differences. Working from an "as is" model will restrict the team's attention to incremental improvement opportunities.

An "as is" model is useful for tracing the symptoms of a problem to its root cause, and exploring ways to resolve the problem, because of the dependent relationship of functions that form the FAST model. Any function on the HOW-

WHY logic path is a logic path function. If the functions along the WHY direction lead into the basic function(s), than they are located on the major logic path. If the WHY path does not lead directly to the basic function, it is a minor logic path. Changing a function on the major logic path will alter or destroy the way the basic function is performed.

Changing a function on a minor logic path will disturb an independent function that enhances the basic function. Supporting functions are usually secondary and exist to achieve the performance levels specified in the objectives or specifications of the basic functions or because a particular approach was chosen to implement the basic function(s).

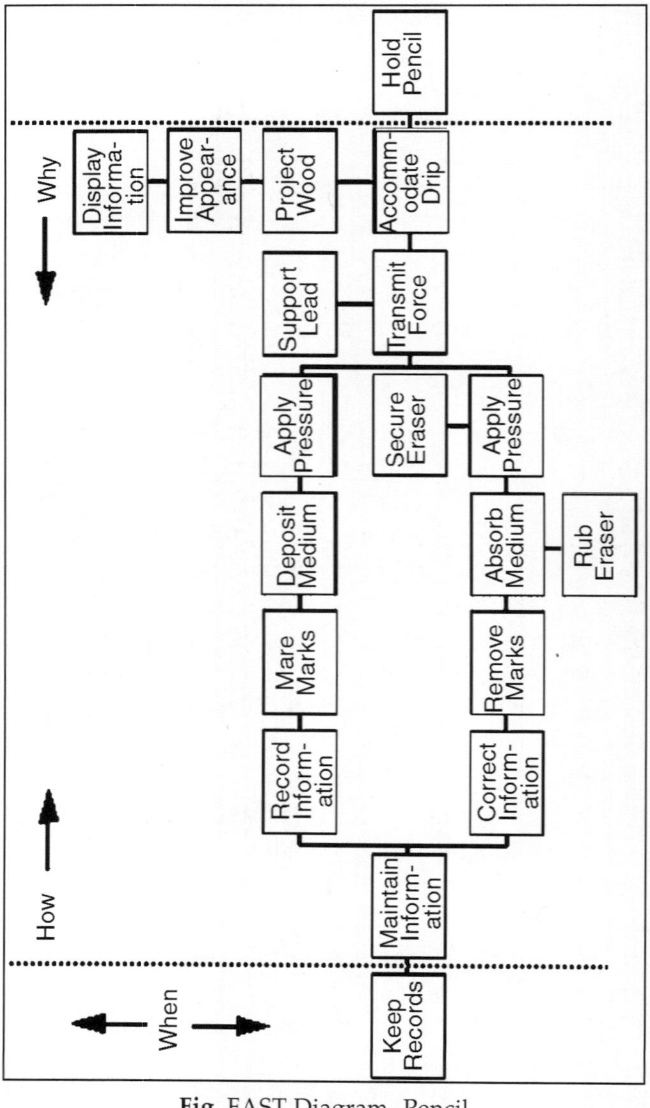

Fig. FAST Diagram- Pencil

Independent functions describe an enhancement or control of a function located on the logic path. They do not depend on another function or method selected to perform that function. Independent functions are located above the logic path functions, and are considered secondary, with respect to the scope, nature, level of the problem, and its logic path. An example of a FAST Diagram for a pencil is.

The next step in the process is to dimension the FAST model or to associate information to its functions. FAST dimensions include, but are not limited to: responsibility, budgets, allocated target costs, estimated costs, actual costs, subsystem groupings, placing inspection and test points, manufacturing processes, positioning design reviews, and others. There are many ways to dimension a FAST model. The two popular ways are called Clustering Functions and the Sensitivity Matrix.

Clustering functions involves drawing boundaries with dotted lines around groups of functions to configure sub-systems. Clustering functions is a good way to illustrate cost reduction targets and assign design-to-cost targets to new design concepts. For cost reduction, a team would develop an "as is" product FAST model, cluster the functions into subsystems, allocate product cost by clustered functions, and assign target costs. During the process of creating the model, customer sensitivity functions can be identified as well as opportunities for significant cost improvements in design and production.

Following the completion of the model, the subsystems can be divided among product development teams assigned to achieve the target cost reductions. The teams can then select cost sensitive sub-systems and expand them by moving that segment of the model to a lower level of abstraction. This exposes the detail components of that assembly and their function/cost contributions.

MANAGING EXTERNAL FORCES

IMPORTANCE OF EXTERNAL FORCES

As we noted, most external forces are beyond the direct control of the marketing organization. By "direct control" we mean marketers lack the power to determine the direction and intensity of a change in these forces. Instead, marketers must treat external forces as something to be monitored and responded to when necessary.

While marketers lack direct control over external forces, in some cases they can exercise a small amount of influence over these factors. For instance, Apple's iPod has played an important role in changing how consumers listen to music, and for some, how they acquire information (*e.g.*, news podcasts). But while Apple is credited with being the catalyst for changing a social behaviour (an external force) they represent just one of several organizations (*e.g.*, music publishers, manufacturers of other music players) and others (*e.g.*, bloggers, podcasters, news media) whose actions were necessary for behaviour to change across a large group. Thus, while one company can market products and services with the intention of changing how a target market behaves, it is nearly impossible for one company alone to control the change.

For marketers the key to dealing with external forces is to engage in continual market research. For larger companies this may involve dedicated research personnel, who watch these factors as part of their day-to-day responsibilities. A research staff dedicated to monitoring external forces may offer marketers the ability to better predict changes and respond well in advance of a change. For example, researchers may be able to predict how the economy (an external force) will change over the next one to two years and through this information allow the marketing organization to respond (*e.g.*, new products, reduced price, etc.). For small organizations that do not have the luxury of market research staff, monitoring change is difficult and often means they react after a change has occurred. However, new innovative products (an external force) are making the monitoring task much easier allowing small companies to respond quicker than in the past.

THE EXTERNAL FORCES FACING MARKETING

For our discussion we will highlight seven important external forces:

- Demographics
- Economic Conditions
- Governmental Environment
- Influential Stakeholders
- Cultural and Societal Change
- Innovation
- Competitors

Each external force is described in detail though these are not presented in order of importance. In fact, the importance of each force may vary depending on the marketing organization and the industry in which they compete. For instance, a company manufacturing technology products may feel innovative forces are more important than demographic changes. While a financial services firm may more aggressively monitor and react to economic conditions.

DEMOGRAPHICS

Demography involves the study of characteristics of a population and how these change over time. The characteristics that are of most interest to marketers fall into two categories:

- *Total Population*: These characteristics take a very broad view of the population as a whole in terms of size (*e.g.*, number of people, number of businesses) and location (*e.g.*, geographic region).

- *Personal Variables*: These characteristics look at how the population is changing based on individual factors such as gender, age, income, level of education, family situation (*e.g.*, single, married, co-habitation), sexual preference, ethnicity, occupation, and social class.

We saw in Part 6: Targeting Markets demographics is a key variable used to segment both consumer and business markets. In particular, demographic variables are an important component in creating customer profiles. These profiles are based on both demographic and non-demographic (*e.g.*, customer behaviour, attitudes, lifestyles) factors and are used for grouping customers into definable market segments from which a marketer then selects its target markets. Since demographics is tied directly to identifying target markets, monitoring how demographics change is critical for making marketing decisions.

Most demographic shifts do not occur rapidly so marketers will not see dramatic changes in a short period of time in the manner that other external forces can impact an organization (*e.g.*, impact of a new law). However, over the long term, demographics can reshape a target market requiring marketing organizations to rework their marketing strategy in an effort to appeal to a changing market.

Adjusting to Demographic Trends

While demographic change occurs slowly, marketers can begin to see indicators of potential change by identifying small trends that may suggest a larger shift over time. By paying close attention to these trends organizations can prepare their long-term marketing strategy to be ready when the shift becomes more apparent.

To illustrate how a marketer may respond, let's consider the demographic characteristic birthrate. In some countries the overall birthrate is declining while the average age of the population is growing (*i.e.*, people living longer). For a company targeting the youth market with sporting products this trend may suggest that in coming years they will see a shrinkage in demand for their products within the youth market as the population of this market declines.

On the other hand demographic data may signal to the company that another market (*i.e.*, older market), which they may not have previously targeted, may hold potential for new products. If it is predicted that the shift will occur over several years the marketer can slowly move into the new market by offering products geared towards older adults.

ECONOMIC CONDITIONS

Since most marketers are engaged in activities designed to entice customers to spend their money, it makes sense that an important external force is economic conditions. Economic analysis looks at how a defined group produces, distributes and consumes goods and services. These groupings can range from those defined very broadly (*e.g.*, country) to those defined narrowly (*e.g.*, small town). Of course the production, distribution and consumption of products are also of high interest to marketers and, in fact, many leading scholars of marketing first studied economics before moving to marketing.

In very simple terms (and with apologies to both marketers and economist) the major difference between the marketer and economist is that marketers are engaged in activity that make things happen to individual customers (*e.g.*, create demand for products) while economists are engaged in activity showing the results marketers' decisions have on a group (*e.g.*, study how much is being spent by certain groups). Additionally, economists whose job it is to study a group may use hundreds of economic variables when assessing how a group is responding.

Marketers tend to evaluate far fewer economic variables preferring to concentrate on those variables that affect spending behaviour of consumers and businesses. The economic conditions of most interest to marketers include:

- *Income*: How much is being earned
- *Spending*: What consumers and businesses are doing with their money
- *Interest Rates*: The cost of borrowing money
- *Inflation*: how prices for products and services are changing
- *Cost of Living*: the financial requirements of living in a certain geographic area
- *Employment Rates*: the percentage of employable people who are working
- *Exchange Rates*: how the value of currencies are changing between countries and regions

Importance of Economic Conditions

For many marketers there is a relationship between level of sales and how customers are doing financially. For most products this relationship is a direct one – as customers' financial condition improves so will selling opportunities for the marketer. A clear example of this can be seen with the sale of luxury products where marketers are likely to see their sales improve as the target market's economic condition improves.

However, other products may see improvement as economic conditions decline. For instance, marketers of business certification programmes (*e.g.*, financial planning, quality management) or career preparation services (*e.g.*, resume development help) may see increased interest in their programmes during weak economic conditions as those who are unemployed or concerned about job stability seek additional credentials to make them more marketable to potential employers.

Whether an organization benefits from improving or declining economic conditions, it is important it monitors changes occurring in the economy in which the organization's target markets are located. In particular, marketers should watch for changing patterns in customer spending which may indicate that a longer term change in the economy is occurring. Changes that extend over a long term (six months or longer) may be part of the business cycle of an economy.

A business cycle is presented as a series of up (economic expansions) and down (economic contractions) measures. During expansion an economy grows and this generally leads to more jobs, higher income and increased customer spending.

However, an economy growing too quickly can present problems of inflation where product prices grow too fast. In this situation, even though customers have higher incomes, they may not be purchasing more since product prices have increased. Such situations are a main reason an economy will contract or see customer spending decrease. If severe this can lead to marketers seeing a major reduction in sales which may indicate the presence of an economic recession (*i.e.*, economic decline).

GOVERNMENTAL ENVIRONMENT

Marketing decisions must be made with an understanding of how they are impacted by international, national, regional and local laws and regulations. For marketers, laws (*i.e.*, acts past by governmental ruling bodies) and regulations (*i.e.*, requirements put in place by governmental agencies) identify rules and procedures that guide certain marketing activities.

Failure to conform to requirements established by the governments and their agencies may result in fines, sanctions or other legal action.

The governmental environment is a difficult external force to monitor for two key reasons. First, the number and variety of laws and regulations can be overwhelming even for the most seasoned marketer.

For instance, in the U.S. alone there are potentially hundreds of laws and regulations that are either directly or indirectly targeted to marketing decisions. The table below provides a sampling of the issues covered by U.S. laws and regulations and the primary marketing decision areas these affect:

Affected Decision Area	Coverage
General	Unfair competition, restraint of trade, environmental
Target Market	Discrimination, online registration, privacy
Product	Product safety, labeling, intellectual property, warranties
Promotion	Deceptive and misleading claims, advertising to children, telemarketing, e-mail spam
Distribution	Tying contracts, exclusive dealerships, transportation safety
Pricing	Price discrimination, predatory pricing, consumer credit purchasing

The second reason the governmental environment proves difficult is due to the complexity inherent in understanding laws and regulations which often makes it impossible for marketers to handle these issues on their own. Seeking legal assistance is necessary (and often costly) for most marketers no matter their size.

Dealing with the Government

In addition to seeking legal assistance, marketing organizations may find value by engaging in either direct discussion between company employees and governmental personnel or indirect discussion through firms hired to serve as a representative for the marketing company (*e.g.*, consultants, lobbyist).

Representatives are particularly important when selling internationally where existing relationships between government personnel and a hired representative can effectively reduce bureaucratic red tape.

In situations where proposed legislation is likely to impact an entire industry, communication with the government may occur through a marketer's participation in an industry trade group. These groups perform many tasks on behalf of their members including maintaining relations with governmental groups to ensure the industry's voice is heard with regard to pending legislation that affects the industry.

Finally, marketers should not view the governmental environment as always erecting obstacles. In many cases laws and regulations present marketing opportunities. For example, the U.S. Federal government recently instituted airline travel regulations limiting the size of liquid, gel and aerosol products that may be carried on a plane. Several companies that produce personal care products (*e.g.*, shaving cream, hair care, toothpaste, etc.) have viewed the new regulations as an opportunity to market their products in new packaging that they promote as being approved for airline travel.

INFLUENTIAL STAKEHOLDERS

Besides dealing with various governmental groups, marketers must also pay close attention to other groups that can affect marketing activity. The most important of these groups are those that have an interest or stake in the company. While such groups are not backed directly by the power of a government they can still command a great deal of power especially in terms of swaying public opinion, which sometimes leads to governmental action.

Influential stakeholders can be divided into two categories:

- *Connected Stakeholders:* These stakeholders consist of groups that regularly interact with the marketing organization and often hold important roles in helping the marketer succeed. Examples include: supply and distribution partners (*e.g.*, distributors, material suppliers), industry standards groups, and support companies (*e.g.*, advertising agencies). To address concerns raised by these groups often requires direct communication by management with the stakeholders.

- *Peripheral Stakeholders:* These stakeholders consist of groups that may not routinely impact the marketer unless a specific issue arises that draws their attention. Examples include: religious organizations, community activists, and cause supporters. To address concerns raised by these groups marketers often use public relations professionals as their first line of communication.

CULTURAL AND SOCIETAL CHANGE

Society is made up of many different cultural groups. Members of a cultural group share similar values and beliefs which are learned and reinforced by others within the same cultural group. These shared values and beliefs, lead members of a cultural group to behave in similar ways (*e.g.*, customs, traditions, likes/dislikes, attitudes, perceptions, etc.).

Cultural groups can be viewed on several levels. At a broad level, a cultural group consists of a very large number who share basic values (*e.g.*, ethnicity, religious affiliation). While looking at the broad level can offer some insight into how a general cultural group behaves, marketers are much more concerned with examining cultural groups at narrower levels where individuals share more specific interests.

Narrow level analysis of cultural groups leads to the study of sub-cultures, which consists of individuals sharing values and beliefs that revolve around special interests. For instance, a large cultural group may exist in a certain region of a country. While they share basic cultural values with others in their country (*e.g.*, sense of patriotism), they may also share values (*e.g.*, work ethic, taste in food, etc.) with those in their region that are not shared consistently throughout the country.

Examining these sub-cultures even more closely will reveal thousands of smaller sub-cultures (*e.g.*, sports interests, type of shopper, music preference, online gaming enthusiast, etc.). It should be evident that a single consumer may belong to many different sub-cultures. It should also be evident that members of a sub-culture sharing similar values are also likely to have similar needs and, this suggests that sub-cultures are natural for market segmentation.

Evolution of Cultural Change

Cultural values and beliefs are not stagnant; these do evolve and change. However the pace of change will differ depending on the level examined. At the broad cultural level changes often evolves slowly. For instance, consider how people in the United States and Japan view the importance of saving money. People in the United States are more inclined to spend their earned income than they are to save resulting in a low personal savings rate for Americans.

Those living in Japan are more concerned with saving and thus show a high personal savings rate. The difference in values towards savings has been consistent for many years and no one expects consumers from either country to alter their values in the near future.

While broad cultures tend to shift values and beliefs slowly, changes within sub-cultures can occur relatively quickly. For instance, the music industry often experiences rapid shifts as a sub-culture of music enthusiasts discovers new artists. The key for marketers targeting sub-cultures is to maintain close contact with these groups through regular marketing research. In this way marketers can see how different sub-cultures behave and also spot trends, which the marketer can capitalize on through new marketing tactics (*e.g.*, new products, new sales channels, added value, etc.).

INNOVATION

Arguably the external force possessing the greatest potential for changing how marketers and industries compete are those associated with innovation. When most people think of innovation they immediately assume it has to do with computers and other high-tech equipment. While the majority of innovative new products rely in some way on computer technology, it is not a requirement for something to be considered innovative.

Instead, an innovation is viewed as anything new that solves needs by offering a significant advantage (*e.g.*, more features, more convenient, easier to use, lower cost, etc.) over existing ways (*e.g.*, products, services). For example, a designer of automobiles may develop a new layout for a car's dashboard using existing products (no new technologies). This new design reduces the amount of time a driver must take his eyes off the road in order to select a new music station. If this new layout is viewed positively by customers, governmental groups and the media it may gain widespread acceptance by other vehicle manufacturers who will make similar designs available in their products.

As noted in the above example, for an innovation to be truly important it must be widely adopted within a targeted group (*e.g.*, within an industry, by a target market). Once adopted an innovation becomes important if it leads to behavioural changes including changing how consumers and business satisfy their needs. These changes present both opportunities and threats to marketers.

For instance, over the last few years several small companies have created productivity software products (*e.g.*, word processing, spreadsheet) that operate over the Internet. These products do not require the software be downloaded to a user's computer. While these innovative products are not new in terms of the features they offer, they are new in terms of convenience in accessing documents from anywhere and the ability to share with others. It remains to be seen whether these products will alter behaviour, though it appears that one leading maker of traditional productivity software, Microsoft, has recognized this as a threat and is expected to respond with its own version of web-based software.

Because of the potential innovation has in affecting products and industries it is no surprise that many marketing organizations direct a significant amount of funds to researching this external force. In fact, in many industries, such as pharmaceuticals and computers, spending on technological research and development represents a significant portion of a company's overall budget.

Innovation in Marketing

Marketers in many industries know that innovation through new product development is vital to remain competitive. But product decisions are not the only areas affected by new developments. Innovation can affect almost all marketing areas. Below is a sampling of how innovation has affected different marketing areas:

Marketing Area	Effect of Innovation
Marketing Research	Creates new ways to conduct research including more sophisticated methods for monitoring and tracking customer behavior and analyzing data.
Targeting Markets	Allows for extreme target marketing where marketing-to-person is replacing mass marketing. For customer service, technology makes it easier to manage relationships and allows for rapid response to customer's needs.
Product	Creates new digital products/services. Incorporation of innovation into existing product/service enhances value by offering improved quality, features & reliability at a lower price.
Promotion	New techniques allow better matching of promotion to customer activity and individualized promotion. Makes it easier for sellers to offer product suggestions and promotional tie-ins.
Distribution	Creates new channels for distribution and transaction (e.g., electronic commerce) that include making it easier for buyers to place orders. Allows more control over inventory management and closer monitoring of product shipment
Pricing	Enables the use of dynamic pricing methods.

Many of the benefits shown above are driven by the evolution of the Internet. The Internet is transforming how all functional areas of an organization perform work. However, it can be argued that no functional area has been more affected than marketing. Throughout the Principles of Marketing Tutorials we have seen evidence of how the Internet has impacted marketing. Over the next decade it is expected that the Internet's effect on marketing will continue to grow and marketers are well served to embrace this.

COMPETITORS

For many marketers the final external force is the one most relevant to immediate day-to-day decision making. While the other external forces we've discussed tend to be examined periodically (or in some cases rarely), monitoring competitor activity is often a daily undertaking.

Monitoring competitors can serve several goals:

- *Competitors as Threats:* The most obvious reason to monitor the competition is to see how they are responding in the same markets in which the marketer operates.
  Many larger companies recognize the importance of keeping tabs on their competition and create specific positions or even departments that focus on gathering and analyzing competitor data. These competitive intelligence programmes mainly employ high-tech methods, and principally the Internet, to locate information about competitors such as news reports, government filings (*e.g.*, patents, stock reports) and changes to competitors' web sites. Even small sized marketers can more easily track competitor actions. For instance, there are several news and information services that will alert a marketer (usually via e-mail) when a competitor is mentioned in the news.
- *Competitors as Partners:* While many may consider competitors as representing the enemy, there are situations where competitors can present opportunities. This happens often to large companies that offer a broad product line serving many target markets. In some markets a company may compete aggressively with another firm but in other markets both firms may be lagging and it may make more sense for both to work together. This can be seen in the computer industry where Apple Inc., which for many years viewed computers built with Intel processors as competitors since these run Microsoft operating systems, has now accepted Intel processors and is building computers powered by this chip.
- *Competitors of Tomorrow*: In many industries and, in particular, those in technology-focused industries where there is heavy emphasis on research and development, the most dangerous competitors are the

ones that have yet to emerge. Because technology-dependent industries, such as computers, consumer electronic and pharmaceuticals, rely heavily on innovative new products, serious competitors can emerge quickly from what seems to be out of nowhere. For instance, the evolution of online video and its impact on the news and entertainment industry grew very rapidly with the introduction of online video services (*e.g.*, YouTube) which was previously an unknown project developed in a garage. However, in less than 18 months it came to dominate the online video industry.

MARKETING PLANNING AND STRATEGY

In particular, we focus attention on the importance of marketing planning with special attention given to the role marketing strategy plays in the planning process.

For marketers planning is an essential task that must be continually undertaken. As we will see, shifting market conditions, including changing customer needs and competitive threats, almost always insure that what worked in the past will not work in the future, thus requiring revisions in how a product is marketed.

Marketing planning is also important since it is often a prerequisite for obtaining funding whether one is a marketer in a large corporation seeking additional money for his or her department or is part of a small startup company looking for initial funding.

To aid in our understanding of planning we introduce a key concept in marketing: the Product Life Cycle. We will see the Product Life Cycle offers valuable insight and guidance for marketing decisions. In this tutorial we also discuss different types of marketing strategy that can be followed to meet marketing objectives. Additionally, we look at how innovative products are adopted within a market and how this impacts marketing planning.

IMPORTANCE OF MARKETING PLANNING

Marketers consider many factors when making decisions. Of course the main factors are those directly associated with how customers (including distribution partners) respond to an organization's marketing efforts, such as how they may react to changes in a product, new advertisements, special pricing promotions, etc.

But when making decisions marketers face other concerns that are not directly customer related. For instance, we have discussed how marketing decisions (*e.g.*, lowering price) may place pressure on other areas of the organization (*e.g.*, production, shipping). Other examples include:

- As we noted in our definition of marketing, decisions must be made with an understanding of the value these provide not only to customers but to the marketing organization. Consequently, marketers must be well aware of how their decisions fit with the overall objectives of the company. For example, a company whose goal is to be the low-price leader may have concerns if the company's marketing department wants to market a very high-end product, since this would go against the reputation and core strengths of the company.

- We showed that marketers' decisions may affect peripheral stakeholders who are not directly connected to the marketing organization but have the potential to impact the organization if issues arise that draw their attention.
- Marketing decisions also directly affect an organization's financial condition. Marketers' efforts generate the funds (*i.e.*, sales) needed for the company to survive, but do so while using company resources, in particular, expenditure of funds. Controls must be put in place to insure the results of what the organization spends through marketing (*i.e.*, return on investment) meet expectations.

Because marketing decisions have both internal and external impact, marketers are wise to make their decisions only after engaging in a careful, disciplined planning process. Marketers who make hasty, off-the-cuff decisions without regard to the implications are taking risks that may lead to problems. Instead, marketing decisions should be made with consideration of how these affect others and the resources (*e.g.*, funds) required to carry out the plan.

THE MARKETING PLAN

The central point in planning for marketing decisions is the Marketing Plan. The plan serves several functions including:

- Forcing marketing personnel to look internally in order to fully understand the results of past marketing decisions.
- Forcing marketing personnel to look externally in order to fully understand the market in which they operate.
- Setting future goals and providing direction for future marketing efforts that everyone within the organization should understand and support.
- Serving as a key component in obtaining funding to pursue new initiatives.

The scope of the Marketing Plan depends on the company and industry. A small technology startup company may, for instance, have a less elaborate plan that is highly flexible (*e.g.*, does not identify exactly where advertising money is spent) to meet the needs of a rapidly changing market. A more established marketing organization, such a large consumer products firm, may create a very structured plan that clearly identifies all activities that take place over a

12-month period. Whether the marketer is creating a short plan intended to cover a narrow timeframe or a full-blown document laying out plans for a year or more, any plan requires undertaking significant market research to better understand the market. With knowledge of the market, the marketer can then begin to build the plan which will include the following key concepts:

- *Organizational Mission*: Represents the guiding force of an organization by identifying the long-run vision for what the organization hopes to achieve. The mission comes from the top leaders of the organization and often remains unchanged for many years.
- *Objectives*: Reflects what the organization expects to achieve with its marketing efforts. As with the mission, objectives also flow from the top of the organization down to the marketing department. Objectives can be in the form of financial goals (*i.e.*, profits) or marketing goals (*e.g.*, achieve certain level of market share).
- *Marketing Strategy:* Achieving objectives requires the marketer engage in marketing decision-making which indicates where resources (*e.g.*, marketing funds) will be directed. However, before spending begins on individual marketing decisions (*e.g.*, where to advertise) the marketer needs to establish a general plan of action that summarizes what will be done to reach the stated objectives.
- *Tactical Programmes*: Marketing strategy sets the stage for specific actions that will take place. Marketing tactics are the day-to-day actions that marketers undertake and involve the major marketing decision areas. As would be expected, this is the key area of the Marketing Plan since it explains exactly what will be done to reach the organization's objectives.
- *Marketing Budget*: Carrying out marketing tactics almost always means that money must be spent. The marketing budget lays out the spending requirements needed to carry out marketing tactics. While the marketing department may request a certain level of funding they feel is required, in the end it is upper-management that will have final say on how much financial support will be offered.

TYPES OF MARKETING STRATEGY

One of the most important concepts of the marketing planning process is the need to develop a cohesive marketing strategy that guides tactical programmes for the marketing decision areas. In marketing there are two levels to strategy formulation: General Marketing Strategies and Decision Area Strategies.

General Marketing Strategies

These set the direction for all marketing efforts by describing, in general terms, how marketing will achieve its objectives. There are many different General Marketing Strategies, though most can be viewed as falling into one of the following categories:

- *Market Expansion*: This strategy looks to grow overall sales in one of two ways:
  - *Grow Sales with Existing Products*: With this approach the marketer seeks to actively increase the overall sales of products the company currently markets. This can be accomplished by: 1) getting existing customers to buy more; 2) getting potential customers to buy (*i.e.*, those who have yet to buy); or 3) selling current products in new markets.
  - *Grow Sales with New Products:* With this approach the marketer seeks to achieve objectives through the introduction of new products. This can be accomplished by: 1) introducing updated versions or refinements to existing products; 2) introducing products that are extensions of current products; or 3) introducing new products not previously marketed.
- *Market Share Growth:* This strategy looks to increase the marketer's overall percentage or share of market. In many cases this can only be accomplished by taking sales away from competitors. Consequently, this strategy often relies on aggressive marketing tactics.
- *Niche Market*: This strategy looks to obtain a commanding position within a certain segment of the overall market. Usually the niche market is much smaller in terms of total customers and sales volume than the overall market. Ideally this strategy looks to have the product viewed as being different from companies targeting the larger market.
- *Status Quo*: This strategy looks to maintain the marketer's current position in the market, such as maintaining the same level of market share.
- *Market Exit*: This strategy looks to remove the product from the organization's product mix. This can be accomplished by: 1) selling the product to another organization, or 2) eliminating the product.

DECISION AREA STRATEGIES

These are used to achieve the General Marketing Strategies by guiding the decisions within important marketing areas (product, pricing, distribution, promotion, target marketing). For example, a General Marketing Strategy that centers on entering a new market with new products may be supported by Decision Area Strategies that include:

- *Target Market Strategy*: Employ segmenting techniques
- *Product Strategy*: Develop new product line

- *Pricing Strategy:* Create price programmes that offer lower pricing versus competitors
- *Distribution Strategy:* Use methods to gain access to important distribution partners that service the target market
- *Promotion Strategy:* create a plan that can quickly build awareness of the product

Achieving the Decision Area Strategies is accomplished through the development of detailed Tactical Programmes for each area. For instance, to meet the Pricing Strategy that lowers cost versus competitors' products, the marketer may employ such tactics as: quantity discounts, trade-in allowances or sales volume incentives to distributors.

PLANNING WITH THE PRODUCT LIFE CYCLE

As we have seen, there are many components, both internal and external, that must be considered within the marketing planning process. In fact, for many marketers creating the Marketing Plan represents one of the most challenging and burdensome tasks they face. Fortunately, over the years marketing academics and professionals have put forth theories, models and other tools that aid planning. Possibly the most widely used planning tool within marketing is the Product Life Cycle (PLC) concept. The basic premise of the PLC is that products go through several stages of "life" with each stage presenting the marketer with different challenges that must be met with different marketing approaches. By understanding a product's position in the PLC, the marketer may be able to develop more effective plans.

There have been several attempts over the years to define the stages that make up the PLC. Unfortunately, the PLC may be different for different products, different markets and different market conditions (*e.g.*, economic forces). Consequently, there is not a one-model-fits-all PLC. Yet there is enough evidence to suggest that most products experience patterns of activity that divide the evolution of the product into five distinct stages. These stages are:

- *Development*: Occurs before the product is released to the market and is principally a time for honing the product offering and preparing the market for product introduction.
- *Introduction*: Product is released to the market and sales begin though often gradually as the market becomes aware of the product.
- *Growth*: If the product is accepted it may reach a stage of rapid growth in sales and in profits.
- *Maturity*: At some point sales of a product may stabilize. For some products the maturity phase can be the longest stage as the product is repeatedly purchased by loyal customers. However, while overall sales may grow year-over-year, percentage sales increases may be small.

- *Decline*: All products eventually see demand decline as customers no longer see value in purchasing the product.

LEVELS OF ANALYSIS OF THE PLC

The Product Life Cycle is commonly referenced in many business publications as a way of describing the current conditions facing a market or product. The fact it is used to describe either markets or individual products points out the need to understand the different levels of analysis for which the PLC can be used. These levels include:

- *Product Category*: This level considers the macro market view for the general category of products that meet a general need. For instance, automobiles would be a general category that meets the need for personal motorized transportation (obviously there are others, such as motorcycles, scooters and trucks but we will focus only on automobiles) and includes hundreds of products. Since the PLC for a product category includes sales for all products, the timeframe for the automotive PLC is quite long with the Introduction stage beginning around 1900.
- *Product Form*: This level looks at product groupings that fall within a product category. The product form contains many different groupings that, taken together, make up the product category. These groupings include products that not only satisfy the general need of the product category, but do so by also offering additional benefits. In our example, hybrid cars would be a product form, since it satisfies the general need for personal motorized transportation and offers additional benefits in the form of fuel efficiency and environmental friendliness. Other product forms in the product category include sports cars, minivans, luxury sedans, etc. Clearly there can be a unique PLC for each form of a product. Marketers are very concerned with analysis at this level since it provides evidence for what is occurring in specific markets and for this reason is considered the most important level of analysis.
- *Individual Brand*: This level concerns the life cycle of a specific brand within a product form. In our example this would include the Toyota Prius. While it may seem marketers would be most concerned with this level, they actually gain more value from analyzing what is happening in the overall market (*i.e.*, product form). For instance, a marketer may make a serious mistake if she assumes the entire market has entered the Decline stage just because her company's brand has seen a sales drop. Doing so may mean a total misread of what is happening in the market and lead to the marketer missing out on additional opportunities if the market for the product form is still growing.

We should note that in most cases the PLC considers what is happening for the total market (*i.e.*, worldwide sales). However, more information could be obtained by applying the concepts of the PLC to individual market segments, such as geographic regions or customer characteristics (*e.g.*, by age, education level, etc.).

ADOPTION OF NEW PRODUCTS

The PLC is tied closely to the concept of Diffusion of Innovation, which explains how information and acceptance of new products spread through a market, innovation is anything new that solves needs by offering a significant advantage over existing methods (*e.g.*, other products) customers use. Innovation can encompass both highly advanced technology products, such as new computer chips, and non-technological products, such as a new soft drink. In fact, the seminal work of the Diffusion of Innovation concept occurred in the 1950s when researchers in the agricultural industry observed how new corn seeds were adopted by farmers in Midwest U.S. states.

For marketers a key concept to emerge from research on new product diffusion is the identification of adopter categories into which members of a market are likely to fall. These categories include:

- *Innovators*: Represent a small percentage of the market that is at the forefront of adopting new products. These people are often viewed as enthusiasts and are eager to try new things, often without regard to price. While a good test ground for new products, marketers find that Innovators often do not remain loyal as they continually seek new products.
- *Early Adopters*: This group contains more members than the Innovator category. They share Innovators' enthusiasm for new products though they tend to be more practical about their decisions. They also are eager to communicate their experiences with the Early Majority (next group) and because of their influence they are important to the future success of the product (*i.e.*, act as opinion leaders).
- *Early Majority*: This represents the beginning of entry into the mass market. The Early Majority account for up to one-third of the overall market. The Early Majority like new things but tend to wait until they have received positive opinions for others (*i.e.*, early adopters) before purchasing. Adoption by the Early Majority is key if a new product is to be profitable. On the other hand, many new products die quickly because they are not accepted beyond early trials by Innovators and Early Adopters and never reach mass market status.
- *Late Majority*: Possibly as large as the Early Majority, this group takes a wait-and-see approach before trying something new. Marketers are likely to see their highest profits once this group starts to purchase.

- *Laggards*: This is the last group to adopt something new and, in fact, may only do so if they have no other choice. Depending on the market this group can be large though because of their reluctance to accept new products marketers are not inclined to direct much attention to them.

Adopter Categories and the PLC

The adopter categories help explain the shape of the life cycle for many products. For instance, consider how a new household cleaning product may become successful. First, Innovators may experience the product during the developmental stage and then become the key targeted customers at the beginning of the Introduction stage. Early Adopters will also be targeted during the Introduction stage and their adoption will determine whether the product makes it to the Growth stage.

If the product survives the Innovator and Early Adopters it moves to the Growth stage where acceptance by the Early Majority means the product is entering the mass market. The product can continue to be successful as it is adopted by the Late Majority and, to a much lesser extent, by Laggards. Eventually product sales decline as Innovators and Early Adopter move to something new and the cycle starts over.

It should be noted that an assumption of a person's placement in a certain adopter category for one product does not imply that person will also occupy the same category for other products.

For example, someone who is an Innovator for one product may be a Laggard for another. However, with research, marketers may find that an individual's adopter classification for one product applies across a similar set of products.

For instance, those classified as Innovators for computer hardware may have a high probability of being categorized the same for computer software. This assumption may be necessary as a software company develops its target marketing strategies in advance of the launch a new product.

Finally, it should be noted that each adopter category may consist of multiple smaller market segments. For example, the Early Majority is made up of smaller markets that can be segmented on variables such as geography, age, income, etc.

THE PLC AND MARKETING PLANNING

With a basic understanding of the PLC, we now turn to how this is used in marketing planning. As we will see, the PLC helps the marketer understand that marketing decisions must change as a product moves from one stage to another. For example, marketers will find that what works when appealing to Innovators in the Introduction stage is different than marketing methods used to attract Early Majority during the Growth stage. For much of the rest of this tutorial we offer a detailed discussion of how the PLC can aid marketing planning. The discussion is presented using the following assumptions and techniques:

- The chief scope of analysis is at the product form level (*i.e.*, what is happening in a specific industry) where we show how certain characteristics of the market change over time. We break down each stage and discuss the market characteristics in terms of:
  - Level of Competition
  - Nuances of the Target Market
  - Available Product Options
  - Average Price Level
  - Promotional Focus
  - Distribution Strategy
  - Total Industry Profits
- While market characteristics are evaluated for the product form, we offer strategy guidance for individual brands that compete within these specific industries.
- While at the general level the PLC is divided into five main stages, we view most stages as consisting of sub-stages that result from noticeable changes in market characteristics.

DEVELOPMENT STAGE

The Product Life Cycle begins long before a product is brought to market. While technically sales do not start until the next stage, marketers must address many of the same issues they will face once the product is launched. Much of what happens in the Development stage follows our discussion of New Product Development in the Managing Products, where market research is the key element in planning. Most of what occurs in this stage is experienced only by companies who are on the forefront of innovation of a new product form. In our discussion, the Development stage is divided into two distinct sub-stages: early and late.

Early Development Stage

Characteristics

- *Competition*: No real competition exists since the product is in early development much of which is in-house and not readily viewable to competitors. However, from a research perspective competitors are now being identified.
- *Target Market*: The target market exists only in market research terms. Possibly a small number of target customers are used to assist with research.

- *Product*: The product exists only in the form of ideas and prototypes. Inventory is not yet available.
- *Prices*: Non-existent unless the company charges research customers a fee to be part of early product testing.
- *Promotion*: Promotion has yet to occur as companies continue to refine the product form and build their marketing plan.
- *Distribution*: Mostly limited to internal analysis of possible distribution alternatives, though there may be some communication with a limited number of distribution partners in order to gauge interest.
- *Profits*: At this stage there are costs only.

Brand Strategy

For firms developing a new product form this stage is primarily concerned with market research. This stage matches the Concept Development and Testing step for New Product Development.

Customers and distribution partners are only involved to aid in information gathering often through focus group research. Because the product form is still in early development the marketer has yet to determine whether the company will move forward with a full product launch.

Late Development Stage

Characteristics

- *Competition*: While a marketer may not face competition in terms of sales, they may face competitive pressure from companies developing similar products, such as competition to acquire materials or technologies for product development, competition to line up product evaluators, and competition to get early word out about the product to the news media. Additionally, competition may exist in the form of other types of products that potential customers currently use to satisfy needs targeted by the new product form. If these competitors are aware that a new product form is being developed, they may increase efforts to sell their product with the intention of reducing the market's need for the new product.
- *Target Market*: Companies may test market the product among a small group of customers or within a selected geographic market.
- *Product*: Companies researching the product form begin to produce small quantities of the product, primarily for testing or to build initial awareness (*e.g.*, for display at trade shows).
- *Prices*: Initial market price is discussed and if there are active test markets the company may be testing different price levels.
- *Promotion*: Promotion often begins prior to product launch as

marketers prime the market. Emphasis may be on public relations in an attempt to encourage the media to discuss the product prior to launch. If a real test market is used the companies may be using several promotional options including advertising and sales promotion.

- *Distribution*: For product sold through distributors, the ground work is being laid to build the distribution network. In some cases distributor education and training will start prior to product launch.
- *Profits*: A small amount of revenue may be generated if real test markets are used, but overall marketers continue to experience substantial costs.

Brand Strategy

Products that have moved to the late stage of development have done so because market research suggests there is strong potential for success. By this point a marketer has a real product (not just ideas) and is in the position to test it in the market.

Consequently, this stage matches the Market Testing step for New Product Development. Firms electing to test their product in real "test markets" will do so using all their marketing tools.

INTRODUCTION STAGE

This stage represents the launch of the new product form by one or more companies. It is done only after the marketer has created a detailed Marketing Plan. In many cases tactical marketing decisions (*i.e.*, product, price, promotion, distribution, target market) have been adjusted as the product has gone through the Development stage. The Introduction stage is divided into two distinct sub-stages: early and late.

Early Introduction Stage

- *Competition*: In many cases, when two or more companies are working to be first to market with a new product form, one company will be out ahead and for a period of time have the market to itself. However, this does not mean there is no competition. The company that launched the product still faces competition from existing products that customers previously purchased in order to satisfy their needs.
- *Target Market*: To establish interest in the market for a new product form marketers will initially target Innovators and to a larger extent Early Adopters.
- *Product*: From the target market's perspective, product options are limited since only one or a very small number of companies are selling products. Because of the uncertainty in whether the product will be accepted by a larger market and because of the expense involved in

producing products in small volume (primarily due to low demand) there are very few product options available.

- *Prices*: In most cases marketers follow a pricing strategy called price skimming in which price is set at a level that is much higher than can be sustained once competitors enter. Price skimming allows the company to recover development and initial marketing costs before the onslaught of competitors eventually lowers price.
- *Promotion*: For products considered to be a leap ahead of existing products, early marketers may have some difficulty explaining how the product satisfies customer's needs. This is particularly an issue with high-tech products. In this situation the marketer must engage in a promotional campaign that is designed to educate the market on the product form and not necessarily push a specific brand. Additional sales promotion may be used to encourage product trial. Also, the sales force may begin a strong push to acquire distributors.
- *Distribution*: Upon product launch marketers continue efforts to build their distributor network. As we saw in the Development stage, the focus of marketers is to find distributors committed to handling the product.
- *Profits*: Marketers often experience low profits and most likely a loss as the cost of acquiring customers (*i.e.*, promotion) is high and marketers also need to pay back development expense.

Brand Strategy

For the early entrants in the market the most important goal is to create awareness for the product form. If customers can see that the product form holds similar characteristics to existing products then the marketer's task is easier since their job becomes one of convincing customers that this new product form is better than what they are currently using.

However, if the product form is significantly different than existing products then the marketers' job may be far more difficult. Under these conditions the marketer must not only make customers aware of the new product but they must also educate customers as to what the product is, how it works and what benefits are derived from its use.

For some products, such as technology products, conveying this message can prove difficult as customers may not fully understand how the product works and, consequently, not see a need for the product.

Whether customers understand the product or not, this stage requires promotional spending directed to addressing the need for customer education and building awareness. Also, education and awareness alone are not enough; customers must often be enticed to try a product through special promotional efforts (*e.g.*, free trials).

Late Introduction Stage

- *Competition*: By this stage any company that was alone in launching the new product form is alone no longer, as it is highly likely at least one competitor has entered the market.
- *Target Market*: Marketers are now engaged heavily in getting a high percentage of Early Adopters to accept the product.
- *Product*: With competitors entering the choices available to customers expand, though the difference between competitors' offerings is often not that significant.
- *Prices*: Product pricing remains high, though any new competitor entering at this stage may attempt to compete with the early entrants by offering a lower relative price.
- *Promotion*: The promotional message is still one designed to educate the market on the benefits of this new product form but with more competition there is a noticeable increase in the use of advertising that highlights a company's brand. Also, personal selling and sales promotion have increased especially targeting the channel of distribution as entrants attempt to secure distributors.
- *Distribution*: The number of distributors continues to increase with many now offering products from several market entrants (which at this point may still be only a few).
- *Profits*: Losses continue to mount due to high marketing cost and the need to recover development expense. Losses may be even higher than anticipated if the market adopts slower than forecast or if more companies enter than expected.

Brand Strategy

Early entrants continue to create awareness and educate customers, but their promotional orientation may shift to a "buy-our-brand" approach if more companies enter the market. Thus, at this stage, marketers begin to position their products with the intention of separating themselves from the competition.

GROWTH STAGE

The Growth stage is characterized by product sales increasing often at a very rapid rate. This is seen by large percentage sales increases over previous periods (*e.g.*, 50 per cent increase in sales from one quarter to the next). This is an indication the product has advanced beyond Early Adopters and is now being purchased by the mass market (*i.e.*, Early Majority).

It is also the stage when early entrants begin to realise profits, though the fact the market is now profitable invariably leads to increased competition. It is also the time in which competitors try to actively position their brand in a way that will separate it from the onslaught of new entrants. For many products the Growth stage is represented by three distinct sub-stages: early, middle and late.

Early Growth Stage

Characteristics:

- *Competition*: Only a few competitors may be in the market as others wait to see whether the mass market will adopt the product. However, competitors selling products customers previously purchased to satisfy needs now addressed by the new product form may be getting very aggressive in their marketing tactics as they sense the new product form to be a threat.
- *Target Market*: Continued focus is on Early Adopters but marketers begin to identify new market segments that contain the Early Majority.
- *Product*: A basic product sold to the Early Adopters remains, but plans are underway to introduce products with different configurations, such as more options (*e.g.*, advanced models) and fewer options (*i.e.*, stripped down model). An expanded product line may be necessary to satisfy many different potential segments of the mass market.
- *Prices*: The average selling price may remain high especially in cases where market demand is strong and only a few competitors have entered.
- *Promotion*: Promotions are broadened with more emphasis on mass promotions and sales promotions that encourage product trial. Also, personal selling and sales promotions to distributors continue as marketers attempt to make inroads into distributors that target the mass market.
- *Distribution*: Marketers look for new distribution channels that enable the product to begin to reach the mass market. For instance, consumer products may look to gain distribution in large discount retailers.
- *Profits*: The early market entrants may begin to experience profits as early development costs have been covered and overall demand is gaining steam.

Brand Strategy

In the early part of the Growth stage marketers are looking to expand the market beyond the Early Adopters and into the mass market using Market Expansion strategies such as: 1) Grow Sales with Existing Products primarily by getting new market segments to buy, and 2) Grow Sales with New Products by introducing new models containing different sets of features.

The latter strategy is used not only to appeal to new customers but also to encourage repeat purchasing by existing customers.

Additionally, greater emphasis is placed on using promotion to continue building awareness and driving interest in the product form. This is due to: 1) the need to reach a broader market, and 2) to maintain an effective "share of voice" (*i.e.*, percentage of all promotions in the market) so the marketer's message is not lost among competitors' increased promotional spending.

MIDDLE GROWTH STAGE

Characteristics:

- Competition: More competitors are attracted to the market as they see the market potential to provide high profits. Competitors selling products customers previously purchased to satisfy needs now addressed by the new product form may be extremely aggressive (may be entering the Maturity stage of their industry's PLC) resulting in major price reductions. This may delay the adoption of the new product form by some Early Majority.
- *Target Market*: The Early Majority sector of the mass market begins to purchase in higher volume and depending on the product, existing customers (*i.e.*, Early Adopters) may be purchasing again. The Late Majority are beginning to become customers.
- *Product*: Companies increase the number of product offerings in order to differentiate themselves from competitors. In most cases new product offerings do improve on the performance or benefits offered by earlier products. However, the target market may begin to feel burdened by too many choices.
- *Prices*: As more competitors enter with more product options prices may begin to fall, though the effect may not be felt as strongly if demand remains strong. Pricing may be somewhat more competitive if large companies with strong financial backing are now entering, or in smaller segments where multiple companies are trying to establish a niche.
- *Promotion*: Emphasis has shifted to heavy advertising and promotions that promote individual brands and not just awareness and education of the product form. Heavy selling and sales promotion continues with distributors.
- *Distribution*: Distribution reaches saturated levels as all possible channels are now handling the product.
- *Profits*: Marketers who were early entrants to the market may begin to see very high profits as demand is increasing while the pricing levels remain fairly strong. Depending on the product, unit cost of production may be dropping as manufacturing levels increase.

Brand Strategy

In the middle part of Growth stage the objective is to continue a Market Expansion strategy, including seeking out new market segments that have not been targeted. This stage is also a time to focus on product positioning. The idea is to use marketing decisions to affect customer's perceptions of a brand by trying to either: 1) separate a brand from other products (*i.e.*, differentiate), or 2) bring a brand closer to competitor's offerings (*i.e.*, equivalency). For the differentiation approach marketers use promotional methods that show why their brand is different while the equivalency approach may suggest that a brand is equal to other brands but offers an advantage, generally on price.

Late-to-market competitors may use a penetration pricing approach to establish a position in the market. Penetration pricing intentionally sets a price that is below long-term pricing in order to capture large share of market. The firm will raise price once the product is established.

Some marketers also determine that it is time to focus on specific segments of the market via a Niche strategy approach.

Characteristics

- *Competition*: As the market begins to see slower growth, companies find themselves in a highly competitive market with fierce battles occurring on some fronts, such as within certain segments, where demand is falling faster than in other segments.
- *Target Market*: The overall market is still growing in terms of sales volume, especially as the product spreads to the Late Majority. But there is some evidence that while sales are increasing it is occurring at a decreasing rate.
- *Product*: With so many competitors offering numerous product options customers feel overwhelmed and confused by the choices available. In cases where customers do not fully understand the product (*e.g.*, technology product) they may feel more comfortable purchasing from top brands or products sold at major distributors.
- *Prices*: The average price is falling rapidly as market growth begins to slow and competitors struggle to maintain their market share. Price wars may break out.
- *Promotion*: Heavy spending on advertising and especially on sales promotions designed to offer incentives to customers to purchase and to re-purchase.
- *Distribution*: With demand beginning to slow, some distributors cut back on the number of products they stock and persuade leading product marketers to offer more incentives to remain with the distributor.
- *Profits*: Marketers begin to see a leveling off of profits as overall

revenue flattens due to slowing demand and falling prices. However, marketing costs still remain high.

Brand Strategy

Many marketers find this to be the most difficult part of the PLC. The late growth stage is a turbulent time with firms fighting just to survive. The turbulence is brought on by the slowing of growth. This is not to say that overall sales are declining but that the percentage of growth from one period to the next is declining. For instance, sales over a three-year period may show an overall increase but it is occurring at a decreasing rate compared to the previous years (*e.g.*, 20 per cent,15 per cent, 10 per cent).

The key objective for a marketer is to remain competitive by maintaining a power position (*e.g.*, leading brand name) or by achieving an insulated position within a niche. Brands may use promotional tactics that keep existing customers happy (*e.g.*, coupons, improved customer service) and entice new customers to try the product (*e.g.*, rebates, extended payment, try-before-you-buy). Distribution partners are encouraged to remain loyal through such actions as special pricing, promotional assistance and special packaging.

MATURITY STAGE

At some point in time sales of the product form slows. Instead of double-digit growth from one period to the next, the industry limps along with low single digit sales increases or worse. There are two key reasons why this occurs. First, the market has become saturated with a large majority of potential customers having already purchased the product. In the case of products that have a long buy-cycle (*i.e.*, time between repeat purchases) the infrequency of repurchase results in slow sales for some time. Second, customers have moved on to purchase other products that are seen as replacements for this product form. In this situation, the growth of the product form may have been interrupted with the introduction of a new product form (*e.g.*, cassette tape players replaced by CD players).

Under these conditions marketers can no longer count on the growth in the overall market as the trigger for increased company sales. This can be best explained with an example.

- *Period 1:* Market Size 100,000 units Market Share 10 per cent Total Company Sales 10,000 units
- *Period 2:* Market Size 200,000 units Market Share 10 per cent Total Company Sales 20,000 units
- *Period 3:* Market Size 200,000 units Market Share 10 per cent Total Company Sales 20,000 units

As shown, during the growth stage (Period 1 to Period 2) a marketer may see product sales increase without the need for an increase in market share (*i.e.*, maintain status quo). In fact, if their market share dropped to 6 per cent in Period 2 they would still realise an overall sales increase (200,000 x 6 per cent = 120,000 units). But once sales have leveled off (Period 3) competitors now find that the only way to increase sales is to either: 1) increase market share, or 2) increase the market size. This, of course, will make things very competitive.

The slowing of market growth is a signal that the product form may have reached the Maturity stage of the PLC. In our discussion the Maturity stage is divided into two distinct sub-stages: early and late.

Early Maturity Stage

Characteristics

- Competition: By far the fiercest competition takes place as marketers move to grab customers from often weakened competitors. At this stage many competitors fail or merge with others.
- Target Market: Little or no growth is occurring as the market is saturated or the target market looks to other product to satisfy their needs. Laggards may start buying but only if they can no longer purchase products they previously purchased to satisfy their needs.
- Product: Many products still exist though some level of product standardization has occurred. Any new models introduced do not lead to major improvements in product performance or benefits offered, but instead offer minor incremental improvements.
- Prices: The average price continues to fall possibly below cost as competitors attempt to remain in market. Price wars occur in many segments.
- Promotion: Heavy competitive advertising and extensive promotions take place with the objective of getting existing customers to switch (for their repeat purchases) and encouraging distributors not to drop from their inventory.
- Distribution: Distributors continue to reduce their inventory and promotional focus for the product form and become very selective on the products they will carry.
- Profits: Industry profits fall rapidly and many firms lose money as they increase spending in hopes of remaining in the market.

Brand Strategy

In the early part of the maturity stage, the key objective is to enact strategies that enable a product to survive in the face of strong competition driven by lessening of demand. In fact, marketers may be happy following a Status Quo strategy that is intended to just maintain their market position.

Unfortunately, this may prove difficult as this stage, often called the "shakeout stage", leads to many products failing or being absorbed by competitors (*i.e.*, companies merge, products are sold).

In order to survive, marketers may need to resort to tactics designed to "steal customers" from others which often involves significant price promotions (*e.g.*, heavy discounting) or strong promotions intended to improve image or solidify a niche. Marketers who have avoided competing on price may be in a better position to weather the storm if they have convinced the market they offer special features that few others offer. This can be the case if they have successfully established a strong position in a niche market.

Extending the PLC

A more likely scenario for companies at this stage is to investigate new ways to grow the market in an effort to extend the growth stage of the PLC. The use of resurgence tactics include such measures as:

- Changing how customers use the product such as: encourage more frequent use or more consumption per usage (*e.g.*, consume 2 units instead of 1 unit); suggest new benefits that can be obtained from using the product (*e.g.*, has added health benefits not previously promoted); or suggest new uses for the product.
- Finding new markets not previously targeted.
- Developing new product options (*i.e.*, product line extensions) that offer more or better features (*e.g.*, easier to use, safer, more attractive) that may get existing customers to re-purchase more quickly then they would normally.
- Heightening interest by changing image through heavy promotion and package redesign.
- Competing with lower priced brands by offering own low price product through private label branding arrangement with distribution partners.

Late Maturity Stage

Characteristics

- *Competition*: The competitive landscape has stabilized with only the survivors remaining often made up of a few market giants and several small niche firms.
- *Target Market*: The market has become saturated for first time buyers and focus is now on getting existing customers to remain loyal.
- *Product*: The introduction of new models is reduced to just a few product performance enhancements, though there may be more stylistic improvements.
- *Prices*: Overall prices stabilize and may rise due to limited competition.

- *Promotion*: Large competitors begin to cut back on expensive promotions designed to attract new customers and focus on reminder promotions to loyal customers.
- *Distribution*: Has stabilized with few new distributors agreeing to handle product. For products sold at retail stores there is a noticeable reduction in shelf space devoted to the product.
- *Profits*: Companies see profits recover as demand stabilizes, pricing rises and overall marketing costs drop.

Brand Strategy

If companies have failed to extend the PLC in the early part of the maturity stage, it is very likely the product form may never again experience growth. Instead the companies will continue to market the product, albeit, with little effort other than making it available to customers who have been purchasing it for some time.

By the late part of the maturity stage the companies that are still selling may no longer consider the product an important product for the future of the company, but this does not mean the product is not important. In fact, it may be very important for the profit it generates (a.k.a. cash cow) which is used to fund new products. Consequently, some attention is still paid to the product but only to insure that it is still available to those who want to purchase.

DECLINE STAGE

A product form has reached this stage when it becomes clear the market is no longer able to sustain itself. Like the Maturity stage, the Decline stage may last a long time especially for products that have been adopted by a large percentage of the market who are not inclined to change how they satisfy their needs (*i.e.*, Laggards). Since the end of the product form is seen as inevitable, there are no sub-stages here.

Characteristics

- *Competition*: As time goes on firms drop out until no one is producing the product.
- *Target Market*: Mostly consists of Laggards who have been loyal to this type of product for a long time and have not moved on to newer products.
- *Product*: No new improvements are introduced and some models are discontinued.
- *Prices*: May be rising as competitors drop out and companies still in the market have little incentive to engage in price competition. Also, there may be a large loyal market they may not be sensitive to price increases. However, some companies looking to get out of market,

but have existing inventory, may drastically markdown product to encourage rapid sales.

- *Promotion*: Companies limit promotions to occasional reminders to loyal customers though overall little is spent.
- *Distribution*: With declining demand distributors are removing products. The marketer may even make the decision to remove the product from unprofitable distributors. Sales may shift to online distribution or via non-traditional channels.
- *Profits*: For companies remaining, profits may be stable and possibly big if this stage takes a long time to play out.

Brand Strategy:

Marketers are faced with Market Exit strategies when they reach the Decline stage. There are two ways marketers can address this. First, companies may consider a "milking" strategy that involves getting the most out of the product in terms of sales without spending any additional funds to support the product. This strategy works best if a sizable market remains that is loyal to the product and not very price sensitive. A customer base with these characteristics allows a marketer to ride through the decline stage for some time while earning sizeable profits. Second, companies may look to sell off or "divest" the product. In some situations this can be done by first investing in the product in order to make the product more attractive to potential buyers.

However, discontinuing a product does not mean a company no longer earns revenue from the product form. Many discontinued products, especially those used in business and industrial settings, will continue to earn money through support services such as selling supplies and service/repair contracts.

CRITICISMS OF THE PLC

As we have seen, the PLC has the ability to offer marketers guidance on strategies and tactics as they manage products through changing market conditions. Unfortunately, the PLC does not offer a perfect model of markets as it contains drawbacks that prevent it from being applicable to all products. Among the problems cited are:

- *Shape of Curve*: Some product forms do not follow the traditional PLC curve. For instance, clothing may go through regular up and down cycles as styles are in fashion then out then in again. Fad products, such as certain toys, may be popular for a period of time only to see sales drop dramatically until a future generation renews interest in the toy.
- *Length of Stages*: The PLC offers little help in determining how long each stage will last. For example, some products can exist in the Maturity stage for decades while others may be there for only a few

months. Consequently, it may be difficult to determine when adjustments to the Marketing Plan are needed to meet the needs of different PLC stages.

- *Competitor Reaction not Predictable*: As we saw, the PLC suggests that competitor response occurs in a somewhat consistent pattern. For example, the PLC says competitors will not engage in strong brand-to-brand competition until a product form has gained a foothold on the market. The logic is that until the market is established it is in the best interest of all competitors to focus on building interest in the product form itself and not on claiming one brand is better than another. However, competitors do not always conform to theoretical models. Some will always compete on brand first and leave it to others to build market interest for the product form. Arguments can also be made that competitors will respond differently than what the PLC suggests on such issues as pricing, number of product options, spending on declining products, to name a few.
- *Impact of External Forces*: The PLC assumes customers' decisions are primarily impacted by the marketing activities of the companies selling in the market. In fact, there are many other factors that can affect a market which are not controlled by marketers. Such factors (*e.g.*, social changes, technological innovation) can lead to changes in market demand at rates that are much more rapid than would occur if only marketing decisions were being changed (*i.e.*, if everything was held constant except for company's marketing decisions).
- *Use for Forecasting*: The impact of external forces makes it difficult to use the PLC as a forecasting tool. For instance, market factors not directly associated with the marketing activities of market competitors, such as economic conditions, may have a greater impact on reducing demand than customers' interest in the product. Consequently, what may be forecasted as a decline in the market signaling a move to the Maturity stage may in fact be the result of declining economic conditions and not a decline in customers' interest in the product. In fact, it is likely demand for the product will recover to growth levels once economic conditions improve. If a marketer follows the strict guidance of the PLC they would conclude that strategies should shift to those of the Maturity stage. Doing so may be an over-reaction that could hurt market position and profitability.
- *Stages Not Seamlessly Connected*: Some high-tech marketers question whether one stage of the PLC naturally will follow another stage. In particular, technology consultant Geoffrey Moore suggests that for high-tech products targeted to business customers a noticeable space or "chasm" occurs between the

Introduction and Growth stages that can only be overcome by significantly altering marketing strategy beyond what is suggested by the PLC.

While not perfect, the PLC is a marketing tool that should be well understood by marketers since its underlying message, that markets are dynamic, supports the need for frequent marketing planning. Also, for many markets the principles presented by the PLC will in fact prove to be very much representative of the conditions they will face in the market.

Finally, the PLC is just one of many models that can assist marketers as they are engaged in the planning process. Most are beyond the scope of this tutorial. For those interested in learning more about these models you are encouraged to consult one or more of the many excellent Marketing Strategy textbooks or trade books.

PURCHASING PROCEDURE

PURCHASE REQUEST

The specifications and number/quantity and delivery of equipment, devices and materials are determined by the department(s) that will be using the product(s) or materials. The Purchasing Department conducts purchase activities based on purchase requests submitted by the/these department(s).

SELECTION OF COMPANIES FOR ESTIMATE SUBMISSION

The Purchasing Department, at its sole discretion, selects companies from which estimates will be sought. Suppliers are selected from the files of "Companies with Previously Established Business Relationships", "Companies from Which Estimates Can Be Requested" and "Products and Suppliers". Selection is made by comprehensivly evaluating such factors as the quality and performance of the equipment, device(s) or materials to be purchased, compatibility with existing facilities, degree of reliability, product requirements including safety, delivery time, the scale of the order, after-sale service and the company's previous business record.

As a rule, Osaka Gas asks several companies to submit estimates. However, only one company may be specified for estimate submission in such special cases as those concerned with industrial property rights, those requiring maximum levels of safety that only one specific supplier can ensure, cases where only one specific supplier can assure compatibility with existing facilities, or in case of urgency.

ESTIMATE REQUEST

As a rule, when requesting an estimate from a company that it has selected,

Osaka Gas will set out a specification from listing Osaka Gas's requirements in respects of quality, performance standard, size, inspection and method of inspection. The selected companies will be asked to submit cost estimates and specifications to Osaka Gas prior to a specified date.

SUBMISSION ESTIMATE

Specification sheets submitted by potential suppliers at their own expense are checked by the Purchasing Department and the department(s) that will be using the product(s), in order to determine whether the required standards are met by the product(s). All products must pass this examination. During this process, Osaka Gas may request additions or changes to the specifications.

NEGOTIATION

After valid cost estimates and specifications have been comprehensively evaluated in respect of price, technical requirements, etc. Osaka Gas will commence negotiation with the company with the most attractive proposal to discuss the amount of the contract and other terms and conditions. The selection of such a company shall be made by Osaka Gas at its sole discretion. Contract terms and conditions will be decided upon mutual agreement.

CONTRACT CONCLUSION

The business will be established upon conclusion of a contract, in the form of a written document if necessary. The obligations and liabilities of Osaka Gas arise only when such contract is concluded.

DELIVERY AND INSPECTION

Delivery dates specified in the contract must be strictly observed. Precise details of the delivery schedule will be agreed between the supplier and the relevant department(s) of Osaka Gas. Delivered equipment, device(s) or materials must pass inspections conducted by the relevant department(s) of Osaka Gas. When deemed significant, an interim inspection may be conducted during the manufacturing process.

PAYMENT

Payment will be made according to the payment terms specified in the contract.

VALUE ANALYSIS

CONCEPT OF VALUE

The value of a product will be interpreted in different ways by different customers. Its common characteristic is a high level of performance, capability, emotional appeal, style, etc. relative to its cost. This can also be expressed as maximizing the function of a product relative to its cost:

Value = (Performance + Capability)/Cost = Function/Cost

Value is not a matter of minimizing cost. In some cases the value of a product can be increased by increasing its function and cost as long as the added function increases more than its added cost. The concept of functional worth can be important. Functional worth is the lowest cost to provide a given function. However, there are less tangible "selling" functions involved in a product to make it of value to a customer.

INTRODUCTION TO VALUE ANALYSIS

Lawrence Miles conceived of Value Analysis (VA) in the 1945 based on the application of function analysis to the component parts of a product. Component cost reduction was an effective and popular way to improve "value" when direct labour and material cost determined the success of a product. The value analysis technique supported cost reduction activities by relating the cost of components to their function contributions.

Value analysis defines a "basic function" as anything that makes the product work or sell. A function that is defined as "basic" cannot change. Secondary functions, also called "supporting functions", described the manner in which the basic function(s) were implemented. Secondary functions could be modified or eliminated to reduce product cost. As VA progressed to larger and more complex products and systems, emphasis shifted to "upstream" product development activities where VA can be more effectively applied to a product before it reaches the production phase. However, as products have become more complex and sophisticated, the technique needed to be adapted to the "systems" approach that is involved in many products today. As a result, value analysis evolved into the "Function Analysis System Technique" (FAST) which is discussed later.

VALUE ANALYSIS METHOD

In all problem solving techniques, we are trying to change a condition by means of a solution that is unique and relevant. If we describe in detail what we are trying to accomplish, we tend to describe a solution and miss the opportunity to engage in divergent thinking about other alternatives. When trying to describe problems that affect us, we become locked in to a course of action without realizing it, because of our own bias. Conversely, the more abstractly we can define the function of what we are trying to accomplish, the more opportunities as suggested, have for divergent thinking.

This high level of abstraction can be achieved by describing what is to be accomplished with a verb and a noun. In this discipline, the verb answers the question, "What is to be done?" or, "What is it to do?" The verb defines the required action. The noun answers the question, "What is it being done to?" The noun tells what is acted upon. Identifying the function by a verb-noun is not as simple a matter as it appears. Identifying the function in the broadest possible terms provides the greatest potential for divergent thinking because it gives the greatest freedom for creatively developing alternatives. A function should be identified as to what is to be accomplished by a solution and not how it is to be accomplished. How the function is identified determines the scope, or range of solutions that can be considered.

That functions designated as "basic" represent the operative function of the item or product and must be maintained and protected. Determining the basic function of single components can be relatively simple. By definition then, functions designated as "basic" will not change, but the way those functions are implemented is open to innovative speculation. As important as the basic function is to the success of any product, the cost to perform that function is inversely proportional to its importance. This is not an absolute rule, but rather an observation of the consumer products market. Few people purchase consumer products based on performance or the lowest cost of basic functions alone.

When purchasing a product it is assumed that the basic function is operative. The customer's attention is then directed to those visible secondary support functions, or product features, which determine the worth of the product. From a product design point of view, products that are perceived to have high value first address the basic function's performance and stress the achievement of all of the performance attributes. Once the basic functions are satisfied, the designer's then address the secondary functions necessary to attract customers. Secondary functions are incorporated in the product as features to support and enhance the basic function and help sell the product. The elimination of secondary functions that are not very important to the customer will reduce product cost and increase value without detracting from the worth of the product.

The cost contribution of the basic function does not, by itself, establish the value of the product. Few products are sold on the basis of their basic function alone. If this were so, the market for "no name" brands would be more popular than it is today. Although the cost contribution of the basic function is relatively small, its loss will cause the loss of the market value of the product. One objective of value analysis or function analysis, to improve value by reducing the cost-function relationship of a product, is achieved by eliminating or combining as many secondary functions as possible.

VALUE ANALYSIS PROCESS

The first step in the value analysis process is to define the problem and its scope. Once this is done, the functions of the product and its items are derived. These functions are classified into "basic" and "secondary" functions. A Cost Function Matrix or Value Analysis Matrix is prepared to identify the cost of providing each function by associating the function with a mechanism or component part of a product. Product functions with a high cost-function ratio are identified as opportunities for further investigation and improvement. Improvement opportunities are then brainstormed, analysed, and selected.

The objective of the Function Cost Matrix approach is to draw the attention of the analysts away from the cost of components and focus their attention on the cost contribution of the functions. The Function Cost Matrix displays the components of the product, and the cost of those components, along the left vertical side of the graph. The top horizontal legend contains the functions performed by those components. Each component is then examined to determine how many functions that component performs, and the cost contributions of those functions.

Detailed cost estimates become more important following function analysis, when evaluating value improvement proposals. The total cost and per cent contribution of the functions of the item under study will guide the team, or analyst, in selecting which functions to select for value improvement analysis. A variation of the Function-Cost Matrix is the Value Analysis Matrix. This matrix was derived from the Quality Function Deployment (QFD) methodology.

It is more powerful in two ways. First, it associates functions back to customer needs or requirements. In doing this, it carries forward an importance rating to associate with these functions based on the original customer needs or requirements. Functions are then related to mechanisms, the same as with the Function-Cost Matrix. Mechanisms are related to functions as either strongly, moderately or weakly supporting the given function. This relationship is noted with the standard QFD relationship symbols. The associated weighting factor is multiplied by customer or function importance and each columns value is added. These totals are normalized to calculate each mechanism's relative weight in satisfying the designated functions. This is where the second difference with the Function-Cost Matrix arises. This mechanism weight can then be used as the basis to allocate the overall item or product cost. The mechanism target costs can be compared with the actual or estimated costs to see where costs are out of line with the value of that mechanism as derived from customer requirements and function analysis.

INTEGRATING QFD WITH FAST

A powerful analysis method is created when FAST is used in conjunction with QFD. QFD enables the uses of the Value Analysis Matrix. An example of a value analysis matrix for the pencil example.

The steps for using these two methodologies are as follows:

1. Capture customer requirements and perform QFD product planning with the product planning matrix. Translate customer needs into directly into verb-noun functions or use a second matrix to translate technical characteristics into verb-noun functions.

2. Prepare a FAST diagram and develop the product concept in conjunction with the QFD concept selection matrix. Review the verb-noun functions in the QFD matrix and assure that they are included in the FAST diagram. Revise verb-noun function descriptions if necessary to assure consistency between the QFD matrix and the FAST diagram.
3. Dimension the system in the FAST diagram into subsystems/assemblies/parts. These are generically referred to as mechanisms.
4. Develop value analysis matrix at system level. The "what's" or system requirements/function in the value analysis matrix are derived from either a customer FAST diagram or by selecting those function statements that correspond to the customer needs or technical characteristics in the product planning matrix. The importance rating is derived from the product planning matrix as well.
5. Complete the value analysis matrix by relating the mechanisms to the customer requirements/functions and calculate the associated weight. Summarize the column weights and normalize to create mechanism weights. Allocate the target cost based on the mechanism weights. This represents the value to the customer based on the customer importance. Compare with either estimated costs based on the product concept or actual costs if available.
6. Identify high cost to value mechanisms/subsystems by comparing the mechanism target costs to the mechanism estimated/actual costs

A product or system such as an automobile contains a great many components and would result in an extremely complex FAST model. The complexity of the process is not governed by the number of components in a product, but the level of abstraction selected to perform the analysis.

With an automobile, a high level of abstraction could contain the major subsystems as the components under study, such as: the power train, chassis, electrical system, passenger compartment, etc. The result of the FAST model and supporting cost analysis might then focus the team's attention on the power train for further analysis.

Moving to a lower level of abstraction, the power train could then be divided into its components for a more detailed analysis. In other words, the concept of decomposition is applied to a FAST model. The initial FAST model will stay at a high level of abstraction. Starting at a higher level of abstraction allows for uncluttered macro analysis of the overall problem until those key functions can be found, isolated, and the key issues identified. If a function is identified for further study. A supporting FAST diagram is then created for that subsystem function. This process of decomposition or moving to lower levels of abstraction could be carried down several levels if appropriate. Once high cost to value mechanisms are identified in the initial system value analysis matrix, the next step is to focus more attention on those mechanisms and associated functions. Dimensioning groups the functions together into those associated with a particular subsystem, assembly or part. The FAST diagram can be expanded into a lower level of abstraction in the area under investigation.

The steps involved are as follows:

- Use QFD to translate higher-level customer needs to subsystem technical characteristics.
- Create FAST diagram at lower level of abstraction for targeted mechanism/subsystem.
- Prepare a FAST diagram and develop the product concept in conjunction with the QFD concept selection matrix
- Dimension the system in the FAST diagram into assemblies/parts or identify the assemblies/parts needed to perform the given function.
- Develop value analysis matrix at a lower level of abstraction for the targeted subsystem. The "what's" or system requirements/function in the value analysis matrix are derived from either a customer FAST diagram or by selecting those function statements that correspond to the customer needs or technical characteristics in the subsystem planning matrix.
- Complete the value analysis matrix and identify high cost to value mechanisms by comparing the mechanism target costs to the mechanism estimated/actual costs

VALUE IMPROVEMENT PROCESS

Performing value analysis or producing the FAST model and analyzing functions with the value analysis matrix are only the first steps in the process. The real work begins with brainstorming, developing and analyzing potential improve-ments in the product.

These subsequent steps are supported by:

- The QFD Concept Selection Matrix is a powerful tool to evaluate various concept and design alternatives based on a set of weighted criteria that ultimately tie back to customer needs.
- Benchmarking competitors and other similar products helps to see new ways functions can be performed and breaks down some of the not-invented-here paradigms.
- Product cost and life cycle cost models support the estimating of cost for the Function-Cost and Value Analysis Matrices and aid in the evaluation of various product concepts.
- Technology evaluation is leads us to new ways that basic functions can be performed in a better or less costly way. Concept development should involve people with a knowledge of new technology development and an open mind to identify how this technology might

relate to product functions that need to be performed. Methods such as the theory of inventive problem solving or TRIZ are useful in this regard.

- Design for Manufacturability/Assembly principles provide guidance on how to better design components and assemblies that are more manufacturable and, as a result, are lower in cost.

Value Analysis or Function Analysis provide the methods to identify the problem and to begin to define the functions that need to be performed. As we proceed in developing a FAST model, implicit in this process is developing a concept of operation for the product which is represented by all of the lower order functions in a FAST diagram. Concept alternatives will be developed through brainstorming, benchmarking other products performing similar functions, and surveying and applying new technology. Since multiple concepts need to be evaluated, we want to use a higher level of abstraction for the FAST model to provide us with the greatest flexibility and a minimum level of effort. Trade studies and technical analysis will be performed to evaluate various product concepts. A concept selection matrix is a good tool to summarize a variety of different data and support making a decision about the preferred concept.

All of these steps may be iterative as a preferred concept evolves and gets more fully developed. In addition, there should be a thorough evaluation of whether all functions are needed or if there is a different way of accomplishing a function as the concept is developed to a lower level of abstraction. When a Function Cost or Value Analysis Matrix is prepared, functions that are out of balance with their worth are identified, further challenging the team to explore different approaches.

5

Credit Risk Management

CREDIT RISK

Credit risk refers to the risk that a borrower will default on any type of debt by failing to make payments which it is obligated to do. The risk is primarily that of the lender and include lost principal and interest, disruption to cash flows, and increased collection costs. The loss may be complete or partial and can arise in a number of circumstances. For example:

- A consumer may fail to make a payment due on a mortgage loan, credit card, line of credit, or other loan
- A company is unable to repay amounts secured by a fixed or floating charge over the assets of the company
- A business or consumer does not pay a trade invoice when due
- A business does not pay an employee's earned wages when due
- A business or government bond issuer does not make a payment on a coupon or principal payment when due
- An insolvent insurance company does not pay a policy obligation
- An insolvent bank won't return funds to a depositor
- A government grants bankruptcy protection to an insolvent consumer or business

To reduce the lender's credit risk, the lender may perform a credit check on the prospective borrower, may require the borrower to take out appropriate insurance, such as mortgage insurance or seek security or guarantees of third parties, besides other possible strategies. In general, the higher the risk, the higher will be the interest rate that the debtor will be asked to pay on the debt.

ASSESSING CREDIT RISK

Significant resources and sophisticated programmes are used to analyze and manage risk. Some companies run a credit risk department whose job is to assess the financial health of their customers, and extend credit (or not) accordingly. They may use in house programmes to advise on avoiding, reducing and transferring risk. They also use third party provided intelligence. Companies like Standard and Poor's, Moody's Analytics, Fitch Ratings, and Dun and Bradstreet provide such information for a fee. Most lenders employ their own models to rank potential and existing customers according to risk, and then apply appropriate strategies.

With products such as unsecured personal loans or mortgages, lenders charge a higher price for higher risk customers and vice versa. With revolving products such as credit cards and overdrafts, risk is controlled through the setting of credit limits. Some products also require security, most commonly in the form of property. Credit scoring models also form part of the framework used by banks or lending institutions grant credit to clients.

For corporate and commercial borrowers, these models generally have qualitative and quantitative sections outlining various aspects of the risk including, but not limited to, operating experience, management expertise, asset quality, and leverage and liquidity ratios, respectively. Once this information has been fully reviewed by credit officers and credit committees, the lender provides the funds subject to the terms and conditions presented within the contract.

Credit risk has been shown to be particularly large and particularly damaging for very large investment projects, so-called megaprojects. This is because such projects are especially prone to end up in what has been called the "debt trap," *i.e.*, a situation where – due to cost overruns, schedule delays, etc. – the costs of servicing debt becomes larger than the revenues available to pay interest on and bring down the debt.

SOVEREIGN RISK

Sovereign risk is the risk of a government becoming unwilling or unable to meet its loan obligations, or reneging on loans it guarantees. Many countries have faced sovereign risk in the late-2000s global recession. The existence of such risk means that creditors should take a two-stage decision process when deciding to lend to a firm based in a foreign country. Firstly one should consider the sovereign risk quality of the country and then consider the firm's credit quality.

Five macroeconomic variables that affect the probability of sovereign debt rescheduling are:

- Debt service ratio
- Import ratio
- Investment ratio
- Variance of export revenue
- Domestic money supply growth

The probability of rescheduling is an increasing function of debt service ratio, import ratio, variance of export revenue and domestic money supply growth. Frenkel, Karmann, Raahish and Scholtens also argue that the likelihood of rescheduling is a decreasing function of investment ratio due to future economic productivity gains. Saunders argues that rescheduling can become more likely if the investment ratio rises as the foreign country could become less dependent on its external creditors and so be less concerned about receiving credit from these countries/investors.

COUNTERPARTY RISK

A counterparty risk, also known as a default risk, is a risk that a counterparty will not pay what it is obligated to do on a bond, credit derivative, trade credit insurance or payment protection insurance contract, or other trade or transaction when it is supposed to. Financial institutions may hedge or take out credit insurance of some sort with a counterparty, which may find themselves unable to pay when required to do so, either due to temporary liquidity issues or longer term systemic reasons.

On the methodological side, counterparty risk can be affected by wrong way risk, namely the risk that different risk factors be correlated in the most harmful direction. Including correlation between the portfolio risk factors and the counterparty default into the methodology is not trivial, see for example Brigo and Pallavicini.

KINDS OF CREDIT RISK MANAGEMENT

Credit risk can be classified in the following way:

- *Credit default risk*—The risk of loss arising from a debtor being unlikely to pay its loan obligations in full or the debtor is more than 90 days past due on any material credit obligation; default risk may impact all credit-sensitive transactions, including loans, securities and derivatives.
- *Concentration risk*—The risk associated with any single exposure or group of exposures with the potential to produce large enough losses to threaten a bank's core operations. It may arise in the form of single name concentration or industry concentration.
- *Country risk*—The risk of loss arising from a sovereign state freezing foreign currency payments (transfer/conversion risk) or when it defaults on its obligations (sovereign risk).

It is said that success has many parents but failure is an orphan. Surely the massive expansion and pervasive influence of derivatives during the last two decades of the twentieth century stands as one of the great success stories of that period. True to form, there are many claimants to the title of first swap arranger.

CREDIT RISK ASSOCIATED WITH TRADING MANAGEMENT

The primary form of credit risk associated with trading in those days was settlement risk. Recognition of this had been driven home painfully by the failure of Bankhaus Herstatt during the trading day on June 26, 1974. Even in the early 1980s, daily turnover in the foreign exchange spot and forward markets was in the hundreds of billions of dollars. Such volumes gave rise to serious concern about the credit risk of such contracts, from the time payment instructions became irrevocable to the time the agreed exchange amount was received. As the new swap dealers were quick to point out, however, settlement on most of their transactions was on a net basis, which meant there was no settlement risk.

Looking beyond the settlement risk issue, there was only limited understanding of the pre-settlement credit implications of term derivative transactions. Some people thought that since there was no exchange of principal on an interest rate swap there was no credit risk. After all, one cannot claim loss of future interest payments on a loan when a borrower defaults. The fact that most credit officers were thoroughly steeped in the historical cost accounting framework was an additional obstacle to a clear understanding of these mark-to-market instruments. Furthermore, derivative volumes were small and counterparties were virtually all investment grade names. These factors combined to make pre-settlement credit exposure a latent and largely ignored risk aspect of derivative trading in the early 1980s.

By 1986, swap market volumes had grown significantly and so had current mark-to-market exposures. Gradually the realisation spread that these positive market values represented material credit risky balance sheet assets similar to corporate and industrial bank loans. As such, counterparties to such trades clearly should be subjected to credit review and transactions should only be done within an approved credit exposure limit. But there was one nagging problem. When making a traditional loan it doesn't require complex mathematical analysis to answer the question "how big is the loan?" The answer to that question is clearly stated in the proposed term sheet. While some would point out that the fair value of a loan fluctuates just as the price of a bond does, historical cost accounting treats the principal amount as fixed.

For swaps, there are two problems. First, they are usually done near par. Initial market values only reflect the slightly off-market impact of a dealer's bid/offer spread. This initial value, however, is only a small fraction of the potential future exposure that may materialise as a deal ages and market conditions change. Thus current exposure, especially current exposure on newly executed deals, is not a realistic measure of the true potential loss from a downgrade or default on the part of the counterparty. Second, market fluctuations lead to constant revisions in the exposure, however measured. Such unstable exposure presented an entirely new dimension of uncertainty that many traditional credit control personnel found difficult to incorporate into their thinking.

The derivative credit exposure issue received added attention when the Basel Committee on Banking Supervision began to develop its initial rules for minimum regulatory capital requirements in 1986 and 1987. The committee realised that the current market values of a bank's derivative contracts did not capture their full potential credit exposure. As a result, they set out to derive reasonably simple rules to calibrate potential increases in such credit exposure, based on volatility in the underlying market data and the resulting impact on fair values of broad categories of trades. The result was the now well-known add-on approach to measuring potential future exposure.

Several comments are in order regarding the structure and parameters of the initial Basel add-on calculation.

a. The approach was intended to be simple to implement so that even small banks with a few hedge contracts could perform the calculation without difficulty.
b. It was only intended to capture the increase in *aggregate* exposure. It was neither proposed nor intended as a satisfactory approach to measuring individual counterparty exposures.
c. It provided only very limited recognition of the tenor of exposure by offering different parameters for contracts with more than or less than one year to maturity.
d. The same add-ons were applied to both at-the-money and away-from-the-money contracts, despite the amortisation towards zero in the value of many contracts as they approach maturity.
e. It treated each transaction in isolation. While this greatly simplified the mechanics of the calculation, it completely ignored the degree of co-variation in value among multiple deals.
f. Recognising that portfolio effects had been ignored, the parameters of the method were calibrated to reflect an assumed average degree of portfolio diversification.
g. While the potential increase in *aggregate* exposure was probably not unreasonable, the *marginal change* in potential exposure from adding or deleting a single deal was highly unreliable and could even be directionally incorrect.

A negative consequence of Basel's add-on method was to provide apparent regulatory sanction for this approach. While adequate for estimating aggregate potential exposure, it was, and is, quite unsuitable when applied at the individual counterparty level or to evaluating the marginal exposure of a new deal.

The essential problem is the implicit assumption of an average degree of diversification. In fact, individual counterparty portfolios exhibit widely differing diversification characteristics. The most obvious and striking example is an offsetting transaction where the market value moves in a directly opposite direction to that of an existing trade in response to changing market conditions.

If the two trades are not legally nettable, the second trade has almost zero impact on potential exposure. If they are legally nettable, then the second trade significantly reduces potential exposure. The add-on approach, however, will produce an unrealistic increase in measured exposure in both cases.

Despite these widely recognised shortcomings, most institutions adopted some variation in the add-on method for tracking and setting limits for counterparty credit exposure. This was driven by the comparative simplicity and modest cost of deploying such a system. Given the huge trading losses experienced in the mid-1980s, market risk was viewed as the most serious issue requiring attention and resources. Building a more sophisticated system for controlling trading credit risk simply was not a serious consideration at most institutions.

While adopting the add-on approach, bank credit departments invariably insisted on more conservative parameters internally than those employed in regulatory capital calculations. Partly this was driven by a recognition of the fact that the purposes for the two calculations were different. Primarily, however, it reflected an inherent distrust among traditional credit officers of these fancy new instruments. By making the numbers larger, it was felt the volumes could be limited and the associated risks constrained. The result tended to be greatly inflated potential exposure estimates that often had only an infinitesimal chance of materialising as actual exposure-at-default in the future.

Another trend in the late 1980s and early 1990s was the legal battle to make netting enforceable under the bankruptcy laws in various countries. The International Swaps and Derivatives Association (then known as the International Swap Dealers Association) (ISDA) lead the way in most countries around the world. ISDA formulated standard contract language and waged multiple campaigns to gain legislative recognition of the enforceability of netting under the terms of such contracts when one party declared bankruptcy.

While we think of netting as the accepted norm today it is still far from universal. Indeed, even in the US netting is of questionable enforceability when dealing with certain types of institutions. Examples are insurance companies and public utilities where bankruptcy claims are adjudicated in some type of state administrative process rather than under the US bankruptcy code or laws governing federally insured financial institutions.

The most frequent circumstance today is for netting to be partially enforceable across relevant sets of transactions. Certain deals are entered into under terms of an enforceable netting agreement. These are nettable against each other but their combined net market value, if negative, cannot be offset against exposure in other nettable pools or against transactions done outside any enforceable netting agreement. This introduces an added layer of complexity to the analysis. It also means that legal contract information must be captured and properly reflected in the calculations if they are to be robust in reflecting the impact of enforceable netting.

CREDIT RISK MANAGEMENT FOR BANKING

The importance of credit risk management for banking is tremendous. Banks and other financial institutions are often faced with risks that are mostly of financial nature. These institutions must balance risks as well as returns. For a bank to have a large consumer base, it must offer loan products that are reasonable enough. However, if the interest rates in loan products are too low, the bank will suffer from losses. In terms of equity, a bank must have substantial amount of capital on its reserve, but not too much that it misses the investment revenue, and not too little that it leads itself to financial instability and to the risk of regulatory non-compliance. Credit risk management, in finance terms, refers to the process of risk assessment that comes in an investment. Risk often comes in investing and in the allocation of capital. The risks must be assessed so as to derive a sound investment decision. Likewise, the assessment of risk is also crucial in coming up with the position to balance risks and returns. Banks are constantly faced with risks. There are certain risks in the process of granting loans to certain clients.

There can be more risks involved if the loan is extended to unworthy debtors. Certain risks may also come when banks offer securities and other forms of investments. The risk of losses that result in the default of payment of the debtors is a kind of risk that must be expected. Because of the exposure of banks to many risks, it is only reasonable for a bank to keep substantial amount of capital to protect its solvency and to maintain its economic stability. The second Basel Accords provides statements of its rules regarding the regulation of the bank's capital allocation in connection with the level of risks the bank is exposed to. The greater the bank is exposed to risks, the greater the amount of capital must be when it comes to its reserves, so as to maintain its solvency and stability. To determine the risks that come with lending and investment practices, banks must assess the risks. Credit risk management must play its role then to help banks be in compliance with Basel II Accord and other regulatory bodies.To manage and assess the risks faced by banks, it is important to make certain estimates, conduct monitoring, and perform reviews of the performance of the bank.

However, because banks are into lending and investing practices, it is relevant to make reviews on loans and to scrutinize and analyse portfolios. Loan reviews and portfolio analysis are crucial then in determining the credit and investment risks.

The complexity and emergence of various securities and derivatives is a factor banks must be active in managing the risks. The credit risk management system used by many banks today has complexity; however, it can help in the assessment of risks by analysing the credits and determining the probability of defaults and risks of losses. Credit risk management for banking is a very useful system, especially if the risks are in line with the survival of banks in the business world.

CREDIT RISK MODEL

EBCRM is a credit scoring method developed by Splett et al. to classify farms. They used borower data provided by the Farm Credit Bank of St. Louis. Instead of using real loan repayment performance classification, loans are classified by the borrower's farm business performance. With an experience-based model, FFSC dependent variables, variables weights, and interval cutoff points were established and a credit score was computed for each loan. An important contribution of their study is the credit scoring method to classify the loans by farm performance measures, *i.e.*, the FFSC financial measures. It initialized the credit risk evaluation from the borrower's side. Five key measure variables are chosen by the farm lending expert panel. They are liquidity, profitability, repayment capacity, and efficiency. For each variable, five interval ranges are defined. Each farm has five scores on liquidity, solvency, profitability, repayment capacity and financial efficiency accordingly. These five scores are weighted to generate a total score between 1 and 5. Then, each farm is grouped to a credit risk class.

Stress Indicators

This study adopts the results from Zech and Pederson (2003) as the stress indicators. The first stress indicator is the Term Debt Coverage Ratio (TDCR). The second stress indicator is the Earned Net Worth Growth Rate (ENWGR). The Term Debt coverage ratio calculation is the standard established by FFSC. Earned net worth growth is calculated as: Similar to Zech and Pederson, the stress indicators are calculated as averages. The averaging of the dependent variables removes some of the year-to-year volatility inherent in farm income and provides a slightly longer-term stress index.

Probability of Default

The most recent statistically based credit risk model is the logistic model estimating the probability of default of 157,853 loans within the Seventh Farm Credit District. They utilized historical financial origination ratios based on underwriting standards to predict the probability of default of different loan types.

The estimated probability of default is mapped into a similar default risk grid of S&P publicly rated firms for appropriate loan pricing. The results indicate that repayment capacity, owner equity and working capital are important determinants of probability of default.

The FRB model defines default as a payment being ninety days or more past due at least once since origination. This is the traditional and widely-applied definition for default. Two classes of default and not-default construct the binary dependent variable. Three origination ratios are used as the independent variables: Capital Debt Repayment Capacity Percentage (CDRC), Owner Equity Percentage (OE), and Working Capital Percentage (WC). The regression results for the overall model show that all three ratios are significant in the model. With equation 4, the probability of default is estimated for each farm. FRB chose a cutoff value of 2 per cent for classifying default. The proposed FCS guidelines reported in their study suggest a cutoff of between 0.26 and 0.52 for BBB-loans. The grouping of three classes for FRB are based on PD cutoffs of 0.50 per cent and 2 per cent.

DATA

This study uses the annual farm data from 2000 through 2004 provided by the Illinois Farm Business and Farm Management (FBFM) Association. FBFM is an informative database with Illinois farmers' financial information. Cost and market values of assets and liabilities are available as well as farm and non-farm income and expenditure data. There are 399 sole proprietors that meet the consistency and field staff validation criteria to be included in a comparative data set over the entire five year sample. Verification procedures included certifications on cost and market asset valuation; income certification; and farm and non-farm cash flow expenditure validation. Previous studies using the FBFM data typically only utilize a 2 year continuous sample. A more consistent analysis result is expected since this study does not include the farms that drop out or enter in the database during a 5-year period. Moreover, the extended sample allows for the testing of model performance in years subsequent to initial credit evaluation and scoring.

The average ENWGR ranged from a low of-1 per cent in 2001 to a high of 5 per cent in 2004, while the average TDRC ranged from 2.74 in 2003 to 21.38 in 2001. The average Z score and the proportion of high risk borrowers for the Altman 1 model are substantially larger than the Z score for the Altman 2 model. This is primarily due to the inclusion of the capital turnover (sales to asset) ratio. Agricultural businesses tend to be more capital intensive and have higher proportions of assets relative to sales. For example, the average ratio for agricultural borrows in the sample is 0.27 whereas in the Altman original study the average was 1.9. Since the coefficient on this ratio is approximately 1.0, the result is a difference of over 1.5 in the calculated Z score and hence, a higher proportion of borrowers classified as high risk. Similar to FRB results, a substantial proportion of borrowers are grouped in the 2 to 2.5 per cent range and thus, a higher proportion of borrowers are classified in the high risk FRB class.

RESULTS

Comparisons of the classification results over the entire 5-year period. Values on the diagonals of each sub matrix indicate the risk categories are similar between the two models. Large inconsistencies occur with the Altman models. For example, 135 of the 813 borrowers classified as high risk for Altman 1 are classified as low risk in the Altman 2 model. Another major discrepancy occurs between the FRB model and Altman 2 model. Almost 10 per cent of the borrowers classified as low risk in the Altman 2 model are classified as high risk in the FRB model. The classification procedures are not standardized across the models. Another method to compare the models is to measure simple correlation coefficients of the raw scores of each model.

The rank correlation among all the models is very strong ranging from-0.79 between EBSCM and Altman 2 to 0.966 between the two Altman models. Indications are that the ranking of farms is similar across the models whereas the distribution and classifications of the models differ. Effective risk rating models should have a strong relationship to future financial performance and be able to identify future financial stress. Two stress measures are calculated in each year-earned net worth growth (ENWGR) and term debt and capital replacement ratio (TDCR). To remove some of the year-to-year variability prevalent in farming, the measures are averaged over a two-year period. The mean values and significant differences of means across credit rating classes for each of the stress indicators are provided. In general, the directional effects are as expected. The low risk models result in stronger earnings and repayment performance in future periods. As expected the significance tends to decline as the prediction time frame lengthens. Poor loan performance is often dictated by extremely stressed conditions. Another approach to assess and compare the models is to establish a stress threshold where the performance ratio is categorized as high risk.

For each of the two ratios, a cutoff threshold is used to separate high risk farms from other farms. The values for ENWGR and TDCR are 0.00 and 1.00 respectively. Credit scores are then used to evaluate the proportion of farms that exceed the threshold in future periods. The mean results and statistical differences based on credit scores in 2000 are reported. Each percentage value represents the proportion of the 399 farms that did not exceed the stress threshold in each respective period. For example, the 32.47 per cent value for ENWGR for 2001-02 indicates that for all farms classified as low risk with the Altman 1 model in 2000, 32.47 per cent of the farms will be below the stress threshold of 0 in 2001-02. Again, the general direction of each of the models is consistent with expectations.

The EBCSM was the only model that exhibited statistical differences in each year for ENWGR. A final comparison among the models involves estimating a simple logit model measuring the relationship between the raw credit score (or PD) and the high risk threshold classifications for each future period. The steeper the curve, the stronger the relationship between the credit score and future financial performance and stress. The agricultural models (EBCSM and FRB) tend to have stronger relationships with both the earnings and repayment stress indicators. The Altman models did not have a strong relationship with future repayment analysis. This is likely due to the inclusion of repayment capacity in the agricultural models and the linkage over time of repayment capacity.

However, the distribution of the scores and classification rules of the models differed. The models tended to be related to short-term future performance, but the relationship declined over time. The Altman models do not perform as well and some inconsistencies occur in classification. This is likely due to the inherent differences of financial ratios between corporate borrowers and agricultural firms. An extension of this analysis would be to re-weight the discriminant function for agricultural purposes.

Operational Risk

In addition to the capital requirements for credit and equity exposures, the proposed rule would assign a specific risk-based capital requirement for operational risk, which is the risk of loss, exclusive of insurance and tax effects, from events "associated with internal fraud; external fraud; employment practices and workplace safety; clients, products, and business practices; damage to physical assets; business disruption and system failures; or execution, delivery and process management". The proposed rule would require banks to "establish and document a process to identify, measure, monitor, and control operational risk in bank products, activities, processes, and systems". Banks must choose a value-at-risk methodology and produce an estimate of operational risk at the one-year 99.9th percentile confidence level. Also, the methodology must cover expected and unexpected operational loss, unless the bank can show that the former is covered by offsets, such as operational risk reserves.

Regulators of Market Discipline

The regulators included market discipline as the third pillar of the proposed rule on the theory that, if banks are required to publicly disclose substantial information regarding their risk management processes, then the potential effect of such disclosures on the market for their securities would encourage them to have strong risk management processes. In adopting the proposed rule, the regulators brushed aside complaints that such disclosure would be too burdensome, not comparable across banks, and likely to be misinterpreted by the public.

For example, with respect to a bank's assessment of credit risk for wholesale exposures, the bank is required to not only describe the definitions, method and data for estimation and validation of each of the risk parameters, it is required to provide, across a number of PD grades, total EAD, exposure weighted ELGD and LDG, and exposure-weighted capital requirements. It is also required to provide a comparison of risk parameter estimates against actual outcomes for both the preceding period and a longer period. This comparison would at a minimum be shown for the wholesale category and each retail category and, where appropriate, the bank should further decompose this to provide analysis of each risk parameter outcomes against estimates.

ORGANISATIONAL OBSTACLES TO IMPROVEMENT MANAGEMENT

A number of organisational obstacles stood in the way of better credit exposure measurement systems. As already mentioned, cost was an important issue, especially when market risk was viewed as the really serious hazard. Most credit officers just wanted to limit an activity they viewed as fraught with risks they didn't understand and that they weren't sure the traders understood either. Perhaps equally serious, there was little support from the business side for the cost of improved credit exposure estimation systems. On reflection, this is not too surprising. Traders live and die on the basis of three things:

a. Accurate pricing;
b. Clear and reliable understanding of their open positions (usually expressed in terms of Greek letter sensitivities); and
c. Realistic assessments of their potential losses (either in the form of a formal value-at-risk (VAR) estimate or, more likely, in terms of their own intuitive understanding of market volatility relative to their open positions).

These three factors are part of their daily lives, of the very air they breathe. Credit risk, on the other hand, seems like a remote contingency with little relevance. Traders usually regard credit risk oversight as a distasteful nuisance, a series of hurdles to be overcome. The point is to get the deals done. If a counterparty's limit is full, the usual attitude is "just raise the limit and let me get on with my job!"

Unfortunately, unsophisticated credit exposure measurement systems tended to intensify the inherent cultural conflict between traders and credit officers. Traders realised that add-on based exposure estimates, at least at the counterparty level, were inconsistent and inflated. They particularly recognised that marginal exposure implications were unreliable. This became painfully obvious when counterparties did offsetting trades to neutralise future changes in their net positions, and the system indicated that these increased credit exposure! All this reinforced traders' cynicism about credit oversight in general. They insisted that they were being constrained by a system that was inconsistent and arbitrary while credit staff were left to defend the indefensible.

Another obstacle to improved systems was limited analytical talent in the risk management side of the organisation. The big financial opportunities were in trading and it was difficult to attract the best quants and system engineers to the risk management side of an institution.

As a result, while the business had little interest in more sophisticated credit exposure measurement, risk management staff often lacked the analytical vision to formulate a better approach. The prevailing attitude on the credit risk side often tended to be, "make the numbers bigger and that will make us safer." Unfortunately, this tended to undermine the credibility of the exposure estimates even among credit approvers. The result was an unhealthy behavioural feedback loop. In effect, outstanding loan balances and potential trading credit exposures were two different currencies with an uncertain exchange rate between them. Each limit approver was required by circumstances to decide how to translate the one to the other. In such a situation, it was impossible to generate consistent credit decisions across the organisation.

IMPETUS FOR CHANGE MANAGEMENT

With all these obstacles, one might ask how did any improvement occur? In some cases there was a fortunate convergence of technical expertise, management vision and institutional emphasis on deploying best practice risk methods. More often than not, however, the impetus for change came at the point when credit availability began to constrain the ability to do business. As long as volume was modest and counterparties were solid investment grade names this was not a serious problem. Credit limits were generally available to cover even the inflated exposure estimates produced by a conservative add-on approach.

Moving into the 1990s, however, volumes continued to grow while smaller and less creditworthy counterparties entered the market. Gradually the old arguments about the exposures "not being real" and the estimates "being inflated" became less compelling. Credit approvers grew more reluctant to approve increased trading credit limits in the face of already large measured exposures for good names and for new exposure to lower quality names. Eventually situations arose where credit officers would say, in effect: "I don't care how inflated the numbers are, I'm not putting my name on an approval bigger than the current limit, period. Justify more realistic estimates and then maybe we can talk." This resulted in a real business incentive for more realistic exposure measurement and a willingness to spend some money to make it happen.

IMPROVEMENT OF EXPOSURE ESTIMATION SYSTEM MANAGEMENT

Given the incentives and resources to build an improved exposure estimation system, it was useful to consider what features were essential and what features, though not essential, were desirable in such a system. This discussion generally came down to the following essential features.

a. *A foundation in historical behaviour.* Generally it was agreed that historical market behaviour should be the foundation on which such a system was built. While some argued for a more conservative "worst case" approach, most recognised the dangers of inflated estimates losing their credibility. This inevitably leads to varied and highly subjective approval standards across the organisation and to an ultimate loss of control over the process.
b. *Proper recognition of offsets and diversification.* Failure to treat the dynamic interaction among trades in a counterparty's portfolio was recognised as the most obvious shortcoming of the add-on approach. This was particularly obvious relative to marginal exposure calculations. An add-on based system would show exposure increasing when a new trade was added even when it actually reduced exposure by offsetting pre-existing imbalances in the counterparty's portfolio. Few things do more to under mine the credibility of a credit risk system than getting the sign of marginal exposure wrong!
c. *Incorporation of market data correlations.* Clearly correlations between pairs of rates and/or prices are among the less stable parameters of market dynamics. Nevertheless, most analysts agreed that incorporating reasonable estimates of such correlations was an important aspect of realistic exposure estimation.
d. *Exposure profiles rather than single loan equivalent amounts.* Another major flaw of the add-on approach was that it gave no insight into the timing of potential future exposure. Sometimes the potential exposures by deal would be "stacked" in the order of their maturity, but this ignores the fact that swap exposures peak in the middle of a contract's life, not at the end. Any credit analyst will say that the timing of when exposure occurs is often central to whether the risk is acceptable. Whatever else it did, a revised trading credit methodology needed to produce insights into the timing of exposure.
e. *Rigorous treatment of netting.* By the 1990s, netting was becoming more widely accepted in law around the world. This made a reliable treatment of netting increasingly important for accurate exposure estimates. Capturing the impact of enforceable netting in the current exposure is easy. The difficult issue is reflecting it in potential future exposure. A minor revision to the Basel capital rules in April of 1995 introduced a very crude way of reflecting the growth in the enforceability of netting. This was based on the portfolio ratio of current net exposure, to the extent netting is deemed enforceable,

versus current gross exposure. Again, while arguably appropriate for an aggregate exposure adjustment, this approach is much too crude to be reliable when applied to individual counterparty portfolios. A more rigorous approach was clearly necessary.

The common thread running through these essential features was an attempt to incorporate all significant structural factors into the exposure estimation process. The goal was to produce results that were conceptually consistent across counterparties and throughout the projection period. Specifically, the probability of the projected potential exposure actually materialising on any relevant future date should be as consistent as is practically possible. It should not matter whether a portfolio contains one deal, a small number of similar deals, or a large and varied range of deals with two-way sensitivities and multiple market drivers. Likewise, the statistical properties of the exposure estimates should not change over the course of a projection as some deals mature and the complexity of the portfolio changes.

FEATURES OF EFFECTIVE RISK MANAGEMENT

The initial goal for improved exposure estimation was simply to get more realistic results on a periodic basis. Daily or even weekly runs were the normal target frequency. This provided a sound basis for setting and managing credit exposure limits. There was an issue of how to provide availability information to traders in order to hold them accountable for complying with the limits. This usually was done by one of two methods.

- A parallel set of limits might be set up on the basis of a much simpler measurement scheme. For example, the old add-on calculations might be used.
- Alternatively, the sophisticated exposure profiles could be imported into the trading limit system. These would be augmented by conservative exposure increases for new deals between updates from batch runs of the more sophisticated exposure estimation system.

In both cases, incremental exposure of new deals would be added to the existing exposure based on fairly simple additive rules and tracked against limits. Such systems would also provide traders with availability reports or what-if capabilities. It was usually the job of a credit limits administration unit to assure that authorised trades between full exposure simulations would only rarely result in excesses when the batch update was run.

Even in the early 1990s, however, a set of more ambitious goals began to emerge. Progress has been made on some of them, but many remain future aspirations even today. Among these longer-term goals were the following.

a. *Real-time updates on a global basis.* The lag between deals being committed and their credit implications being reflected in the limit system has long been recognised as a source of additional risk. It has generally been necessary to settle for one of two compromises in this area. Global real-time exposure capture can be accomplished if the metrics used are quite simple. Such an approach is used for some products by at least a couple of dozen banks today, usually for foreign exchange trading. Alternatively, a sophisticated measurement method can be combined with real-time deal capture at the local trading room level if the exposure calculations are integrated with the front-office dealing system. This is more common in the fixed income derivative area. Combining global real-time deal capture with sophisticated measurement techniques to answer availability queries remains a future aspiration.

b. *What-if capabilities linked to the front-office booking systems.* Ideally the limits system should be closely integrated with the front office trading environment. Traders should not have to do double entry to determine availability. Often a counterparty will have sufficient availability that a full what-if check is unnecessary. Visual inspection will assure that a proposed deal can be accommodated within the limit. If a full what-if simulation is needed, however, it should be possible for the exposure engine to pick up the necessary details from the front office trading system.

c. *"Trading floor response times" using sophisticated measurement methods.* Anyone who has been there knows that "trading floor response times" usually means almost instantaneous. Especially in the foreign exchange trading arena, response time requirements are extremely short, usually two to three seconds. The computational complexity traditionally required to produce acceptably robust exposure measures has, to date, been impossible to reconcile with these demanding response times on a commercially acceptable basis.

d. *Exposure decomposition and "wrong-way exposure" reporting.* As described above, measuring exposure consistently and reliably is an important goal. It also is important, however, to be able to dissect the portfolio imbalances that give rise to such exposure.This can be done by recording the impact on exposure of controlled deviations in individual market variables from their expected paths. This conveys the type of market events that would drive exposure higher and is an important guide to what types of trades would be risk reducing for a given counterparty.

   Proper organisation of such results also allows risk managers to determine which counterparties will exhibit rising exposure in response to an unfolding market event such as a big currency devaluation or a commodity price shift.

   Combining such sensitivities with user-specified wrong-way exposures also can be very useful. This allows reporting that highlights those counterparties who are likely to exhibit weakened credit status in response to the very same market events that result in increased exposure.

e. *Optimal professional counterparty selection.* Market makers in derivatives are deal takers when it comes to their end-users.Clients have a fundamental risk to hedge and come to the dealer to take an offsetting position. When professional market makers need to hedge their own open market positions, however, they are deal givers. They will need to pay away the bid or offer spread to the other professional market maker with whom they place the trade. At that moment, there is almost free credit risk reduction available to the market risk hedger. By choosing one professional counterparty potential credit exposure may be reduced, whereas choosing another counterparty will result in a potential credit exposure increase. Careful risk source sensitivity analysis and exposition can provide the necessary information to make the appropriate risk reducing choices as these opportunities arises.

f. *Marginal credit cost implications of a new transaction.* This can reasonably be called the Holy Grail of desired functionality. Today exposure is estimated only as a measure to compare to approved limits. As long as a trader is within limit, there is no other impact on incentives or behaviour. In effect, traders are compensated for maximising gross trading profits subject to constraints in the form of market risk and credit risk limits. If marginal exposure could be calculated accurately in a few seconds, it would be possible to present traders with the incremental credit charge associated with a proposed trade. This would mean the spread on the trade would have to cover this charge before the trader realised a net profit. In effect, it would allow market makers to compensate traders on the basis of maximising risk-adjusted profits. In the process, it would bring traders' incentives into much closer alignment with the goals of the institution.

MITIGATING CREDIT RISK MANAGEMENT

Lenders mitigate credit risk using several methods:

- *Risk-based pricing*: Lenders generally charge a higher interest rate to borrowers who are more likely to default, a practice called risk-based pricing. Lenders consider factors relating to the loan such as loan purpose, credit rating, and loan-to-value ratio and estimates the effect on yield (credit spread).
- *Covenants:* Lenders may write stipulations on the borrower, called covenants, into loan agreements:
- Periodically report its financial condition
- Refrain from paying dividends, repurchasing shares, borrowing further,

or other specific, voluntary actions that negatively affect the company's financial position

- Repay the loan in full, at the lender's request, in certain events such as changes in the borrower's debt-to-equity ratio or interest coverage ratio
- *Credit insurance and credit derivatives*: Lenders and bond holders may hedge their credit risk by purchasing credit insurance or credit derivatives. These contracts transfer the risk from the lender to the seller (insurer) in exchange for payment. The most common credit derivative is the credit default swap.
- *Tightening:* Lenders can reduce credit risk by reducing the amount of credit extended, either in total or to certain borrowers. For example, a distributor selling its products to a troubled retailer may attempt to lessen credit risk by reducing payment terms from net 30 to net 15.
- *Diversification:* Lenders to a small number of borrowers (or kinds of borrower) face a high degree of unsystematic credit risk, called concentration risk. Lenders reduce this risk by diversifying the borrower pool.
- *Deposit insurance:* Many governments establish deposit insurance to guarantee bank deposits of insolvent banks. Such protection discourages consumers from withdrawing money when a bank is becoming insolvent, to avoid a bank run, and encourages consumers to hold their savings in the banking system instead of in cash.

ACHIEVING ESSENTIAL MEASUREMENT

There are three potential approaches to achieving the essential objectives needed for consistent exposure estimation.

a. *Monte Carlo simulation with full revaluation.* This involves revaluing all uncompleted terms and conditions for every deal at multiple future dates under several thousand hypothetical sets of market conditions. Needless to say, this is very computationally intensive. Depending on the complexity and volume of the deals in the portfolio, it typically takes several hours to process all the desired exposure profiles. In some cases, the processing time exceeds the available daily window and can only be run on weekends. While this is analytically the most robust approach, the computing power and processing time required often make it impractical for day-to-day use. This has given rise to a search for alternatives that offer almost the same reliability with considerably less computational burden.

b. *Monte Carlo with grid-based pricing.* The most obvious alternative to full-valuation Monte Carlo is one that simplifies the generation of hypothetical future values of the transactions. An attractive approach is to use grid-based pricing. In this method, a small number of full valuations are performed for every deal at every future simulation date based on controlled deviations from the status quo evolution of market variables. These results are saved and reused in the subsequent Monte Carlo step. Instead of performing full revaluations for each of several thousand hypothetical market scenarios, prices are derived by interpolation off the price grid. The interpolations are based on where the market variables in a given scenario fall relative to the controlled changes used to construct the grid. The grid may be more or less complex, incorporating different numbers of market drivers for a given deal. Likewise the interpolation methods may vary in complexity from linear to quadratic or higher order approximations to the value surface. Obviously the more complex the interpolation the smaller the gain in computational efficiency. How complex to make the calculation is a matter of time and budget resources and is also affected by the complexity of the trades involved. In general, however, grid-based pricing can make the update process several times faster than full valuation Monte Carlo. The scenario specific transaction values are not as precise in the grid-based pricing approach as they are using full revaluation. It is important to realise, however, that the characteristics of the hypothetical future market conditions are themselves subject to considerable uncertainty. As a former associate of mine once said, it is easy to refine within the margin of error. Doing so gains little in the way of actual precision and often creates serious operational and maintenance issues.

c. *Advanced analytic approximation.* Within the past two years, advanced analytic methods have been developed that provide remarkably robust approximations to the results of full-blown Monte Carlo simulations. While not foolproof, these methods usually give results that fall within the range produced by Monte Carlo simulations with small versus large numbers of draws. Certain ill conditioned combinations of a small number of trades can lead to non-trivial errors. As a result, periodic Monte Carlo runs are important to catch such situations in those rare instances where they arise.

SIMULATION-BASED EXPOSURE ESTIMATION MANAGEMENT

Given the advances of the past ten years, there is little excuse for any institution with significant derivative activity to operate with nothing but add-on style credit exposure estimates for internal measurement and control. Saying that, there are three distinct levels of sophistication in the application of simulation-based exposure estimates.

1. *As an overnight supplement to less sophisticated measures.* This is where most institutions are today. Daily trading activity is controlled by fairly unsophisticated measures at least relative to newly booked transactions. Even if sophisticated exposure profiles are calculated periodically and fed back into the trading limit system, deals done between updates are typically assessed in a much simpler fashion. This inevitably leads to overstated exposure and may result in turning away deals that could be done within limit if more sophisticated exposure estimates were available on a timelier basis. Such a system also cannot offer meaningful insight into the marginal impact of a proposed trade. Nevertheless, it is a giant step beyond having nothing but addon based exposure estimates. Properly configured, such batch systems also can provide valuable portfolio concentration and risk source sensitivity information. A key success factor is making such information available to relevant decision-makers in multiple locations.
2. *Intra-day simulated exposure updates for new trades.* This approach requires capturing new trades as they are made and transferring them to a central exposure evaluation system. Once received centrally the counterparty exposure profile or profiles affected by a new deal are updated in the background. Depending on the size of the portfolios affected, and the volume of trades being processed in this way the latency is likely to be from a few minutes to an hour or longer. The advantage of this approach is that portfolio effects are reflected faster than with nothing but batch updates of the simulations. Also, if a counterparty's exposure is close to the limit, it is possible to configure such a system to allow a small number of what-if simulations based on proposed new deals. While not able to support a large volume of what-if enquiries, this limited capability can provide support for booking risk-reducing deals that would otherwise be denied based on limit excesses. While this may seem like a small departure from the first configuration, there is a major difference. To achieve intra-day updates requires moving from a batch to an event driven system architecture. Sufficient trade details need to be captured to allow the simulations to run and exposure updates need to be made while new limit enquiries and transactions are taking place. This requires a significant revamping of the entire process when starting from a batch mode approach. Given the rather modest improvement in business functionality, the cost of such a change is often viewed as excessive.
3. *Use of simulation-based exposure for what-if limit checking and pricing implications.* This is the last "desirable feature" described

previously. If accurate simulation-based exposure could be performed on a what-if basis in a matter of seconds, it would offer significant advantages. By providing an accurate estimate of the amount and timing of incremental exposure, reflecting all major effects of offsets and diversification, this would be the basis for reasonable estimates of the cost of the associated incremental credit risk. In addition to creating a minimum spread for exposure increasing deals, such a system would encourage aggressive pricing for exposure reducing deals. Traders' performance could be measured on the basis of risk adjusted returns not gross trading profit. Until the development of the advanced analytical approximation methods described above, this aspiration was commercially impractical. While such a system could have been built technically using Monte Carlo techniques, the cost in hardware and support has heretofore made it commercially impractical. With such methods, such a system becomes far more commercially justifiable.

FUTURE TRENDS IN RISK INFORMATION

Today most risk information is used to make high-level resource allocation decisions using some variation of risk adjusted return on capital (RAROC), or to enforce risk limit controls. Most tactical decisions are still made on the basis of limited local information. Loans and other traditional credit facilities are evaluated on the basis of the financial strength of the obligor with only limited attention paid to portfolio implications. Derivative trades are priced based on how the contract fits the current market risk imbalances and, to a lesser extent, the credit worthiness and sophistication of the counterparty. In neither case are facilities available to assess broader portfolio risk implications. A number of capabilities already available, however, support an expectation of considerable progress along these lines in coming years.

a. *Massive expansion in communication capacity.* The current sad financial state of the telecommunications industry is a reflection of significant excess capacity. This is largely a reflection of massive expansion combined with slower than expected penetration of broadband access among consumers in industrial countries. Such penetration eventually will occur, however, driven in significant measure by access to on-demand streaming video. In that setting, voice, text and numerical data will be minor portions of the total information flow. This will facilitate the much greater communication volume required to provide real-time updates and what-if enquiries to support thousands of daily decisions.
b. *Evolving semantic standards based on Extensible Mark-up Language.*

Extensible mark-up language (XML) has rapidly been accepted as the syntax for self-describing messages. To be practical, however, XML must be supplemented with a series of semantic conventions relevant to specific types of information. Financial products mark-up language (FpML) is one such effort in the financial derivatives arena and there are several others in related fields. Development of these semantic standards is a slow and laborious process. The task is magnified by the need to build a critical core of institutional support through consensus. Progress is being made, however, and such protocols can be expected to be an important tool supporting, real-time, event-driven data exchange in coming years.

c. *Browser-based information access capabilities.* An essential feature of an effective risk information system is not just reliable source data and sound analytics, but effective delivery of the resulting information. To realise the potential of risk information to improve tactical decisions requires that such results be delivered to many thousands of staff members. Furthermore, it must be tailored to their particular job needs and responsibilities as well as their personally preferred means of absorbing information. Finally, it must be possible to upgrade the system with added or modified functionality on a continuing basis without excessive coordination problems between the central server and the remote users' desktops. Fortunately, the rise of the Internet offers technology that is ideally suited to address this problem.

d. *Robust approximations to Monte Carlo results.* As noted earlier, recently developed techniques offer the prospect for robust approximations to the results of computationally intense Monte Carlo runs for a small fraction of the processing resources. Deployment of such methods would avoid the need for two measurement systems, one robust but slow and the other crude but fast. Such capabilities would also support risk adjusted pricing by supplying traders with the marginal cost of risk *before* a quote is given to the client. This carries the potential for a major overhaul in how traders' performance is evaluated and their compensation is determined.

6

Risk Management in Insurance Sector

Risks, it seems, is embedded in a contemporary, worldwide culture. It has been widely accepted that risk and uncertainty exist whenever the future is unknown. Nowadays, while the society is widely viewed as 'knowledge society, it is also commonly recognized as 'risky society' or 'uncertain society' Ericson and Doyle. Jaeger et al. point out compared with the risks in the past, today many risks are "eco-systemic" and global, and there is a growing public awareness of common risks around the globe. Therefore, risk is concerned by the modern society increasingly.

While humankind has struggled through the ages to cope with and address risks and uncertainties, there are extensive literatures reflecting their efforts to understand risks and uncertainties. Many economists have recognized that uncertainty is central in economic analysis, but early attempts to formalize this dimension were unsuccessful. Daniel Bernoulli, Adam Smith and Bohm-Bawerk are usually cited for their initial contribution.

Nowadays, scholars commonly use uncertainty to define risk. One of the representative views could be Harrington and Niehaus's definition to risk, according to them, at its most general level, risk is used to describe any situation were there is uncertainty about what outcome will occur. Ericson and Doyle share the similar view with them, they further that risk is It refers to the systemic risks that can occur at a local level but are cumulative surrounded by uncertainty, which is the lack of secure knowledge about an unwanted outcome.

There is a growing realization that in a risky world there is potential for gain as well as loss, for example, Australian/New Zealand Standard for Risk Management (AS/NZS 4360:1995) define risk as, "Risk – the chance of something happening that will have an impact upon objectives. It is measured in terms of consequences and likelihood.". This definition implies that risk may entail both upside as well as downside impacts. Association of Insurance and Risk Managers in Industry and Commerce (AIRMIC) shows its agreement with this view, it says that in all types of undertaking there is the potential for events and consequences that constitute opportunities for benefits (upside) or threats to success (downside).

It is helpful to understand risks by knowing scholars' classification to risks. Traditionally, textbooks on risk management and insurance have distinguished between pure and speculative risks. A pure risk in the situation where there is a chance of loss but no chance of gain; and speculative risks when the situation which has chances to bring about loss or gain. Pure risks are always distasteful, for example, a fire which could burn down the house; but speculative risks posses some attractive features, for instance, gamblers could have chance to win although they may lose. To distinguish these two kinds of risks is very important. For example, for the insurers who insure risks for profits will only accept pure risks which only could yield loss, but for the gamblers, although they tend to be risk taking, but they might not gamble on the pure risks which will never bring gains.

Another important classification distinguishes risks between diversifiable and non-diversifiable risks. Diversifiable risk could be reduced through pooling or risk-sharing agreements, but non-diversifiable risks can not be reduced effectively through these mechanisms. For example, drought could be diversified worldwide, but worldwide depression can be diversified. The distinction between diversifiable and non-diversifiable risks is important in insurance and risk management field because it affects the usefulness of pooling or risk-sharing agreements.

PRINCIPLES OF INSURANCE

UTMOST GOOD FAITH (UBERRIMAE FIDES)

As a client it is your duty to disclose all material facts to the risk being covered. A material fact is a fact which would influence the mind of a prudent underwriter in deciding whether to accept a risk for insurance and on what terms. The duty to disclose operates at the time of inception, at renewal and at any point mid term.

INDEMNITY

On the happening of an event insured against, the Insured will be placed in the same monetary position that he/she occupied immediately before the event taking place.

In the event of a claim the insured must:

- Prove that the event occurred
- Prove that a monetary loss has occurred
- Transfer any rights which he/she may have for recovery from another source to the Insurer, if he/she has been fully indemnified.

SUBROGATION

The right of an insurer which has paid a claim under a policy to step into the shoes of the insured so as to exercise in his name all rights he might have with regard to the recovery of the loss which was the subject of the relevant claim paid under the policy up to the amount of that paid claim. The insurer's subrogation rights may be qualified in the policy.

In the context of insurance subrogation is a feature of the principle of indemnity and therefore only applies to contracts of indemnity so that it does not apply to life assurance or personal accident policies. It is intended to prevent an insured recovering more than the indemnity he receives under his insurance and enables his insurer to recover or reduce its loss.

CONTRIBUTION

The right of an insurer to call on other insurers similarly, but not necessarily equally, liable to the same insured to share the loss of an indemnity payment *i.e.* a travel policy may have overlapping cover with the contents part of a household policy. The principle of contribution allows the insured to make a claim against one insurer who then has the right to call on any other insurers liable for the loss to share the claim payment.

INSURABLE INTEREST

If an insured wishes to enforce a contract of insurance before the Courts he must have an insurable interest in the subject matter of the insurance, which is to say that he stands to benefit from its preservation and will suffer from its loss. In non-marine insurances, the insured must have insurable interest when the policy is taken out and also at the date of loss giving rise to a claim under the policy.

PROXIMATE CAUSE

An insurer will only be liable to pay a claim under an insurance contract if the loss that gives rise to the claim was proximately caused by an insured peril. This means that the loss must be directly attributed to an insured peril without any break in the chain of causation.

TYPES OF INSURANCE

Any risk that can be quantified can potentially be insured. Specific kinds of risk that may give rise to claims are known as "perils". An insurance policy will set out in detail which perils are covered by the policy and which are not. A single policy may cover risks in one or more of the categories. For example, auto insurance would typically cover both property risk and liability risk. A homeowner's insurance policy in the U.S. typically includes property insurance covering damage to the home and the owner's belongings, liability insurance covering certain legal claims against the owner, and even a small amount of coverage for medical expenses of guests who are injured on the owner's property. Business insurance can be any kind of insurance that protects businesses against risks.

Some principal subtypes of business insurance are:

- The various kinds of professional liability insurance, also called professional indemnity insurance; and
- The business owner's policy, which bundles into one policy many of the kinds of coverage that a business owner needs, in a way analogous to how homeowners insurance bundles the coverages that a homeowner needs.

AUTO INSURANCE

Auto insurance protects you against financial loss if you have an accident. It is a contract between the insured and the insurance company. You agree to pay the premium and the insurance company agrees to pay losses as defined in the policy.

Auto insurance provides property, liability and medical coverage:

- Property coverage pays for damage to or theft of the car.
- Liability coverage pays for the legal responsibility to others for bodily injury or property damage.
- Medical coverage pays for the cost of treating injuries, rehabilitation and sometimes lost wages and funeral expenses.

An auto insurance policy comprises six kinds of coverage. Most countries require you to buy some, but not all, of these coverages. If you're financing a car, the lender may also have requirements. Most auto policies are for six months to a year. In the United States, the insurance company should notify you by mail when it's time to renew the policy and to pay the premium.

HOME INSURANCE

Home insurance provides compensation for damage or destruction of a home from disasters. In some geographical areas, the standard insurances exclude certain types of disasters, such as flood and earthquakes, that require additional coverage. Maintenance-related problems are the homeowners' responsibility.

The policy may include inventory, or this can be bought as a separate policy, especially for people who rent housing. In some countries, insurers offer a package which may include liability and legal responsibility for injuries and property damage caused by members of the household, including pets.

HEALTH

Health insurance policies by the National Health Service in the United Kingdom or other publicly-funded health programmes will cover the cost of medical treatments. Dental insurance, like medical insurance, is coverage for individuals to protect them against dental costs. In the U.S., dental insurance is often part of an employer's benefits package, along with health insurance.

ACCIDENT, SICKNESS AND UNEMPLOYMENT INSURANCE

- Disability insurance policies provide financial support in the event the policyholder is unable to work because of disabling illness or injury. It provides monthly support to help pay such obligations as mortgage loans and credit cards.
- Disability overhead insurance allows business owners to cover the overhead expenses of their business while they are unable to work.
- Total permanent disability insurance provides benefits when a person is permanently disabled and can no longer work in their profession, often taken as an adjunct to life insurance.
- Workers' compensation insurance replaces all or part of a worker's wages lost and accompanying medical expenses incurred because of a job-related injury.

CASUALTY

Casualty insurance insures against accidents, not necessarily tied to any specific property:

- Crime insurance is a form of casualty insurance that covers the policyholder against losses arising from the criminal acts of third parties. For example, a company can obtain crime insurance to cover losses arising from theft or embezzlement.
- Political risk insurance is a form of casualty insurance that can be taken out by businesses with operations in countries in which there is a risk that revolution or other political conditions will result in a loss.

LIFE

Life insurance provides a monetary benefit to a decedent's family or other designated beneficiary, and may specifically provide for income to an insured person's family, burial, funeral and other final expenses. Life insurance policies often allow the option of having the proceeds paid to the beneficiary either in a lump sum cash payment or an annuity. Annuities provide a stream of payments and are generally classified as insurance because they are issued by insurance companies and regulated as insurance and require the same kinds of actuarial and investment management expertise that life insurance requires.

Annuities and pensions that pay a benefit for life are sometimes regarded as insurance against the possibility that a retiree will outlive his or her financial resources. In that sense, they are the complement of life insurance and, from an underwriting perspective, are the mirror image of life insurance. Certain life insurance contracts accumulate cash values, which may be taken by the insured if the policy is surrendered or which may be borrowed against. Some policies, such as annuities and endowment policies, are financial instruments to accumulate or liquidate wealth when it is needed. In many countries, such as the U.S. and the UK, the tax law provides that the interest on this cash value is not taxable under certain circumstances. This leads to widespread use of life insurance as a tax-efficient method of saving as well as protection in the event of early death.

In U.S., the tax on interest income on life insurance policies and annuities is generally deferred. However, in some cases the benefit derived from tax deferral may be offset by a low return. This depends upon the insuring company, the type of policy and other variables. Moreover, other income tax saving vehicles may be better alternatives for value accumulation.

PROPERTY

Property insurance provides protection against risks to property, such as fire, theft or weather damage. This includes specialized forms of insurance such as fire insurance, flood insurance, earthquake insurance, home insurance, inland marine insurance or boiler insurance.

- Automobile insurance, known in the UK as motor insurance, is probably the most common form of insurance and may cover both legal liability claims against the driver and loss of or damage to the insured's vehicle itself. Throughout the United States an auto insurance policy is required to legally operate a motor vehicle on public roads. In some jurisdictions, bodily injury compensation for automobile accident victims has been changed to a no-fault system, which reduces or eliminates the ability to sue for compensation but provides automatic eligibility for benefits. Credit card companies insure against damage on rented cars.
  - Driving School Insurance provides cover for any authorized driver whilst undergoing tuition, cover also unlike other motor policies provides cover for instructor liability where both the pupil and driving instructor are equally liable in the event of a claim.
- Aviation insurance insures against hull, spares, deductibles, hull wear and liability risks.
- Boiler insurance insures against accidental physical damage to equipment or machinery.
- Builder's risk insurance insures against the risk of physical loss or damage to property during construction. Builder's risk insurance is typically written on an "all risk" basis covering damage due to any cause not otherwise expressly excluded. Builder's risk insurance is coverage that protects a person's or organization's insurable interest in materials,

fixtures and/or equipment being used in the construction or renovation of a building or structure should those items sustain physical loss or damage from a covered cause.

- Crop insurance "Farmers use crop insurance to reduce or manage various risks associated with growing crops. Such risks include crop loss or damage caused by weather, hail, drought, frost damage, insects, or disease, for instance."
- Earthquake insurance is a form of property insurance that pays the policyholder in the event of an earthquake that causes damage to the property. Most ordinary homeowners insurance policies do not cover earthquake damage. Most earthquake insurance policies feature a high deductible. Rates depend on location and the probability of an earthquake, as well as the construction of the home.
- A fidelity bond is a form of casualty insurance that covers policyholders for losses that they incur as a result of fraudulent acts by specified individuals. It usually insures a business for losses caused by the dishonest acts of its employees.
- Flood insurance protects against property loss due to flooding. Many insurers in the U.S. do not provide flood insurance in some portions of the country. In response to this, the federal government created the National Flood Insurance Programme which serves as the insurer of last resort.
- Home insurance, also commonly called hazard insurance or homeowners insurance, is the type of property insurance that covers private homes.
- Landlord insurance covers residential and commercial properties which are rented to others. Most homeowner's insurance covers only owner-occupied homes.
- Marine insurance and marine cargo insurance cover the loss or damage of ships at sea or on inland waterways, and of cargo in transit, regardless of the method of transit. When the owner of the cargo and the carrier are separate corporations, marine cargo insurance typically compensates the owner of cargo for losses sustained from fire, shipwreck, etc., but excludes losses that can be recovered from the carrier or the carrier's insurance. Many marine insurance underwriters will include "time element" coverage in such policies, which extends the indemnity to cover loss of profit and other business expenses attributable to the delay caused by a covered loss.
- Surety bond insurance is a three party insurance guaranteeing the performance of the principal.
- Terrorism insurance provides protection against any loss or damage caused by terrorist activities.

- Volcano insurance is an insurance that covers volcano damage in Hawaii.
- Windstorm insurance is an insurance covering the damage that can be caused by hurricanes and tropical cyclones.

LIABILITY

Liability insurance is a very broad superset that covers legal claims against the insured. Many types of insurance include an aspect of liability coverage. For example, a homeowner's insurance policy will normally include liability coverage which protects the insured in the event of a claim brought by someone who slips and falls on the property; automobile insurance also includes an aspect of liability insurance that indemnifies against the harm that a crashing car can cause to others' lives, health, or property.

The protection offered by a liability insurance policy is twofold: a legal defence in the event of a lawsuit commenced against the policyholder and indemnification with respect to a settlement or court verdict.

Liability policies typically cover only the negligence of the insured, and will not apply to results of wilful or intentional acts by the insured:

- Public liability insurance covers a business against claims should its operations injure a member of the public or damage their property in some way.
- Directors and officers liability insurance protects an organization from costs associated with litigation resulting from mistakes made by directors and officers for which they are liable. In the industry, it is usually called "D&O" for short.
- Environmental liability insurance protects the insured from bodily injury, property damage and cleanup costs as a result of the dispersal, release or escape of pollutants.
- Errors and omissions insurance.
- Prize indemnity insurance protects the insured from giving away a large prize at a specific event. Examples would include offering prizes to contestants who can make a half-court shot at a basketball game, or a hole-in-one at a golf tournament.
- Professional liability insurance, also called professional indemnity insurance, protects insured professionals such as architectural corporation and medical practice against potential negligence claims made by their patients/clients. Professional liability insurance may take on different names depending on the profession. For example, professional liability insurance in reference to the medical profession may be called malpractice insurance. Notaries public may take out errors and omissions insurance. Other potential E&O policyholders include, for example, real estate brokers, Insurance agents, home inspectors, appraisers, and web site developers.

CREDIT

Credit insurance repays some or all of a loan when certain things happen to the borrower such as unemployment, disability, or death:

- Mortgage insurance insures the lender against default by the borrower. Mortgage insurance is a form of credit insurance, although the name credit insurance more often is used to refer to policies that cover other kinds of debt.
- Many credit cards offer payment protection plans which are a form of credit insurance.

OTHER TYPES

- All-risk insurance is an insurance that covers a wide-range of incidents and perils, except those noted in the policy. All-risk insurance is different from peril-specific insurance that cover losses from only those perils listed in the policy. In car insurance, all-risk policy includes also the damages caused by the own driver.
- Collateral protection insurance or CPI, insures property held as collateral for loans made by lending institutions.
- Defence Base Act Workers' compensation or DBA Insurance provides coverage for civilian workers hired by the government to perform contracts outside the U.S. and Canada. DBA is required for all U.S. citizens, U.S. residents, U.S. Green Card holders, and all employees or subcontractors hired on overseas government contracts. Depending on the country, Foreign Nationals must also be covered under DBA. This coverage typically includes expenses related to medical treatment and loss of wages, as well as disability and death benefits.
- Expatriate insurance provides individuals and organizations operating outside of their home country with protection for automobiles, property, health, liability and business pursuits.
- Financial loss insurance or Business Interruption Insurance protects individuals and companies against various financial risks. For example, a business might purchase coverage to protect it from loss of sales if a fire in a factory prevented it from carrying out its business for a time. Insurance might also cover the failure of a creditor to pay money it owes to the insured. This type of insurance is frequently referred to as "business interruption insurance." Fidelity bonds and surety bonds are included in this category, although these products provide a benefit to a third party in the event the insured party fails to perform its obligations under a contract with the obligee.
- Kidnap and ransom insurance
- Legal Expenses Insurance covers policyholders against the potential costs of legal action against an institution or an individual.

- Locked funds insurance is a little-known hybrid insurance policy jointly issued by governments and banks. It is used to protect public funds from tamper by unauthorized parties. In special cases, a government may authorize its use in protecting semi-private funds which are liable to tamper. The terms of this type of insurance are usually very strict. Therefore it is used only in extreme cases where maximum security of funds is required.
- Media Insurance is designed to cover professionals that engage in film, video and TV production.
- Nuclear incident insurance covers damages resulting from an incident involving radioactive materials and is generally arranged at the national level.
- Pet insurance insures pets against accidents and illnesses - some companies cover routine/wellness care and burial, as well.
- Pollution Insurance which consists of first-party coverage for contamination of insured property either by external or on-site sources. Coverage for liability to third parties arising from contamination of air, water, or land due to the sudden and accidental release of hazardous materials from the insured site. The policy usually covers the costs of cleanup and may include coverage for releases from underground storage tanks. Intentional acts are specifically excluded.
- Purchase insurance is aimed at providing protection on the products people purchase. Purchase insurance can cover individual purchase protection, warranties, guarantees, care plans and even mobile phone insurance. Such insurance is normally very limited in the scope of problems that are covered by the policy.
- Title insurance provides a guarantee that title to real property is vested in the purchaser and/or mortgagee, free and clear of liens or encumbrances. It is usually issued in conjunction with a search of the public records performed at the time of a real estate transaction.
- Travel insurance is an insurance cover taken by those who travel abroad, which covers certain losses such as medical expenses, loss of personal belongings, travel delay, personal liabilities, etc.

INSURANCE FINANCING VEHICLES

- Fraternal insurance is provided on a cooperative basis by fraternal benefit societies or other social organizations.
- No-fault insurance is a type of insurance policy where insureds are indemnified by their own insurer regardless of fault in the incident.
- Protected Self-Insurance is an alternative risk financing mechanism in which an organization retains the mathematically calculated cost

of risk within the organization and transfers the catastrophic risk with specific and aggregate limits to an insurer so the maximum total cost of the programme is known. A properly designed and underwritten Protected Self-Insurance Programme reduces and stabilizes the cost of insurance and provides valuable risk management information.

- Retrospectively Rated Insurance is a method of establishing a premium on large commercial accounts. The final premium is based on the insured's actual loss experience during the policy term, sometimes subject to a minimum and maximum premium, with the final premium determined by a formula. Under this plan, the current year's premium is based partially on the current year's losses, although the premium adjustments may take months or years beyond the current year's expiration date. The rating formula is guaranteed in the insurance contract. Formula: retrospective premium = converted loss + basic premium × tax multiplier. Numerous variations of this formula have been developed and are in use.
- Formal self insurance is the deliberate decision to pay for otherwise insurable losses out of one's own money. This can be done on a formal basis by establishing a separate fund into which funds are deposited on a periodic basis, or by simply forgoing the purchase of available insurance and paying out-of-pocket. Self insurance is usually used to pay for high-frequency, low-severity losses. Such losses, if covered by conventional insurance, mean having to pay a premium that includes loadings for the company's general expenses, cost of putting the policy on the books, acquisition expenses, premium taxes, and contingencies. While this is true for all insurance, for small, frequent losses the transaction costs may exceed the benefit of volatility reduction that insurance otherwise affords.
- Reinsurance is a type of insurance purchased by insurance companies or self-insured employers to protect against unexpected losses. Financial reinsurance is a form of reinsurance that is primarily used for capital management rather than to transfer insurance risk.
- Social insurance can be many things to many people in many countries. But a summary of its essence is that it is a collection of insurance coverages, plus retirement savings, that requires participation by all citizens. By forcing everyone in society to be a policyholder and pay premiums, it ensures that everyone can become a claimant when or if he/she needs to. Along the way this inevitably becomes related to other concepts such as the justice system and the welfare state. This is a large, complicated topic that engenders tremendous debate:
  - National Insurance

  - Social safety net
  - Social security
  - Social Security debate
  - Social Security
  - Social welfare provision
- Stop-loss insurance provides protection against catastrophic or unpredictable losses. It is purchased by organizations who do not want to assume 100 per cent of the liability for losses arising from the plans. Under a stop-loss policy, the insurance company becomes liable for losses that exceed certain limits called deductibles.

CLOSED COMMUNITY SELF-INSURANCE

Some communities prefer to create virtual insurance amongst themselves by other means than contractual risk transfer, which assigns explicit numerical values to risk. A number of religious groups, including the Amish and some Muslim groups, depend on support provided by their communities when disasters strike. The risk presented by any given person is assumed collectively by the community who all bear the cost of rebuilding lost property and supporting people whose needs are suddenly greater after a loss of some kind. In supportive communities where others can be trusted to follow community leaders, this tacit form of insurance can work. In this manner the community can even out the extreme differences in insurability that exist among its members. Some further justification is also provided by invoking the moral hazard of explicit insurance contracts.

In the United Kingdom, The Crown did not insure property such as government buildings. If a government building was damaged, the cost of repair would be met from public funds because, in the long run, this was cheaper than paying insurance premiums. Since many UK government buildings have been sold to property companies, and rented back, this arrangement is now less common and may have disappeared altogether.

LIFE INSURANCE PRODUCTS

TERM ASSURANCE

Based on the benefit patterns the traditional Life Insurance products can be categorised into the following types:

- Term Insurance
- Whole Life Insurance
- Endowment Insurance
- Annuities

Term Insurance provides for life insurance protection for the selected term only. In case the person dies during the term, the benefits are payable under the policy and in case of his survival till the end of the selected term the policy normally expires without any benefit becoming payable.

Term insurance may be regarded as temporary insurance and is more nearly comparable with "Property and Casualty insurance" contracts than the other forms of Life insurance contracts.

WHOLE OF LIFE ASSURANCE

As the name suggests, the whole life insurance policies are intended to provide Life Insurance protection over one's lifetime. The essence of whole life insurance is that it provides for payment of the assured amount upon the insured's death regardless of when it occurs. Under these policies, the payment of the assured sum is a certainty in contrast to the term insurance contracts. Only the time of payment of the assured sum is an uncertainty.

Whole life policies can be either participating type or non-participating type. Participating type policies are those which are entitled to a share in the distributable surplus of the Life Insurance company, whereby the cash value of the policy can go up, with the announcement of bonus/ dividend. Non-participating policies have the same benefit throughout the life of the policy.

There can be the following types of whole life policies:

- Ordinary Whole Life Insurance
- Limited Payment Whole Life Insurance
- Convertible Whole Life Insurance

ENDOWMENT ASSURANCE

These are the most commonly sold policies. These policies assure that the benefits under the policy will be paid on the death of the life insured during the selected term or on his survival to the end of the term. Hence the assured benefits are payable either on the date of maturity or on death of the life insured, if earlier.

Endowment policies assist in providing for the payment of a lump sum amount for a specific purpose, say, provision for retirement, meeting the needs of the child etc. The money required for the purpose will be built up whether the person is alive till that date or not. Like whole life insurance policies, endowment policies can also be of participating and non-participating types.

ANNUITIES

An annuity is a series of periodic payments. An annuity contract is an insurance policy, under which the annuity provider agrees to pay the purchaser of annuity a series of regular periodical payments for a fixed period or during someone's life time.

Classification of Annuities:

- The number of lives covered

  - Single
  - Joint
- The beginning of the payment of annuity
  - Immediate annuity
  - Deferred annuity
- Method of premium payment
  - Single premium
  - Regular installment

NON TRADITIONAL COVERS

Universal Life Insurance is another non-traditional type of Life Insurance introduced in the United States in the year 1979, which had an adjustable face value, floating interest rates based on market conditions and unbundling of savings and protection elements of Life Insurance.

After paying an initial minimum premium, policy owners may thereafter pay whatever amount and at whatever times they wish, or even skip premium payments, provided the cash value will cover policy charges. Similarly they had the option to raise or reduce the face value of the Insurance policy. For increasing the insurance coverage proof of continued insurability was insisted.

Under this type of policy, the policyholder pays an initial premium, which should not be less than a minimum for the given face value and the attained age of the Life to be Insured. From this premium payment, the mortality charge for the first period and the expenses charges will be deducted and the balance will be the policy's cash value. To this cash value a certain interest will be credited at the end of the period.

LIMITATIONS OF INSURANCE SECTOR

An important conclusion emerging from the preceding discussion is that a large proportion of the population in India does not have the choice of facilities available to the workforce of the formal sector. The large number of separate networks of providers tends to make for reduce inefficiency and the choice among providers: only a limited set of providers is offered to a given employee.

A majority of the large public and private establishments are either self-insuring or provide reimbursement plans to their employees. These employers may be more than willing to switch over to private third party insurance, should it become available. This is particularly true for the large-scale enterprises which provide their own clinics and personnel. Given that the employee demand for quality treatment and specialists' care is increasing rapidly, these enterprises would find it worth their while to switch to an insurance structure.

REFORMING ESIS AND CGHS

Although the number of beneficiaries of the ESIS has grown modestly over time, enrolment has not kept pace with growth in the GIC, the organised sector or even the number of low-wage workers that the ESIS is supposed to cover. For reasons discussed above, employees have been reluctant to avail themselves of the ESIS facilities. Here again, the argument of improving quality of services offered under the ESIS holds.

Numerous studies have shown that the providers of treatment at ESIS and CGHS facilities do not have adequate incentive to exert themselves. These facilities generally suffer from low provider morale, understating and equipment shortages. Improvements in the quality of services offered by these facilities can be effected by decentralising the decision-making process and introducing reforms in financing norms. An incentive may be provided by allowing the facilities to charge user fees—even if the fees are paid by the government on the basis of the patient-load factor. An alternative strategy might be to merge the two systems of facilities with the rest of the public health system.

Lack of Incentive for Cost Optimisation

There are important signs that health insurance in India is causing a 'moral hazard' problem. In a health insurance setting, the hazard can be of two types: insurance may induce individuals either to take fewer precautions to avoid the need for treatment or to use more health services when they fall ill. Both actions tend to increase health expenditures. Increased spending when illness is the main phenomenon observed in health markets: patients and health care providers both respond to the presence of insurance by increasing the level of spending on health care. In some cases this increased spending may be socially desirable, such as spending on essential primary care or underutilised, expensive inpatient treatment. In other cases it may lead to increasing levels of inappropriate care, unnecessary treatment, excessive laboratory tests or overcharging. This moral hazard may be reduced by changing incentives either on the demand side or on the supply side.

The current structure of insurance offered in India generally steers clear of cost-sharing. While substantial cost-sharing may reduce access to medicare, low levels of cost-sharing may deter unnecessary treatment. Furthermore, if consumers do not face at least some out of pocket expenditure on health care, they may not have sufficient incentive to avoid the most expensive facilities, or the most extensive set of diagnostic tests. Results from other countries suggest that even nominal fees would discourage a significant amount of use. Charging higher fees or higher co-payment for more expensive facilities will encourage consumers to get referrals and become better informed about the necessity of treatment.

The lack of a governmental focus on curative care has led to almost unregulated growth in the private medical system. Phadke describes some of these problems: substandard but expensive private medical education, lack of continuing medical education and training for doctors in the private sector, irrational drug use, unnecessary medical interventions, lack of regulation and standardisation of nursing homes, etc. These features often inflate costs for the health system as well as for consumers.

Nor are supply side incentives being used to constrain expenditures. As a matter of fact, the GIC subsidiaries indirectly encourage expensive corporate hospital treatment by not devoting enough attention to the appropriateness of claims. Our reading is that it may be easier to get reimbursement if one is treated in one of these expensive and well known facilities rather than in a lesser one.

So far as the monitoring of claims is concerned the GIC subsidiaries appear to be more preoccupied with whether services are being provided with pre-existing conditions than to whether or not the fees paid are justifiable or the facility used by the claimant is qualified and the treatment appropriate. As more expensive and more complex procedures are increasingly being resorted to, it will be important for the insurers to play a more active role in claims monitoring and fraud detection. Computerising the entire claims processing system would facilitate this.

THE CONCEPT OF RISK

People express risk in different ways. To some, it is the chance or possibility of loss, to others, its may be uncertain situations or deviations or what statisticians call dispersions from the expectations. Different authors on the subject have defined risk differently. However, in most of the terminology the term risk includes exposure to adverse situations. The indeterminateness of outcome is one of the basic criteria to define a risk situation. Also, when the outcome is indeterminate, there is a possibility that some of them may be adverse and therefore need special emphasis. Let us have a look at the popular definitions of risk.

According to the Dictionary risk refers to the possibility that something unpleasant or dangerous might happen.

"Risk is a condition in which there is a possibility of an adverse deviation from a desired outcome that is expected or hoped for."

"At its most general level, risk is used to describe any situation where there is uncertainty about what outcome will occur. This is obviously risky."

The degree of risk refers to the likelihood of occurrence of an event. It is a measure of accuracy with which the outcome of a chance event can be predicted.

In most of the risky situations, two elements are commonly found:

1. The outcome is uncertain *i.e.* there is a possibility that one or other(s) may occur. Therefore, logically, there are at least two possible outcomes for a given situation.

2. Out of the possible outcomes, one is unfavourable or not liked by the individual or the analyst.

PERILS

A peril refers to the cause of loss or the contingency that may cause a loss. In literary sense, it means the serious and immediate danger. Perils refer to the immediate causes of loss. Perils may be general or specific *e.g.* fire may affect assets like building, automobile, machinery, equipment and also, humans. Collusion may cause damage to the automobile resulting in a financial loss.

HAZARDS

Hazards are the conditions that increase the severity of loss or the conditions affecting perils. These are the conditions that create or increase the severity of losses. Economic slow down is a peril that may cause a loss to the business, but it is also a hazard that may cause a heart attack or mental shock to the proprietor of the business. Hazards can be classified as follows:

(1) Physical Hazards—Property Conditions—consists of those physical properties that increase the chance of loss from the various perils. *E.g.* stocking crackers in a packed commercial complex increases the peril of fire.

(2) Intangible Hazards—Attitudes and Culture—Intangible hazards are more or less psychological in nature. These can be further classified as follows:

   (a) Moral Hazard—Fraud—These refer to the increase in the possibility or severity of loss emanating from the intention to deceive or cheat. For example—putting fire to a factory running in losses. With an intention to make benefit out of exaggerated claims, deliberately indulging into automobile collusion or damaging it or tendency on part of the doctor to go for unnecessary checks when they are not required, since the insurance company will reimburse the loss.

   (b) Morale Hazard—Indifference—It is the attitude of indifference to take care of the property on the premise that the loss will be indemnified by the insurance company. So, it is the carelessness or indifference to a loss because of the existence of insurance contract. For example—smoking in an oil refinery, careless driving etc.

   (c) Societal Hazards—Legal and Cultural—these refer to the increase in the frequency and severity of loss arising from legal doctrine or societal customs and structure. For example, the construction or the possibility of demolition of buildings in unauthorised colonies.

TYPES OF RISKS

Financial and Non-Financial Risks

Financial risk involves the simultaneous existence of three important elements in a risky situation— (a) that someone is adversely affected by the happening of an event, (b) the assets or income is likely to be exposed to a financial loss from the occurrence of the event and (c) the peril can cause the loss. When the possibility of a financial loss does not exist, the situation can be referred to as non-financial in nature. Financial risks are more particular in nature.

Individual and Group Risks

A risk is said to be a group risk or fundamental risk if it affects the economy-or its participants on a macro basis. These are impersonal in origin and consequence. They affect most of the social segments or the entire population. These risk factors may be socio-economic or political or natural calamities *e.g.* earthquakes, floods, wars, unemployment or situations like 11th September attack on U.S. etc.

Individual/particular risks are confined to individual identities or small groups. Thefts, robbery, fire etc. are risks that are particular in nature. Some of these risks are insurable. The methods of handling fundamental and particular risks differ by their very nature *e.g.* Social insurance programmes may be undertaken by the government to handle fundamental risks. Similarly, an individual to prevent against the adverse consequences of fire may buy fire insurance policy.

Pure and Speculative Risks

Pure risk situations are those where there is a possibility of loss or no loss. There is no gain to the individual or the organisation. For example, a car can meet with an accident or it may not meet with an accident. If an insurance policy is bought for the purpose, then if accident does not occur, there is no gain to the insured. Contrarily, if the accident occurs, the insurance company will indemnify the loss. Speculative risks are those where there is possibility of gain as well as loss. The element of gain is inherent or structured in such a situation. For example—if you invest in a stock market, you may either gain or lose on stocks.

Static and Dynamic Risks

Dynamic risks are those resulting from the changes in the economy or the environment. These risk factors mainly refer to the macro economic variables like inflation, income and output levels, and technology changes. Dynamic risks emanate from the economic environment and therefore, these are difficult to anticipate and quantify. Contrary to this, static risks are more or less predictable and are not affected by the economic conditions. The possibility of loss in a business or unemployment after undergoing a professional qualification, loss due to act of others etc. are static and accordingly suitable for insurance.

Quantifiable and Non-quantifiable Risks

The risk which can be measured like financial risks are known to be quantifiable while the situations which may result in repercussions like tension or loss of peace are called as non-quantifiable.

Personal Risks

These are the risks that directly affect the individual's capability to earn income. Personal risks can be classified into the following types:

(a) Premature death—death of the bread earner with unfulfilled or unprovided financial obligations.
(b) Old age—it refers to the risk of not having sufficient income at the age of retirement or the age becoming so that there is a possibility that the individual may not be able to earn the livelihood.
(c) Sickness or disability—the risk of poor heath or disability of a person to earn the means of survival. *E.g.* the possibility of damage of limbs of a driver due to an accident.
(d) Unemployment—the risk of unemployment due to socio-economic factors resulting in financial insecurity

Property Risks

These are the risks to the persons in possession of the property being damaged or lost. The immovables like land and building being damaged due to flood, earthquake or fire—the movables like appliances and personal assets being destroyed due to fire or stolen.

The losses may be direct or indirect/consequential. A direct loss implies the visible financial loss to the property due to mishappenings. Whereas, the indirect ones are the losses arising from the occurrence of an incident resulting in direct/physical damages or loss. The loss to crops due to flood is a direct loss— the destruction of the growing power is a consequential one.

Liability Risks

These are the risks arising out of the intentional or unintentional injury to the persons or damages to their properties through negligence or carelessness. Liability risks generally arise from the law. *e.g.* liability of the employer under the workmen's compensation law or other labour laws in India. In addition to the above categories, risks may also arise due to the failure of others. For example, the financial loss arising from the non-performance or standard performance in a contract—in engineering/construction contracts.

Losses and Methods of Handling Pure Risk

The various methods of handling pure risk depend upon the nature of losses. The losses from pure risk in an organisation may be categorised as follows:

Direct Losses and Indirect Losses

- Damage to Assets
- Injury/Illness to Employees
- Liability Claims and Defence Costs
- Loss of Normal Profit (net cash flow)
- Continuing and Extra Operating Expense
- Higher Cost of Funds
- Foregone Investment
- Bankruptcy Costs
- (legal fees)

Although the various techniques of risk management have been discussed at length in the following chapter, the following discussion will give you a brief idea of how the risk can be handled:

- Avoidance—avoid the risk or the circumstances which may lead to losses. For example—not to visit border areas at the time of war tensions. Avoid manufacturing and marketing a product of which patent/copyright is doubtful.
- Loss Control
- Loss Prevention—Reduce Loss Frequency—for example not to smoke in a factory producing inflammable products, getting training before driving etc.
- Loss Reduction—Lower Loss Severity—deployment of fire fighting equipment, first aid boxes etc.
- Retention—to retain in full or part of the risk. A risk is said to be actively retained if the individual is fully aware of the risk and its implications and prefers to retain it. On the contrary it is said to be passive, if the individual is ignorant of the risk or there is carelessness on part of the exposed.
- Transfer—to transfer the risk to another individual or organisation either by:
- Contractual Agreements—insurance, derivatives, diversification strategies etc.
- Corporatising—converting the sole proprietor/partnership business into a company from an organisation. It is well known that in case of

a proprietor firm, the proprietor is individually liable in an unlimited sense and in case of partnership firm, the partners are jointly and severally liable which is also in the nature of unlimited liability. However, in case of companies the liability of the shareholders is generally limited to the extent of capital contributed by them.

RISK MANAGEMENT PROCESS

The role of risk management

The future is largely unknown. Most business decision-making takes place on the basic of expectations about the future. Making a decision on the basis of assumptions, expectations, estimates and forecasts of future events involves taking risks.

Risk has been described as the "sugar and salt of life". This implies that risk can have an upside as well downside. People take risk in order to achieve some goal they would otherwise not have reached without taking that risk.

On the other hand, risk can mean that some danger or loss may be involved in carrying out an activity and therefore, care has to be taken to avoid that loss. This is where Risk Management is important, in that it can be used to protect against loss or danger arising from a risky activity.

Definition

Risk management is an integrated process of delineating specific areas or risk, developing a comprehensive plan, integrating the plan, and conducting ongoing evaluation.

The Process

The risk management process involves the following logical steps.

1. Defining the objectives of the risk management exercise
2. Identifying the risk exposures
3. Evaluating the exposures
4. Critical analysis of risk management alternatives and selecting one of them
5. Implementation and review.

The job of risk management can, therefore, be broken down into three elements, which follow each other in a logical sequence:

A. Risk analysis
B. Risk control
C. Risk financing

Because the conditions under which firms operate change, the risk management process has a necessity to be dynamic. All three elements of the process have therefore to be continuing reassessment and monitoring of the results. A Risk Manger's believe that "prevention is better than cure". It is better not to have suffered a loss than to suffer and collect under an insurance policy. Insurance does not compensate for all losses; for example, time spent dealing with the claim loss of client base and reputation. There is also a growing body of evidence to suggest that a significant proportion of firms never fully recover from the effects of a major loss and have to be wound-up within a short time even if fully insured.

A. Risk Analysis

The first step in the process is to analyse the risk to which an organisation may be exposed. Risk analysis has to prime elements—the identification of risk and its evaluation.

Risk Identification

Risk Identification requires knowledge of the organisation, the market in which it operates, the legal, social, economic, political, and climatic environment in which it does it's business, it's financial strengths and weakness, its vulnerability to unplanned losses, the manufacturing processes, and the management systems and business mechanism by which it operates.

Any failure at this stage to identify risk may cause a major loss for the organisation.

Risk identification provides the foundation for risk management. The various methods of risk identification are:

- Checklist Method
- Financial Statement Method
- Flowchart Method
- On-site Inspections
- Interactions with Others
- Contract Analysis
- Statistical Records of Losses

Risk Evaluation

Risk Evaluation breaks down into two parts, the assessment of:

- the probability of loss occurring, and
- its severity

The probability analysis tells us the various possibilities of the perceived scenarios for a given set of circumstances. The severity refers to the direct and indirect measurable impact of the scenarios being analysed.

B. Risk Control

Risk control covers all those measures aimed at avoiding, eliminating or reducing the chances of loss-producing events occurring, or limiting the severity of the losses that do happen. Here, one is seeking to change the conditions that bring about loss-producing events or increase their severity. Though some measures call for little more than common sense, often considerable technical knowledge is required, for which the risk manager will need to turn to experts in the particular field.

Risk can be controlled either by avoidance or by controlling losses. Avoidance implies that either a certain loss exposure is not acquired or an existing one is abandoned.

Loss control can be exercised in two ways.

(a) One way is to enhance and monitor the level of precautions taken to minimise the losses due to exposures.

(b) Another is to control and minimise the risk operations, internal risk control techniques include diversification and/or investments in getting information of loss exposures so as to control them.

The internal risk control measures generally employed are (a) diversification and (b) investment in information. The operational measures fro risk control in an organisation includes—(a) increased precautions and (b) reduced level of activity.

C. Risk Financing

When the risk exposure for an orgamsation exceeds the maximum limit that the organisation can bear, it becomes necessary to either transfer or reduce risk.

However, there is cost involved in both of these exercises. If the method adopted is insurance, the consequential impact on taxes and profits also becomes important. Risk Financing, therefore, refers to the manner in which the risk control measures that have been implemented shall be financed.

It has to be recognised that in the long run an organisation will have to pay for its own losses. The primary objective of risk financing is to spread more evenly over time cost of risk in order to reduce the financial strain and possible insolvency which random concurrency of large losses may cause. The secondary objective is to minimise risk costs.

Essentially an organisation can finance its risk cost in three ways:

- Losses may be charged as they occur to current operating costs; or
- Ex-ante provision may be made for losses, either through the purchase insurance or by building up a contingency found to which losses can be charged; or
- When losses occur they may be financed with loans, which are repaid over the next few months or years.

RISK FINANCING TECHNIQUES

Risk financing includes the following alternatives:

Risk Retention

Risk retention implies that the losses arising due to a risk exposure shall be retained or assumed by the party or the organisation. Risk retention is generally a deliberate decision for business organisations inherited with the following characteristics:

(a) The consequential losses are small;

(b) Losses are shown as operating expenses or can be funded with retained profits.

Of the various techniques of risk retention, self-insurance and captive insurance and the popular ones.

Self-Insurance

Self-insurance is one of the forms of planned retention by which the part or full of the exposure arising due to a risk factor is retained by the firm. Self-insurance programmes differ from the other programmes in the sense of the formal arrangements made. It acts as an alternative to buying insurance in the market or when a part of the claim is not insured in the commercial market. It may be done by keeping aside funds to meet insurable losses. The main reason for self insurance is that the organisation believes it has large funds to finance losses and the opportunity cost of transfer is less than the cost of insurance.

Benefits of Self-insurance

(a) Saves transaction costs—it helps to save cost in the form of amount payable to insurer for overheads and profits, commissions and taxes and the social loading (arising from the statutory requirements) inherent in the premium.

(b) Accuracy of predictions—the risk managers in the organisation think that they are better judges of the adverse exposures and can estimate better than the insurers.

(c) Investment of funds—since insurance companies invest large chunk of funds m various securities and the returns arising therefrom is not reflected in the rates charged by the insurers, the cost reduction becomes obvious for the insured.

(d) Minimisation of disputes—self-managed funds enhances satisfaction to the insured and reduces the conflicts in claims settlement. Also, there is a direct incentive to reduce and control the risk of loss.

Captive Insurance

Captive insurance companies represent a special case of risk retention. A captive insurance company is an entity created and controlled by a parent, whose main purpose is to provide insurance to its corporate owner. The ideology behind this method is that the parent company may save in terms of overhead costs and profits which would otherwise be charged by the insurance company. Also, the insured companies claim premiums as expenses, which may lead to advantages in terms of differential cash flows. These captives may either be pure captives or group captives.

A pure captive is an insurance company established by the parent (generally into non-insurance business) organisation to provide insurance cover to itself or its subsidiary or affiliated organisations.

Group captives are those formed by a group 'of companies for providing insurance cover to control their respective and collective risks. In U.S. terminology these are also known as "trade association insurance companies."

Motives Behind Captives

(a) Optimised loss prevenlion benefits—The benefits enduring from loss prevention are available directly to the insured.
(b) Economies of scale—Groups with several subsidiaries can enjoy the benefit of perfectly tailored insurances products made available to cover risks.
(c) Non-availability' of insurance—Captives provide to cover risk exposures for which covers are otherwise not available in the market.
(d) Stability of earnings—The captives reduce the chances of adverse impact of sudden fluctuations in profits on the firm.
(e) Cost and tax advantages—Obviously, as said earlier, captives reduce cost of risk financing and provide gains in the regime of differential taxes.

Risk Transfer

Risk transfer implies that the exposed party transfers whole or part of the losses consequential to risk exposure to another party for a cost.

The insurance contracts fundamentally involve risk transfers. Apart from the insurance device, there are certain other techniques by which the risk may be transferred.

(a) Insurance—Insurance is a contractual transfer of risk. The insurance company agrees to in demnify the losses arising out an occurrence pre-determined and charges some cost for this act, called as premium. The insurance method of risk transfer is most appropriate when the severity of losses is very high.'° Since the important constraint. *i.e.* the cost of transfer prevails, the suitability of this method depends upon the size of the organisation and affordability.
(b) Non-insurance transfers—Out of the various methods of non-insurance risk transfers, the most common are:
   (i) Hold-harmless agreements or indemnity agreements are the contractual relationships specifying that all losses shall be borne

by the designated party *e.g.* a landlord contracting that all losses shall be borne by the tenant. These agreements by themselves do not reduce original risk. The form and jurisdiction of hold harmless agreements varies from contract to contract.

(ii) Incorporation is another method by which, for example, the sole proprietorship firm or partnership firm can convert themselves into companies and reduce the liability on them. To quote, the liability of a proprietorship firm is unlimited compared to that of a company limited by shares—the liability of the members is limited to the extent of capital contributed by them.

(iii) Hedging can be used to transfer speculative risk. The popular of the instruments used in hedging are derivative contracts.

(iv) Diversification across business or geographic locations justified or coupled with synergies or economies of scale can also significantly reduce risk in aggregate.

ORGANISING INSURANCE BUSINESS

Legal Frame Work with Respect to Insurance

Insurance is a federal subject in India. Two statutes primarily regulate the insurance business— (a) Insurance Act 1938 and (b) Insurance and Regulatory Development Authority Act, 1999. The Insurance business is classified into four classes—(1) Life Insurance, (2) Fire, (3) Marine and (4) Miscellaneous insurance. Life Insurers transact life insurance business and General Insurers transact the rest. Apart from this, GIC and its subsidiaries are regulated by General Insurance Business (Nationalization) Act, 1972 and LIC of India being regulated by The Life Insurance Corporation Act 1956.

Need for Regulation

The regulator of insurance business in India is IRDA constituted by the IRDA Act, 1999. Regulation of Insurance business provides the insurance market with direction, management control and correction. Insurance, generally, all over the world is widely regulated. This is because of the following reasons:

(a) Widespread severe impact of insurer solvency. Since solvency ensures that insurance transactions are certain ad predictable, promotion and maintenance of insurer solvency are at the heart of all regulatory activity. Insureds are generally incapable of self-protection and if the insurance company becomes insolvent, the results may be disastrous. Insurance generally mobilise savings and therefore they bear a kind of fiduciary relationship as that of a banker and customer, and therefore, it requires public regulation.

(b) Unequal knowledge and bargaining power of the buyers arid seller—

insurance contacts are complex and the insurance itself is an intangible product.

(c) Insurance pricing is—typical and unique and requires estimation before the costs are fully known.

(d) Social welfare—insurance by definition is a sound device and optimally should be made available to public at large without discrimination.

Indian Contract Act, 1872

Insurance contracts are agreements between insurance companies and insured for the purpose of transferring from insured to the insurer a part of the risk of loss arising out of contingent event.

Therefore all the provisions of Indian Contract Act, 1872, in general are applicable to insurance contracts.

Under Section 10 of the Indian Contract Act, following conditions are necessary to form a valid contract:

(a) Agreement between two parties
(b) Lawful object
(c) Capacity to contract
(d) Legal purpose
(e) Consideration
(f) Possibility of performance etc.

Insurance Act, 1938

This Act was passed in 1938 and was brought into force from 1st July 1939.

Afterwards, the Acy has been amended a number of times including those in 1950 and 1968. Important Provisions in the Act relate to:

(A) Conduct of Insurance Business (Part—II)
  (1) Registration and licensing of insurance
  (2) Accounts and Audit
  (3) Licensing of agents and surveyors
  (4) Submitting of returns
  (5) Investment norms
  (6) Amalgamation and transfer of insurance business
  (7) Authority's control over management.

(B) Insurance Association of India Councils of the Association and Committees thereof (Part IIA)

(C) Tariff Advisory Committees and control of tariff rates (Part IIB)

(D) Solvency Margin, Advance Payment of premium and restrictions on the opening of a new place of business (Part IIC)

(E) Provident Societies (Part III) Registration, working, Investment norms, liquidation etc.

(F) Mutual insurance companies and co-operative life insurance societies (Part IV) Working capital norms, loans, membership, deposits etc

(G) Reinsurance (Part WA)

(H) Penalties (Part V).

Section 2c of the Act prohibits persons to carry on insurance business until he is –

(a) A public company.

(b) A registered society under

(c) A body corporate incorporated under the law of any country outside India not being in the nature of a private company. However, the central government is empowered to exempt any insurer or any person for the purpose of carrying on the business of granting superannuation allowances and annuities as per Section 2(111(c) or for the purpose of carrying general insurance business. Exempted insurer after the promulgation of IRDA Act, 1999 only Indian Insurance company can carry insurance business.

Licensing conditions

Only Indian Insurance companies to be granted licenses: Under the Act, it is mandatory that only an Indian insurance company can carry on an insurance business in India. An Indian insurance company is a company registered under the Companies Act 1956 where the aggregate foreign equity shareholding does not exceed 26 per cent and whose sole purpose is to carry on a life, general or reinsurance business.

TWO-STAGE LICENSING PROCESS

Stage 1—Requisition for Registration

An application has to be made to the Authority with all the prescribed disclosure norms. Some of the important items cover

1. Promoter's back-ground, financial strength, share-holders' agreement and reasons for entering the sector.
2. Director's back-ground.
3. Capital structure, initial and future.
4. Financial projections for 5 years.
5. Scenario Building and Sensitivity analyses.
6. Rural and social sector strategy.

There is no provision for appeal in the event of a second rejection. A revised application is permissible by the applicant company only after 2 years with an additional condition that this will be with a new set of promoters or for a different class of insurance business.

Stage 2—Application for Registration

After the requisition is granted by the Authority, the applicant is required to make an application for registration.

Information to be disclosed includes:

- Proof of paid-up capital of ₹ 100 crore.
- Proof of deposit.
- Marketing and distribution information. This should include information on Market Research. Product information, Distribution Strategy and Details, Sales promotion, Customer service.
- Operations: Information should cover underwriting, information technology, internal controls, Personnel.
- Investment Information on investment Philosophy, Strategy and ground level arrangements.
- Reinsurance: Information on Approach and Terms.
- Expenditure: This should include a description of the manner in which the expenses of administration have been estimated. These expenses will have to be distinguished between first year and renewal, fixed and variable. The proposed expenses as a per cent of premium at levels of operational offices; supervisory offices and head office.

Licensing Criteria

Some of the important parameters include:

- Promoter and directors' background
- Promoter financial strength
- Volume of business and earning prospects
- Rural and social sector focus
- Product profit
- Capital structure
- Actuarial and professional expertise
- Infrastructure
- Public interest

Other Licensing Issues

An appeal can be made to the Central Government against the decision of Authority, which shall be final. The applicant company can submit, a new application only after two years with the additional condition that it has to be with a new set of promoters or for a different class of insurance business. The Authority will grant more licenses to applicants for life and health insurance than general insurance. Licenses expire on the 31st day of March each year and have to be renewed each year.

Capital Requirement and Foreign Stake

Minimum paid-up equity capital required for a life insurance is ₹ 100 crore and for a reinsurer ₹ 200 crore. The capital contributed can only be in the form of equity shares as preference shares cannot be issued. The incumbent, LIC, would be required to increase its equity share capital from the existing ₹ 5 crore to ₹ 100 crore within a period of six months from the date of commencement of the IRDA Act. Also, the four GIC subsidiaries would have to increase the equity share capital to ₹ 100 crore from ₹ 40 crore are resent. The GIC will not be required to bring in additional capital since its present capital base is Es. 215 crore.

Accounts and Returns

An insurer is required to keep a separate account of all receipts and payments in respect of each class of insurance *viz.*, Fire, Marine and miscellaneous Insurance. Every insurer is required to prepare, at the expiration of each financial year, in the prescribed forms,

(a) a balance sheet

(b) a profit and loss account

(c) a revenue account for each class of insurance business

These accounts are required to be audited annually by an auditor and printed and four copies to be furnished as returns to the IRDA within 6 months from the close of the financial year. Every Insurer is required to furnish to the authority a certified copy of the minutes of the proceedings of every General Meeting, within 30 days from the holding of the meeting. The Insurance Rules framed under the Act provide that the following items of information shall be maintained in respect of each class of business:

- A record of cover notes specifying the identification number, name of party, dates of commencement and expiry, type of cover granted, the amount of premium and cross- reference to the policy.
- A record of policies, which should be serially numbered, listing all policies issued, entered in chronological order, stating the number of policy, date of commencement and expiry of risk, name/s of the insured, premium received, cross reference to the relevant bank Guarantee or deposit and the nature of risk granted, cross reference to any cover-note issued prior to the issue to the policy and cross-reference to any endorsement passed subsequent to the issue of the policy.
- A record of premiums showing, according to chronological order or receipt of premiums, date of receipt, the amount, and name of party from whom received and with cross- reference to policy number.
- A record of endorsements mentioning the policy number to which attached, dates of commencement and expiry of the endorsement, the type of endorsement and the additional premium charged or refund due and cross reference to the premium register.
- A record of bank guarantees and deposits giving particulars of the party, amount and conditions of guarantee or deposits and cross-reference to the relevant policy or policies.

- A record of claims intimate mentioning name of claimant, giving reference to policy number, date of intimation of claim, interest covered, nature and cause of the loss or damage, pro visional estimate of loss, amount at which settled, date of settlement of claim, recoveries from salvage or otherwise and whether surveyed. Two separate records, one relating to claims intimated and the other relating to claims paid, may be maintained if there is ad equate cross referring of information between them and if the information required under this clause is readily available from them taken together.

The rules framed under the Insurance Act, 1938 also provide that the following items of information shall be maintained for the business of the insurer as a whole.

(i) A register of agents.
(ii) A record of business procured by each agent and the amount of commission paid thereon.
(iii) Records of employees including field workers.
(iv) Cash book and disbursement book.
(v) A record of investments and assets.
(vi) Records of insurance companies with which common and facultative reinsurance arrangements of reinsurance treaties are entered into.
(vii) Record of facultative reinsurance ceded and accepted.

Further, the Rules provide that receipts for payments received shall be maintained in a systematic manner and documents used for assuming risk are serially numbered and field accordingly.

The documents relating to claims settled, including copies of any survey of loss assessment reports, shall be maintained as follows:

(i) in respect of every loss or damage on which a claim of less than Its. 5,000 has been made, for a period of three years:
(ii) in respect of every loss or damage on which a claim of ₹ 5,000 or more but less than rupees ₹ 20,000 has been made, for a period of five years:
(iii) in respect of every loss or damage on which a claim of ₹ 20,000 or more but less than rupees one lakh has been made, for a period of seven years
(iv) in respect of every loss or damage on which a claim of rupees one lakh or more has been made, for a period of twelve years; such period being counted from the date on which the claim is settled.

Investments

Every insurer is required to invest his assets only in those investments approved under the provisions. Returns in the prescribed form are to be submitted to the Authority showing as at 31st March of the preceding year, the investments made out of assets.

Limitation on: Expenses of Management

The Act prescribes maximum limits of expenses of management including commission that may be incurred by the insurer. The percentages are prescribed in relation to the total gross direct business written by the insurer in India. These provisions do not apply to the General Insurance Corporation of India.

Prohibition of Rebates

No person shall allow or offer to allow as an inducement to any person to take out insurance arty rebate of the whole or part of commission payable or any rebate of the premium shown in the policy. Any person making default in complying with these provisions shall be punishable with fine which may extend to five hundred rupees.

Powers of Investigation

The Central Government may at anytime, by order £n writing, direct the Authority or any other person specified in the order, to investigate the affairs of any insurer and report to the Central Government.

Advance Payment of Premium

No insurer shall assume any risk unless and until the premium is received in advance or is guaranteed to be paid or a deposit is made in advance in the prescribed manner.

This rule of advance payment of premium may be relaxed in circumstances specified in the rules framed under the Act.

Licensing of Surveyor or Loss Assessor

A surveyor or a loss assessor must hold a valid licence, which is subject to renewal after a period of 5 years. Before admitting a claim exceeding ₹ 20,000 a general insurance company needs to obtain a report on the loss that has occurred from the surveyor or loss assessor.

Penalties

The Act has laid down penalties for contravention of the following provisions:

- Failure to maintain solvency margins.
- Failure to comply with investment norms.
- Failure to carry out rural and social sector obligations.
- Making a false statement or furnishing a false document.
- Failure to comply with the directions of the Authority.
- Failure to furnish documents, statements and returns required by the Act.

Tariff Advisory Committee

The Tariff Advisory Committee (TAC) established under the Act is empowered to control and regulate the rates, terms, etc. that may be offered by insurers in respect of any risk or of any category of risks.

It is provided that in fixing, amending or modifying such rates etc. the Committee shall try to ensure as far as possible that there is no unfair discrimination between risks of essentially the same hazard and also that consideration is given to past and prospective loss experience. Every insurer is required to make payment to the TAC of the prescribed annual fees.

List of Existing Tariff Business Controlled by TAC

Fire : All India Fire Tariff, Petrochemical Tariff, Industrial All Risks Tariff, Consequential Loss (fire) Tariff

Marine: Marine Hull Tariff, Fishing Vessels Tariff, Tea Tariff

Engineering: Contractor's All Risk Tariff (CAR), Contractors Plant and Machinery Tariff (CPM), Electronic Equipments Insurance Tariff (EEI), Machinery Breakdown Tariff (MB), Civil Engineering Completed Risks Tariff (CECR), Storage cum Erection Tariff (SCE), Loss of Profit, Boiler and Pressure Vessels Tariff, Deterioration of Stocks (Potato) Tariff etc.

Motor: All India Motor Tariff

Miscellaneous: Workmen Compensation Tariff.

RISKS IN INSURANCE INDUSTRY

This section is set out to analyze the risks and uncertainties from the lens of different business lines. Ericson and Doyle argue that each line poses unique problems of uncertainty regarding the scientific knowledge available, underwriting decisions, administration, loss prevention, claim management, reinsurance, and investment. As a result, each line entails different approach to risk, attributions of responsibility for risk, and abilities to respond to uncertainty.

The nature of an insurance operation is to accept risks faced by its policyholders in exchange for a premium. In this sense, risks which others do not want to retain are transferred into the insurers' business system. Therefore, insurers are undoubtedly exposed to a variety of risks. For example, a life insurer may be exposed to longevity risk by offering annuity products – if people begin to live longer, life insurer may does not have enough provision to meet the increased liabilities, because the insurer underestimated the premiums. Or it may be exposed to mortality risk by offering death coverage due to policyholders die earlier than they were estimated. For example, Legal and General has the sensitivity analysis in its annual report, it is illustrated that the firm was exposed to the risks of longevity(for annuity product) and mortality (for protection product) at the same time, if people live longer, the company would be better off on protection product but worse off on annuity product. But they won't be balance each other, in total, the company would be worse off if people live longer. Thus, same risk factors may lead to different sides of influences to firms' different business lines; one should view the firm's risk holistically.

Likewise, in the line of general insurance, examples are extensive. For the liability insurance, in which insurer has the obligation to pay compensation for harm suffered by third parties; the insurer is exposed to the risk that its policyholders pose harm to third parties. The case could be more complicated if that harm could only be found after a long period. *E.g.* scientists suggests the usage of mobile phone may bring about brain cancer to people, thus insurers which offer product liabilities to mobile phone manufacturers might be posed to big risks when years later mobile phone users begin to sue for claims.

Classification of Risks Faced by Insurance Companies

In managing risks in insurance business, it is helpful to classify risks. Many studies have described in detail the risks that insurance companies are exposed to. According to KPMG, the risks insurers are exposed to at company level could be summarized as: pure underwriting risk, underwriting management risk, credit risk, reinsurance risk, operational risk, investment risk, liquidity risk, matching risk, expenses risk, lapses risk and provisioning risk. Financial Services Authority (FSA) classifies risks as *market risks*: the risk consists of interest rate risks and currency risks etc, which could lead to the prices of the firm's investment declining; *credit risks*, the risks of the market value of the assets declines; *operational risks*, the risk that the operations of the insurers do not work as intended, *insurance technical risks*, the risks specific to the insurance industry; *liquidity risk*, that the assets that need to be liquidated in order to pay claims are not in fact easily available; and*group risk*: that the comes from the insurer being part of a wider group (FSA).

WHY RISK MANAGEMENT IN INSURANCE INDUSTRY?

Insurance is about reduction of risk and protection against the financial loss of adverse events. An insurance company, 'by sharing such losses amongst a large pool, reduce the risk faced by the individual party to the insurer'. The nature of an insurance company operation is to undertake the risk of its policyholders in return for a premium, and insurance companies have to those risks as so to make profits.

The essential elements of the insurance company risk management process include the 'pooling and diversification of the risk, controlling exposure and obtaining appropriate reinsurance protection. According to the study conducted by KPMG in most insolvencies, the cause has not been due to a single factor, but rather to a combination of both internal and external factors. A frequent reason for insurance company failure is a combination of poor quality of management and inadequate risk management procedures dealing with the key risks to which the company is exposed. This highlights the need for adequate internal models to assist in the risk management process.

Risk management procedures, and the overall quality of management, are critical factors and, together with adequacy of financial resources these factors are of primary importance in protecting an insurance undertaking against insolvency. In addition, an effective risk management process should cover all key elements of the business cycle and, most importantly, adequately manage the risks to which the company is exposed. Consideration of the wider risk management practice, systems and controls is beyond the scope of this study. The main features of the business cycle are underwriting, investment management, claims management, control over expenses, and the reinsurance (and for reinsurers, retrocession) programme.

Tillinghast conducted a survey about the enterprise risk management in the insurance industry. It shows that, in reality, there is a steadily increasing interest in, and use of, ERM by insurers. Insurers are adopting ERM because of its compelling promise to make stronger, more competitive businesses. It will help them balance their policyholders' need for financial strength with their shareholders' demand for attractive returns coupled with consistent bottom-line and top-line growth. Insurers are taking aggressive steps to integrate ERM into their businesses through the sound institutional practices of appointing CROs and creating ERM committees.

RISK MANAGEMENT PROCESS

RISK IDENTIFICATION

Risk identification is the first stage of the risk assessment process. It is a systematic, thorough attempt to list the possible future states of the world that the firm may experience which may be adverse. In other words risk identification is the process by which organizations discover what may happen in the future, how it may happen, and what the consequences may be. Risk identification is a battle against a lack of understanding and imagination: its purpose is to guard organizations against unpleasant surprises.

It is necessary to ensure that a comprehensive risk identification process is carried out, including the consideration of low frequency/high severity risks. Once the individual risk profiles have been defined, it will be necessary to combine them into one risk profile for the organization.

This combination of individual risk profiles needs to allow for the various inter- relationships of the individual risk profiles. For example, risks that are uncorrelated will need less capital in total than the sum of the capital required for each individual risk.

Control

This is an important and rapidly evolving area in the risk management field. Mitigation techniques are becoming increasingly sophisticated and wide ranging. Successfully applied, they can reduce the expected costs and/or reduce the likelihood of loss. They can, therefore, materially impact the profile of any given risk.

Financing

Risk financing is about planning and procedures to make money available to pay for losses.

Organizing risk management

Responding to the new comprehensive risk management approach, a company needs a dedicated and expertise to handle 'the complexity of controlling and managing risks across the company'. As a result, a co-ordination of the various elements of integrated risk management, a person in some organization title as CRO (Chief Risk Officer), is emerging.

Besides the role of the coordination among separate company departments, the CRO should take the responsibility of promoting the integrated risk management programme to management as well as communicating goals and results to the board. One study carried out by Liebenberg and Hoyt shows that 'firm with greater financial leverage and more likely to appoint a CRO'. Consequently, it can be argued that the appointment of a CRO shows a signal of a good risk management and internal control practice.

RISK MANAGEMENT BY INSURANCE FIRMS

Cummins, Phillips, and Smith (CPS) analyze the factors that motivate both life and property-liability insurance firms to participate in derivatives markets as well as the drivers of the volume of derivatives transactions for insurers that decide to participate. Based on 1994 data, CPS find that about 10.9 per cent of life insurers and 6.9 per cent of property-liability insurers use derivatives. However, usage is much more widespread in the largest size quartile, where 34.4 per cent of life and 21.1 per cent of property-liability insurers are active in derivatives markets.

The transactions volume for life insurers far exceeds that of property-liability insurers. The transactions volume for life insurers is concentrated in bond and interest rate derivatives, as expected if insurers are using derivatives to hedge interest rate (duration and convexity) risk. Life insurers also show significant activity in foreign currency derivatives, consistent with the argument that insurers use derivatives to manage exchange rate risk. The leading categories of derivatives transactions for property-liability insurers include equity call options, foreign currency contracts, and bond and interest rate derivatives, again consistent with the management of price volatility, foreign exchange rate risk, and interest rate risk.

Following Gunther and Siems, CPS conduct a multivariate probit analysis of the decision by insurers to participate in derivatives markets and a lognormal regression analysis investigating the volume of derivatives transactions by insurers. The authors investigate both decisions as they argue hedging is not costless, either in terms of fixed or variable costs. Thus, if the participation decision is driven by fixed costs, only firms with high enough levels of risk exposure, for example, due to a high tolerance for risk per unit of expected return, would find it worthwhile to enter the derivatives market. However, conditional on being active in derivatives, firms/managers with high appetites for risk will generally hedge less at the margin to the extent that each additional unit imposes marginal costs in the form of risk premiums. As evidence in support of this hypothesis, the authors report that many of the risk measures employed in the study often display exactly the opposite signs in the participation and volume regressions. This suggests that among firms having a large enough exposure to warrant participation in derivatives markets, those with the largest exposures are less willing to incur the marginal cost associated with eliminating the exposure.

The participation investigation in the CPS analysis also provides a considerable amount of support for the hypothesis that insurers hedge to maximize value. They present evidence consistent with the use of derivatives to reduce the expected costs of financial distress. For example, the decision to use derivatives is inversely related to the capital-to-asset ratio for both life and property-liability insurers. CPS also provide evidence consistent with the use of derivatives by insurers to hedge asset volatility, liquidity, and exchange rate risks. They find significant regression coefficients on several variables related to asset risk exposure such as the proportions of assets in privately placed bonds and collateralized mortgage obligations. Life insurers appear to use derivatives to manage interest rate risk and the risk from embedded options present in their individual life insurance and GIC liabilities. There is also some evidence that tax considerations play a role in motivating derivatives market participation decisions by insurers.

RISK MANAGEMENT BY NON-INSURANCE FIRMS

A major study investigating the question of the "motive" for risk management is by Tufano, who looks at managerial compensation schemes and hedge ratios in the gold mining industry to determine whether risk management is motivated by value maximization or managerial risk aversion. Tufano argues that risk-averse managers whose compensation comes in large part through acquiring shares in the firm will want to hedge their risk. Such a policy would not necessarily benefit diversified shareholders. Tufano contrasts these managers with managers who earn a relatively large portion of their compensation through stock options. In this situation managers can walk away from the options should the firm do poorly, but if the firm does well their positions will provide high payoffs. With this form of incentive compensation, even risk-averse managers would be more willing to tolerate gold price, and therefore earnings, volatility and thus would find hedging to be less advantageous. Tufano's empirical evidence suggests that managers with high option holdings manage risk less than those with high stock holdings consistent with the managerial risk-aversion hypothesis of risk management. Tufano finds almost no evidence in favour of the various rationales that would make risk management a value-maximizing decision.

Contrary to Tufano's results, some authors have provided evidence that is more consistent with the value-maximization theories of risk management. Numerous authors have investigated whether firms engage in risk management in an effort to reduce the probability of incurring financial distress costs. An early study by Wall and Pringle found support for the hypothesis as they report that firms with lower credit ratings are more likely than higher-rated firms to use interest rate swaps.

Other authors have considered the more general question of whether the firm's capital structure is related to the likelihood that the firm will engage in risk management via derivatives contracting. The evidence presented in these studies is mixed. For example, neither Mian nor Nance, Smith, and Smithson report any evidence to suggest that derivatives trading is related to the capital structure of the firm. A more recent study by Geczy, Minton, and Schrand investigates the relationship between the capital structure of the firm and the decision to manage foreign currency exposures using derivatives. This study differs from its predecessors by recognizing the simultaneity of a firm's capital structure and risk-management decisions. Even after controlling for simultaneity, however, the authors conclude that there does not appear to be a relationship between a firm's capital structure and the decision to use derivatives.

Two exceptions to these studies of non-financial firms are Dolde and Graham and Rogers. Dolde finds a significant relationship between risk management and the leverage of the firm after controlling for the firm's underlying exposure to various financial risks. Graham and Rogers, like Geczy, et.al., investigate the hedging and debt policy decisions of the firm using a simultaneous equations approach. They find that the use of derivatives is positively related to firm leverage. Thus, these authors find evidence to suggest highly levered firms appear more likely to use derivatives to avoid the expected costs of financial distress; or as Graham and Rogers argue, firms that use derivatives can maintain higher leverage ratios and maximize firm value by increasing their interest-expense tax deductions.

The evidence from studies investigating the decision by non-insurance financial firms to use derivatives as a way to avoid financial distress costs is also mixed. Sinkey and Carter provide weak evidence that the capital structure and risk-management decisions of U.S. commercial banks are related. Gunther and Siems, who also analyze U.S. banks, report no significant relationship between the decision to use derivatives and the capital structure of the bank. Focusing only on banks that are active in derivatives markets, Gunther and Siems find that banks reporting a higher volume of derivatives activity also have higher capital ratios. This result is in fact inconsistent with the financial distress hypothesis, at least as it is usually defined in the literature.

Mixed evidence has also been presented on the use of derivatives to lower the firm's expected tax burden. In their study of non-financial companies, Nance, Smith, and Smithson find that firms with higher investment tax credits are more likely to engage in derivative transactions. In an analysis of firms reported on Compustat, Graham and Smith conclude that approximately 50 per cent of the firms in their sample face convex tax schedules and therefore have an incentive to reduce the volatility of their income stream. However, in a subsequent study, Graham and Rogers use a similar methodology to estimate the convexity of the tax schedule for a large sample of firms across many industries and are unable to find any relationship between derivative holdings and tax convexity.

A number of authors have found strong evidence documenting that firms use derivatives to reduce the variability of their income stream and thus help to ensure that adequate internal funds are available to take advantage of attractive investments. Gay and Nam, for example, provide results consistent with the hypothesis that non-financial firms with both low levels of liquidity and high growth opportunities tend to hedge more. This finding is consistent with managers trying to mitigate the need to seek costly external funds to finance positive net present value projects. Other authors have found similar results.

For example, Geczy, Minton, and Schrand and Nance, Smith, and Smithson both found that companies with less liquidity or companies that use less preferred stock, as opposed to using straight debt, are more likely to use derivatives to avoid shocks to the internal capital resources. A recent study by Ahmed, Beatty, and Takeda investigating 152 U.S. commercial banks also finds support for the costly external finance hypothesis.

INSURANCE OF RISK MANAGEMENT

Recognizing and assessing areas at risk in your business is the beginning. Once a risk issue is discovered, a strategy must be devised to manage that risk. Among the treatments are avoiding the risk, accepting (retaining) the risk, reducing (mitigating) the negative effect of the risk and risk transfer. Risk transfer is accomplished through risk management insurance. A well rounded risk management strategy will utilize each of these treatments where applicable. Risk transfer through risk management insurance is a common method of obtaining financial protection against potential loss. Our risk management consultants can help you identify insurable risk areas. Moreover, we will show you how to minimize your risk management insurance cost through correct use of all available treatment options and through educational initiatives proven to reduce events that result in loss.

GLOBAL INSURANCE INDUSTRY

Global insurance premiums grew by 9.7 per cent in 2004 to reach $3.3 trillion. This follows 11.7 per cent growth in the previous year. Life insurance premiums grew by 9.8 per cent during the year, thanks to rising demand for annuity and pension products. Non-life insurance premiums grew by 9.4 per cent, as premium rates increased. Over the past decade, global insurance premiums rose by more than a half as annual growth fluctuated between 2 per cent and 10 per cent. Advanced economies account for the bulk of global insurance. With premium income of $1,217 billion in 2004, North America was the most important region, followed by the EU (at $1,198 billion) and Japan (at $492 billion). The top four countries accounted for nearly two-thirds of premiums in 2004. The United States and Japan alone accounted for a half of world insurance premiums, much higher than their 7 per cent share of the global population. Emerging markets accounted for over 85 per cent of the world's population but generated only 10 per cent of premiums. The volume of UK insurance business totaled $295 billion in 2004 or 9.1 per cent of global premiums.

INSURANCE COMPANIES

Financial stability and strength of an insurance company should be a major consideration when purchasing an insurance contract. An insurance premium paid currently provides coverage for losses that might arise many years in the future. For that reason, the viability of the insurance carrier is very important. In recent years, a number of insurance companies have become insolvent, leaving their policyholders with no coverage (or coverage only from a government-backed insurance pool or other arrangement with less attractive payouts for losses). A number of independent rating agencies, such as Best's, Fitch, Standard and Poor's, and Moody's Investors Service, provide information and rate the financial viability of insurance companies.

Accounting Definition

An operational definition of insurance is that it is:

- The benefit provided by a particular kind of indemnity contract, called an insurance policy;

- In which the insurer promises to pay on behalf of or to indemnify another party, called a policyholder or insured;
- That protects the insured against loss caused by those perils subject to the indemnity in exchange for consideration known as an insurance premium.
- That is issued by one of several kinds of legal entities (stock insurance company, mutual insurance company, reciprocal, or Lloyd's syndicate, for example), any of which may be called an insurer;

In recent years this kind of operational definition proved inadequate as a result of contracts that had the form but not the substance of insurance. The essence of insurance is the transfer of risk from the insured to one or more insurers. How much risk a contract actually transfers proved to be at the heart of the controversy. This issue arose most clearly in reinsurance, where the use of Financial Reinsurance to reengineer insurer balance sheets under US GAAP became fashionable during the 1980s. The accounting profession raised serious concerns about the use of reinsurance in which little if any actual risk was transferred, and went on to address the issue in FAS 113, cited above. While on its face, FAS 113 is limited to accounting for reinsurance transactions, the guidance it contains is generally conceded to be equally applicable to US GAAP accounting for insurance transactions executed by commercial enterprises.

Requirement of Risk Transfer

FAS 113 contains two tests, called the '9a and 9b tests,' that collectively require that a contract create a reasonable chance of a significant loss to the underwriter for it to be considered insurance. Indemnification of the ceding enterprise against loss or liability relating to insurance risk in reinsurance of short-duration contracts requires both of the following, unless the condition in paragraph 11 is met:

a. The reinsurer assumes significant insurance risk under the reinsured portions of the underlying insurance contracts.
b. It is reasonably possible that the reinsurer may realize a significant loss from the transaction.

Paragraph 10 of FAS 113 makes clear that the 9a and 9b tests are based on comparing the present value of all costs to the PV of all income streams. FAS gives no guidance on the choice of a discount rate on which to base such a calculation, other than to say that all outcomes tested should use the same rate. Statement of Statutory Accounting Principles ("SSAP") 62, issued by the National Association of Insurance Commissioners, applies to so-called 'statutory accounting'-the accounting for insurance enterprises to conform with regulation. Paragraph 12 of SSAP 62 is nearly identical to the FAS 113 test, while paragraph 14, which is otherwise very similar to paragraph 10 of FAS 113, additionally contains a justification for the use of a single fixed rate for discounting purposes. The choice of an "reasonable and appropriate" discount rate is left as a matter of judgement.

"Safe Harbour" Exemptions

The analysis of reasonableness and significance is an estimate of the probability of different gain or loss outcomes under different loss scenarios. It takes time and resources to perform the analysis, which constitutes a burden without value where risk transfer is reasonably self-evident. Guidance exists for insurers and reinsurers, whose CEO's and CFO's attest annually as to the reinsurance agreements their firms undertake. The American Academy of Actuaries, for instance, identifies three categories of contract as outside the requirement of attestation:

- Pre-1994 contracts. The attestation requirement only applies to contracts that were entered into, renewed or amended on or after 1 January 1994. Prior contracts need not be analyzed.
- Inactive contracts. If there are no premiums due nor losses payable, and the insurer is not taking any credit for the reinsurance, determining risk transfer is irrelevant.
- Where risk transfer is "reasonably self-evident."
- "Risk transfer is reasonably self-evident in most traditional per-risk or per-occurrence excess of loss reinsurance contracts. For these contracts, a predetermined amount of premium is paid and the reinsurer assumes nearly all or all of the potential variability in the underlying losses, and it is evident from reading the basic terms of the contract that the reinsurer can incur a significant loss. In many cases, there is no aggregate limit on the reinsurer's loss. The existence of certain experience-based contract terms, such as experience accounts, profit commissions, and additional premiums, generally reduce the amount of risk transfer and make it less likely that risk transfer is reasonably self-evident."— "Reinsurance Attestation Supplement 20-1: Risk Transfer Testing Practice Note,"

American Academy of Actuaries, *November 2005.*

No Brightline Test

Neither FAS 113 nor SAP 62 defines the terms *reasonable* or *significant*. Ideally, one would like to be able to substitute values for both terms. It would be much simpler if one could apply a test of an X per cent chance of a loss of Y per cent or greater. Such tests have been proposed, including one famously attributed to an SEC official who is said to have opined in an after lunch talk that a 10 per cent chance of a 10 per cent loss was sufficient to establish both reasonableness and significance. Indeed, many insurers and reinsurers still apply this 10/10" test as a benchmark for risk transfer testing. It should be obvious that an attempt to use any numerical rule such as the 10/10 test will quickly run into problems. Implicit in the test is keeping the 10/10 that either are upper bonds for the comment made by the SEC official therefore, the rest of this paragraph doesn't apply.

Suppose a contract has a 1 per cent chance of a 10,000 per cent loss? It should be reasonably self-evident that such a contract is insurance, but it fails one half of the 10/10 test. It does not appear that any brightline test of reasonableness nor significance can be constructed. Excess of loss contracts, like those commonly used for umbrella and general liability insurance, or to insure against property losses, will typically have a low ratio of premium paid to maximum loss recoverable. This ratio (expressed as a percentage), commonly called the *rate on line* for historical reasons related to underwriting practices at Lloyd's of London, will typically be low for contracts that contain reasonably self-evident risk transfer. As the ratio increases to approximate the present value of the limit of coverage, self-evidence decreases and disappears. Contracts with low rates on line may survive modest features that limit the amount of risk transferred. As rates on line increase, such risk limiting features become increasingly important.

Features of Risk Limiting

An insurance policy should not contain provisions that allow one side or the other to unilaterally void the contract in exchange for benefit. Provisions that void the contract for failure to perform or for fraud or material misrepresentation are ordinary and acceptable. The policy should have a term of not more than about three years.

This is not a hard and fast rule. Contracts of over five years duration are classified as 'long-term,' which can impact the accounting treatment, and can obviously introduce the possibility that over the entire term of the contract, no actual risk will transfer. The coverage provided by the contract need not cease at the end of the term (*e.g.*, the contract can cover occurrences as opposed to claims made or claims paid).

The contract should be considered to include any other agreements, written or oral, that confer rights, create obligations, or create benefits on the part of either or both parties. Ideally, the contract should contain an 'Entire Agreement' clause that assures there are no undisclosed written or oral side agreements that confer rights, create obligations, or create benefits on the part of either or both parties. If such rights, obligations or benefits exist, they must be factored into the tests of reasonableness and significance. The contract should not contain arbitrary limitations on timing of payments. Provisions that assure both parties of time to properly present and consider claims are acceptable provided they are commercially reasonable and customary. Provisions that expressly create actual or notional accounts that accrue actual or notional interest suggest that the contract contains, in fact, a deposit.

Provisions for additional or return premium do not, in and of themselves, render a contract something other than insurance. However, it should be unlikely that either a return or additional premium provision be triggered, and neither party should have discretion regarding the timing of such triggering. All of the events that would give rise to claims under the contract cannot have materialized prior to the inception of the contract. If this "all events" test is not met, then the contract is considered to be a retroactive contract, for which the accounting treatment becomes complex.

7

Financial Engineering and Risk Management Products

The techniques just described can seldom accomplish all of management's objectives. To add to management's arsenal of tools to manage the risk associated with adverse changes in currency exchange rates, interest rates, and commodity prices, a host of risk management products have been devised by financial engineers. J. D. Finnerty, a professorat Fordham University, "Financial Engineering in Corporate Finance: An Overview," appearing in the Winter 1988 issue of Financial Management, defined "financial engineering" as follows: Financial engineering involves the design, the develop-ment, and the implementation of innovative financial instruments and processes, and the formulation of creative solutions to problems in finance.

Financial engineers work closely with a client firm to first identify and measure the potential exposure to risk and then create a solution to obtain a desired outcome. Some financial engineers specialize in the quantitative analysis of determining the exposure to risk. Others are responsible for coming up with what may be an innovative and creative solution. Still others are involved with the practical aspects of implementing the solution. Financial engineering usually requires the services of accountants, lawyers, tax specialists, analysts, modeling professionals, programmers, and information specialists. Financial engineering is a sign of the times—as volatility of prices and interest and currency exchange rates increases, so does the risk of potential loss faced by corporations, and, therefore, the need for outside expertise to manage the risk of potential loss.

The efficacy of financial engineering depends on modern methods of communication and the interfacing of communications and computers for the dissemination of information on various financial and commodity markets. Modern technology in the networking of computers allows multiple users to tap the same data base and use the same spreadsheet financial models for rapid analysis in preparing timely and effective recommendations to clients, both internal and external.

One interesting example of the technological impact of computers and telecommunications on financial markets is "programme trading." Stock market index futures are used by portfolio managers as insurance, or protection, against a falling market.

Suppose that a mutual fund manager is worried about a falloff in the stock market. By shorting the index futures, any falloff in the stock market, which creates portfolio losses, is compensated by profits made in the index futures. Programme trading is the exploitation of discrepancies between the price of stock market index futures and the underlying market value of the stocks represented by these futures.

Speed of execution of orders, computerized matching of buy and sell orders, buying and selling of "baskets" of securities, and rapid analysis of the complex mathematics associated with identifying pricing discrepancies are necessary technological preconditions for the existence of programme trading. Stock market index futures can be viewed as a financial tool, devised by financial engineers for stock portfolio managers to protect themselves against volatility in stock prices. But financial engineers are also hard at work devising innovative and creative ways for individuals and firms to increase their yield on investments. By examining the spread between index futures and the underlying value of the basket of securities, financial engineers can provide the necessary information and the means to buy one and short the other, locking in a superior return over investing in other securities such as Treasury bills. This particular financial tool, created by financial engineers to protect portfolio managers against adverse changes in stock prices, is also exploited by financial engineers to enhance the return on investment for investors.

The irony of the situation is that the exploitation of a financial instrument to enhance yield may also be responsible for increasing the volatility of stock prices. If this is the case, then the medicine is both treating and contributing to the disease.

The ability to gather information promptly and accurately, and disseminate the information immediately throughout the world can be considered a risk management tool. This, too, may be responsible for increased volatility. A manager of a chocolate factory who first learned about a cocoa crop failure in West Africa in the nineteenth century from a captain of a sailing vessel probably had sufficient time to act on this information to protect his company's interest in cocoa beans before his competitors learned about it.

His individual buying of cocoa beans would probably not affect the market to any great degree. The slow dissemination of the information about the crop failure allows for an orderly adjustment of prices. Nathan Rothschild supposedly learned of the defeat of Napoleon at Waterloo by homing pigeon. This allowed him to buy depressed stocks in London before anyone else knew of the allied victory and sell them when everyone else knew.

Leaving aside the moral implications of having sole access to vital information, the buying and selling by Rothschild probably reduced the volatility in the London stock market because his buying occurred when everyone was selling and his selling occurred when everyone was buying. In today's world, all those who deal in cocoa beans and stocks and everything else are tapped into the same source of news. No one has a timing advantage, which means that all act in unison, and by so doing, increase the volatility of prices.

RISK MANAGEMENT STRATEGIC CONSIDERATIONS

A U.S. based company sells a product for a million British pounds, to be paid in six months, with a current exchange rate of $1.80 per pound. The financial advisors to the company feel that the pound is likely to fluctuate in a range of $1.70 to $1.90 per pound. A futures contract can be purchased to guarantee conversion at $1.78 per pound, indicating some negative feelings about the prospects for the pound by those selling futures. What should be done?

There are two pure strategies: do nothing or hedge everything. The do nothing approach is simple—do nothing. In six months, the pound might be worth $1.70, meaning that the company will receive $100,000 less than what it anticipated when the goods were sold for 1 million pounds. The hedge everything approach is just as simple. This would commit the company to honouring a futures contract that would, in effect, lock the proceeds from the sale of goods at $1,780,000. Many financial managers subscribe to the latter course of action because a fully hedged portfolio "let's them sleep peacefully at night." The cost of a futures contract is small, being the brokerage fee associated with buying the contract.

So the peaceful sleep costs the company little, unless, of course, one wants to overlook the loss of opportunity gain associated with the pound moving up to $1.90. In this case, the true cost of the peaceful night's sleep could escalate from the small brokerage fee up to about $100,000. This is a very expensive tranquilizer. A less expensive tranquilizer might be a futures option to establish a minimum exchange rate for a million pounds, while letting the company benefit if the British pound gains in value.

This costs more in the form of an upfront premium than a futures contract, but there may be offsetting opportunity gains associated with a strengthening British pound that could justify the extra cost. Between these two extremes are all sorts of mixed strategies where the individual hedge does not cover the entire million pounds, or where the strike, or option price, does not match the current exchange rate. The key question is which of these myriad of possibilities does one follow? Utility theory allows the mathematical modeling of risk aversion, or fear, on the part of managers.

What kind of a disaster awaits the company if the pound should fall to $1.70? Suppose this sale has a profit element of $300,000 with the pound at $1.80.

The worst that can happen is that the profit element is reduced to $200,000. That may be acceptable given that, by doing nothing, the profit element may grow as large as $400,000 if the pound rises in value to $1.90. On the other hand, perhaps the profit element in the transaction is not the main concern to the manager. Perhaps, the receipt of the $1.8 million is crucial for the firm continuing as a going concern.

Suppose that approximately $1.78 million must be dedicated to repaying a loan and bankruptcy looms if the company does not repay the loan in full. Now there is no question that the company had better lock in the $1.78 million through a futures contract; the financial officer has good reason to buy a futures contract to guarantee a peaceful night's slumber. No manager actually knows the future price of a commodity or the exchange rate of a currency. If so, he or she would be better off giving up his or her position and taking a speculative position in the asset.

But managers do know the consequences if the price of a commodity, the interest rate on a loan, or the exchange rate of a currency reaches certain levels. These thresholds of financial pain vary with the circumstances of every company, and with the perceptions of every executive. As an example, a public bus company consumes an enormous quantity of diesel fuel oil. The last thing the bus depot manager wants is to have to go before the town budget committee and beg for more money because diesel fuel costs have gone beyond his budgetary allotment. Risk management provides the financial means, such as a range forward, to avoid this pain. The fact that he might end up paying more for fuel if it falls below the floor rate is not of any great concern; the manager is still within his budgetary limit.

Pain is on the side of high prices, not low prices. He may forego the opportunity to enjoy lower prices in order to avoid the pain of paying higher prices. A manager of the fuel purchases for an airline cannot afford to pay more for jet fuel than some stipulated amount. On the other hand, he has no authority for paying upfront premiums for protection. A market maker in the jet fuel offers the airline a participating forward where the airline will not pay more than a ceiling price on the purchase of jet fuel.

However, when the price of jet fuel is less than the ceiling price, the airline pays some premium over the market price. For instance, the price of jet fuel may be adjusted upward by half the difference between the spot and ceiling prices. This, of course, is the hidden premium for this risk management product because, in the world of finance, there is no free lunch. In this case, there are two pains.

One is the pain associated with jet fuel prices escalating above a certain level. Pain is also in requesting upfront premium fees to pay for this risk management product. The financial engineers created a remedy for both pains by devising the participating forward contract. Financial engineers or market makers stand between the oil producers and the oil consumers. An oil producer has a large amount of debt. He cannot afford to have oil fall below a certain price because he will not generate the earnings necessary to repay his loans. He is an obvious candidate for entering into some sort of arrangement that fixes the price at which he can sell his oil. The bus company and the airline and a host of other companies want to fix their cost of oil products. A financial engineer has to devise hedging tools not just in crude oil but also in gasoline, heating oil, and other petroleum products. Once these financial tools are developed, a market maker can stand between the various parties making up the oil industry fixing revenue, fixing cost, to everyone's heart's content, even devising clever schemes to hide the premiums.

With financial engineers creating futures in crude oil, gasoline, heating oil, and jet fuel, a market maker can now approach an oil refiner and induce him to sell futures in gasoline and heating oil and buy futures in crude oil and fix his margin. That is, the refinery operator can lock in his operational profit margin through risk management products. When risk management is used in ways that lock in profit margins, it is sometimes referred to as economic management. An example of economic management is a copper mining company wanting to borrow funds to expand its capacity. Lenders are wary of the project because of the inherent volatility in copper prices.

A falling copper price will jeopardize the repayment of the loans. To combat this risk, the copper mine operator can use a risk management product to enter into a swap that stabilizes the price he is going to receive for his copper production. Since the economic risk of a falling copper price is no longer of concern to the bankers, they offer a floating rate interest loan to finance the mine project. Now it is the copper mine operator's turn to worry about the financial risk of a rising floating rate interest destroying his profitability, now that his revenue is fixed by virtue of the copper swap. To accommodate the mine operator's perception of risk, another risk management product, an interest rate swap, can be set up to fix the rate of interest.

If by chance, different currencies were involved between the selling of the copper and the financing of the loan, a currency swap can also be part of the picture. With both the copper price and the interest rate, along with any possible currency exchanges involved with the project, fixed, the projected cash flow can be sufficiently stabilized to proceed with the development of the mine. The economic risks associated with the project were addressed by an assortment of risk management products. Once in place, they made the project financially viable.

Another example of economic management is a U.S. exporter competing in the global market. His non-U.S. based competitors quote in different currencies. The U.S. exporter quotes only in dollars. He perceives this to be a competitive disadvantage. One way to address the marketing risk of not satisfying the needs of customers is to enter into currency exchange rate swaptions, or other financial instruments, based on estimates of sales in these currencies. If these currency exchange risk management products can be properly designed, a company can quote in different currencies and not be exposed to a currency exchange loss.

SYNTHETICS

Finally, the financial engineers can set up synthetic instruments. Synthetics use risk management products not directly related to the underlying asset. The use of currency exchange futures to hedge interest rate positions and vice versa are examples of synthetic instruments. Suppose that there is no way to hedge against currency X. However, in tracking past movements of currency X, and comparing these movements with those of currency Y, it is noted that there is good correlation between the two. That is to say, the two currencies move more or less in tandem. If there is a market for risk management products in currency Y, then it is possible for financial engineers to devise a hedging vehicle for currency X using risk management products based on currency Y. The problem here is that future movements of currency X may not correlate, or be in tandem, with currency Y.

In which case, the hedge may not only be ineffective, but may be a financial disaster. One example of a synthetic instrument that failed to perform as intended was the use of heating oil futures as a synthetic hedge for jet fuel futures by airlines before the development of jet fuel futures. The synthetic instrument had previously shown a good degree of correlation between the prices of heating oil and jet fuel. Their respective prices more or less moved in tandem. Unfortunately, one day the two diverged. Jet fuel prices went up and heating oil futures went down. Not only did the heating oil futures fail to provide any protection against rising jet fuel prices, but the heating oil futures themselves were liquidated at a loss.

MODELING AND MANAGEMENT JUDGEMENT

To manage risk, management must first have an assessment of its exposure to a particular risk. A financial reporting and control system could have a projection of the financial statement and balance sheet projection of a company set up using nominal values for those currency exchange rates, interest rates and commodity prices that are of importance in the operation of a company.

This does not have to be an integral part of an financial reporting and control system *per se*. It could be done on a spreadsheet where a single change in the value of one of these key variables can be transmitted throughout the income statement and balance sheet in such a way that management can see the associated impact of a change on reported profitability and cash flow. The company is now in a position to play what if scenarios for different values of the key variables whose volatility can be addressed by risk management products. By keeping all variables at their nominal value and adjusting one at a time for likely changes in value, exposure to risk can be quantified for each variable and ranked in importance. Such an analysis can also lead to determining those values of key variables that approach a threshold of financial pain. That is, if the floating interest rate rose to a certain level, if a particular currency exchange rate fell to some other level, if the price of an important commodity rose or fell to another level, then the earnings would not be sufficient to satisfy the cash needs of the company.

This defines the threshold of financial pain. Presumably, management is willing to pay for some degree of coverage to avoid the threshold of financial pain. If the spreadsheet is designed to handle futures and options, and this is no small task, then it would be possible for management to compare a futures with a call from the point of view of avoiding financial pain for a given cost. A sophisticated spreadsheet may be able to provide information for management on how much coverage, and what form of coverage, should be taken to financially safeguard the company. A simulation is a very large number of what if scenarios. This, too, can be used as a risk management tool in deciding on the requisite degree of coverage.

Simulations have been used to sort out the efficacy of various hedging programmes relying on historic price fluctuations. The problem with this approach is the underlying assumption that the past is a prelude to the future. The fact that a specific hedging programme worked best in the last five years is no guarantee that it is the best choice for the coming year. Several companies have developed an in-house capability to analyse their exposure to risk and measure the effectiveness of various hedging techniques.

Other companies rely on outside vendors who sell systems that are adaptable to the particulars of a company. Some of these systems are dedicated to handling currency exchange risk, because this is a risk faced by all global companies. Others cover a broader range of currency, interest, and commodity risks. Some confine their output to exposure to risk and tracking of hedges in place. Others provide analysis of alternatives, and some are better described as decision support systems because their output offers suggested optimal risk management strategies. There are about thirty software companies offering risk management systems. In addition, certain banks offer tracking and analysis systems to their clients. Regardless of the nature of the software systems, the simplicity or complexity of what if spreadsheet models, or the nature of other computer aids, their purpose is to provide quantitative data to decision makers.

There is little question that a well-designed quantitative model improves the quality of decisions. The designing of such models enhances the understanding of the participants in the inner financial workings of a corporation. On the other hand, models cannot run companies unless human judgement can be reduced to a series of 0's and 1's, the language of computers. Judgement is more than 0's and 1's. Judgement is required in "what if" analysis because there must be management inputs on the perceived direction rates or prices may take in orchestrating the what if scenarios. Judgement is necessary in assessing volatility.

Volatility itself must be judged by people because volatility is not predictable. Periods of calm with relative stability in prices or rates follow and precede periods of tumult. Management judgement is required in deciding on what must be avoided; that is, what is the threshold of financial pain for a company. Judgement also comes into play in deciding the degree and cost of the risk management product coverage necessary to avoid this pain.

The final decision on which risk management programme to implement must be made by management. No computer programme can perceive the world better than a human mind, which, after all, is also the programmer of the computer. Therefore, risk management, like all management functions, is ultimately as effective as the people making the decisions.

RISK MANAGEMENT ACCOUNTING ISSUES

FASB 52 sets forth a series of conditions for accounting for currency exchange futures as hedges, avoiding having to "mark to market" the value of a futures on the last day of each accounting period. Mark-to-market gains and losses flow through the income statement, which adds to the volatility of earnings. Managers take a dim view of the mark-to-market accounting treatment of futures because of its unpredictable impact on earnings.

Earnings, in the mind of many managers, should reflect the result of operations and not be distorted by the "snapshot" valuation of futures contracts. FASB 52 also accords the same accounting treatment to currency exchange forward contracts as to currency exchange futures contracts. In 1984, FASB 80, "Accounting for Futures Contracts," was issued to deal with futures contracts for other than currency such as stock index, commodities, and interest rates. FASB 80 defers the loss or gain of a futures contract if the company owns, or is liable for, the delivery of the underlying asset.

The gain or loss of a futures contract can also be deferred if there is a legally enforceable obligation to make or accept delivery of the underlying asset. And the third criterion for deferring a gain or loss is entering into a futures or forward contract on the basis of an anticipated transaction. This transaction need not be legally enforceable. In other words, if in management's judgement, there is sufficient probability of some transaction occurring to warrant entering into a futures or forward contract, and even if there is nothing legally binding to enforce the consummation of the contract, the gains and losses of the associated futures or forward contract can be deferred. Under FASB 52, deferral of gains and losses can occur only if the currency exchange forward or futures contract reduces the risk of loss of a specified transaction. FASB 80 has a much broader interpretation of the conditions permitting deferral of gains and losses associated with other forms of futures and forward contracts. In particular, hedging based on anticipated transactions, in addition to exposure to risk of existing conditions and firm commitments, is permitted deferral of gains and losses.

Mark to market, or the immediate recognition of gains and losses associated with non-currency-exchange futures and forward contracts, is required only when the futures and forward contract cannot be related to any underlying or anticipated exposure to risk. In essence, FASB 52, which applies only to currency exchange futures and forward contracts, and FASB 80, which applies to all other futures and forward contracts, are inconsistent in the accounting treatment of futures and forward contracts. This, not surprisingly, has sparked a continuing controversy among accounting professionals.

Neither FASB 52 nor FASB 80 addresses options. In 1984, the American Institute of Certified Public Accountants (AICPA) began to study this issue, which led to the publication of the "Options Issues Paper" in 1986. The paper tends to apply the principles underlying FASB 80, rather than FASB 52, to options. That is, using options to hedge against anticipated happenings should be treated similar to the treatment of futures and forward contracts in FASB 80. The "Options Issues Paper" has neither been endorsed by the Securities and Exchange Commission nor has there been follow-up in the form of a published FASB statement.

Therefore, the issue of accounting for options is essentially yet to be fully resolved. Hedge accounting frequently has the effect of shifting reported gains or losses from one period to another. Given that the rules of accounting for hedges involving options are still evolving, management must be accordingly cautious on their approach to accounting for hedges. In 1990, FASB 105, "Disclosure of Information about Financial Instruments with Off-Balance-Sheet Risk and Financial Instruments with Concentrations of Credit Risk," came into effect. Futures, options, and financial swaps fall within the definition of a financial instrument as set forth by FASB 105.

The purpose of FASB 105 is not to specify accounting principles applicable to these financial instruments. Its purpose is footnote disclosure of the off-balance sheet risk associated with certain financial instruments and also concentrations of credit risk. Off-balance-sheet risk is the risk of an accounting loss that exceeds the amount recognized as an asset or liability on the balance sheet. Prior to FASB 105, a company could have entered into a speculative futures contract that might have resulted in a potential loss far exceeding the amount of investment that would be recorded on the balance sheet. No further special accounting or disclosure was required. Normal accounting treatment would handle any gain or loss attributed to the futures contract. With the adoption of FASB 105, footnote disclosure is now required if a company takes a speculative position in a financial instrument that can result in a loss exceeding the acquisition or carrying cost of the financial instrument.

FASB 105 describes the nature of the footnote disclosure and also requires disclosure of credit risk where financial instruments are concentrated by geographic regions, industries, or customer groups that have common exposure to adverse economic developments. The 1990 annual report of the Coca-Cola Company contains these required footnote disclosures. The company's exposure to credit risk of its associated bottlers and customers. Note the reference to outstanding interest rate swaps.

NOTE 4 TO COCA-COLA 1990 ANNUAL REPORT

Finance Subsidiary. Coca-Cola Financial Corporation (CCFC) provides loans and other forms of financing to Coca-Cola bottlers and customers for the acqui-sition of sales-related equipment and for other business purposes.

The approximate contractual maturities of finance receivables for the five years succeeding December 31, 1990, are as follows in thousands):

1991	$38,199	1992	30,609
1993	20,156	1994	11,290
1995	7,111		

These amounts do not reflect possible prepayments or renewals. Finance receivables include amounts due from Johnston of $56 million and $59 million at December 31, 1990 and 1989, respectively. At December 31, 1990, CCFC had outstanding interest rate swap agreements which effectively change CCFCs' float-ing interest exposure on $60 million of commercial paper to a fixed rate of approximately 8.2 per cent. Note 7 of the same annual report, discloses non-U. S. dollar denominated debts, which are acting as hedges against the company's investments in these countries. Note 8 discloses that the company has entered into a substantial amount of foreign currency exchange and interest rate contracts, which are subject to the risk of loss if there is a change in rates. Because "such changes would generally be offset by opposite effects on the items being hedged," there is no speculative aspect associated with these financial instruments.

NOTES 7 AND 8 TO COCA-COLA 1990 ANNUAL REPORT

Notes outstanding at December 31, 1990, were issued outside the United States and are redeemable at the Company's option under certain condition related to U.S. and foreign tax laws. The 5 ¾ per cent notes due to April 24, 1996, are donominated in Japanese yen and the 5 ¾ per cent notes due March 25, 1998, are denominated in German marks. Portions of such notes have been swapped for U.S. dollar, Swiss franc and Belgian franc denominated liabilities.

The Company has designated such foreign currency borrowing as hedges against its net investments in those respective countries. Other long-term debt consists of various mortgages and notes with maturity dates ranging from 1991 to 2013. Interest on a portion of this debt varies with the changes in the prime rate, and the weighted average interest rate applicable to the remainder is approximately 12.7 per cent.

Maturities of long-term debt for the five years succeeding December 31, 1990, are as follows (in thousand):

1991	$97,272	1992	78,353
1993	24,750	1994	14,103
1995	8,009		

The various restrictions, none of which are presently significant to the Company. At December 31, 1990, the Company is contingently liable for guarantees of indebtedness owed by third parties of $139 million, of which $82 million, is related to independent bottling licensees. Interest paid was approximately $233 million, $319 mil-lion and $250 million in 1990, 1989 and 1988, respectively.

Financial Instruments. The Company has various financial instruments with off-balance-sheet risk for the primary purpose of reducing its exposure to fluctuations in foreign currency exchange rates and interest rates. White these financial instruments are subject to the risk that market rates may change subsequent to the acquisition of the financial instrument, such changes would generally be offset by opposite effects on the items being hedged.

The Company's financial instruments typically mature within one year of origination and are transacted at rates which reflect the market rate at the date of contract. At December 31, 1990, the Company had $1.3 billion of foreign currency financial instruments, substantially all of which were forward exchange contracts to purchase or sell foreign currency (primarily French francs, German marks and Japanese yen). These instruments were employed to hedge balance sheet and transactional exposure.

TAX ACCOUNTING

There is a question whether gains and losses associated with futures and options purchased for a business purpose ought to be treated, for tax purposes, as ordinary income or as capital gains. If treated as ordinary income, losses associated with futures and options reduce the company's overall tax liability. If treated as capital gains or losses, capital losses can only be netted against capital gains. Because most companies have little in capital gains, the effect is little, or no, tax loss benefit for net losses associated with futures and options. In other words, a gain associated with a futures or option would be taxed as a capital gain. A loss associated with futures or options can only be netted against a capital gain. If there are no offsetting capital gains, the loss remains on the books as a capital loss and cannot be used to reduce taxes currently. Basically, a company finds itself paying taxes on net gains of holding positions in futures and options, but not being able to shield income if there are net losses associated with futures and options. This is sometimes termed as "asymmetric" treatment of gains and losses. The tax treatment of futures and options acquired for business purposes has traditionally been to match gains or losses against ordinary income.

However, in 1988, the Supreme Court made a decision with regard to the Arkansas Best case, which has been interpreted by the Internal Revenue Service to mean that such gains or losses should be treated as capital gains or losses. This has opened up Pandora's box, as the IRS audits past corporate income tax returns and recasts the tax treatment of futures and options, as well as forwards and swaps. These tax adjustments have been estimated by one expert to be $2 billion. Congressional legislation is required to clear up the situation.

RISK MANAGEMENT FOR OPTION MARKET MAKERS

The role of market makers in options is to have a balanced position in options with little exposed risk. They are not in the options market to assume a risk. Their role is to be intermediaries in the exchange of risk between two parties. In this role, they may have to assume some risk in order to complete a deal.

Then they take action to neutralize, or hedge, the risk assumed in putting the deal together. A hedged portfolio of options may no longer be fully hedged because the price of the underlying asset changes. Price changes in the underlying asset can transform out-of-the-money options to in-the-money ones and vice versa. As a matter of interest, option market makers themselves have a risk management challenge in maintaining a neutral position and living off commissions and bid-ask spreads between buyers and sellers of options.

To do this, they depend on a world of Greek letters. Delta is the price sensitivity of an option to price changes of the underlying asset. When an option is deeply out of the money, a move in the price of the underlying asset has little or no effect on its price (delta = 0). For an option deep in the money, there is an exact one-for-one relationship between its price and the price of the underlying asset. On a per unit basis, as the price goes up by one, the value of a call would also increase by one (delta = 1). For puts that are in the money, an increase in the underlying value of the asset reduces their value by one (delta =-1). The delta associated with a short call in the money would be-1 and the delta associated with a short put in the money would be +1. For options where the market price is approaching the exercise price, there is an intermediate, not a one-for-one, relationship between changes in underlying value and in the value of the option. Therefore, delta values vary between 0 and 1 for long calls and short puts, and between 0 and-1 for short calls and long puts. The net risk of a dealer's exposure to options on the same underlying tangible or intangible asset can be quantified by totaling the deltas of all the options.

A "delta neutral" portfolio of options would be one where the sum of all deltas is near zero. However, there are complications associated with maintaining a delta neutral portfolio of options because, as just discussed, the delta of an option varies with the underlying price of the asset. The rate of change of delta with respect to changes in the price of the underlying value is measured by gamma. Theta measures the erosion of an options premium as the expiration date nears. Theta can be positive or negative depending on whether there is a long and short position.

Rho measures the sensitivity of the option's price to changes in interest rates, whereas kappa, or vega (not a Greek letter, but an old Chevy car model) measures the change in an option's price with respect to changes to the volatility of the price of the underlying asset. Needless to say, delta, gamma, theta, kappa or vega, and rho measures of a portfolio of options are not calculated by hand. In addition, there are other Greek letters in a dealer's lexicon—beta trading is used by option traders to take advantage of similar financial instruments having diverging volatility, whereas omega is the risk associated with a buyer or seller of an option where the accounting of the option will be in a different currency than the option.

OPTIONS IN FUTURES

In addition, financial engineers have originated futures options. Calls and puts can be exercised calling for the delivery or sale of the underlying asset. Futures options are puts and calls on futures. A review of the U.S. financial press shows that one can buy and sell puts and calls on futures of U.S. Treasury notes and bonds, various currencies with both American and European variants including a cross trade between German marks and Japanese yen, various agricultural products, metals, various stock indices, and crude oil and oil products. Settlement of futures options is in cash, not a delivery or acceptance of an underlying asset. A futures option out of the money at the time of expiration is worthless.

EXCHANGE FOR PHYSICALS

There should be a strong linkage between an expiring futures contract and the cash price of the physical asset for futures to be effective as a hedging tool. Very few expiring futures end up with an exchange of physical assets. Usually, a long position is liquidated by selling the futures and a short position is liquidated by buying futures. But the possibility of a long position ending up with the physical possession of the underlying asset ensures that expiring prices and cash prices are very close to one another.

For instance, an expiring copper future could end up with a change in ownership as 25,000 pounds of copper. The copper futures market has an associated warehouse holding a sufficient quantity of copper of the specified purity to provide for a change of ownership between the owner of an expiring futures contract and its seller. Oil is a much less "homogenous" market than copper. The cash market in crude oil is based on commonly traded types of oil such as Saudi Arabian Light, North Sea, and West Texas Intermediate.

The futures in crude oil traded on the New York Mercantile Exchange calls for delivery "at any pipeline or storage facility with pipeline access to Arco, Cushing Storage, or Texaco Trading and Transportation Inc...." In the world of oil, this is a rather limited transformation of "paper" barrels to "wet" barrels. To take into account the wide variety of grades of oil and time and place of delivery, the financial engineers devised exchange for physicals (EFPs). EFPs extend the circumstances surrounding delivery of futures by permitting buyers and sellers of futures to agree to the exact buyer and seller, the nature of the crude oil, and place, volume, time, and other details of delivery. Payment is made by exchanging long and short positions in expiring futures.

BACKWARDATION AND CONTANGO

The relationship between the futures and the cash markets determines whether a market is in backwardation or contango. When a futures contract is selling for less than the current cash price, the market is said to be in backwardation.

Using oil as an example, a backwardation market permits an oil company to sell a part of its inventory that is to be refined in the future in the cash market and buy a, say, two-month future. In two month's time, the "paper" barrel is transformed to a "wet" barrel through an EFP, if necessary, to process the oil. This would only occur if the discount for the futures compared to the cash price is sufficient to make this a profitable transaction. In calculating this profitability, one must bear in mind that an oil company can invest the cash proceeds of selling oil in inventory in an interest-bearing security. There are also transfer, shipping, and other costs involved with the delivery of the futures, or the EFP, that have to be taken into account.

A contango market is one where there is a premium on the futures in relation to the cash price. If the premium on the futures contract is large enough, and if there is sufficient storage capacity at the oil company refinery, it may be to the oil company's advantage to buy extra oil in the cash market and short a futures contract.

On the maturing of the futures contract, the oil company delivers the oil rather than making a cash settlement. The spread between the cash and futures market has to be sufficient to cover the storage costs and the interest costs of investing in what amounts to extra inventory.

CAPS, FLOORS, AND COLLARS

Calls and puts have a finite life usually measured in months. Rarely do their expiration times exceed one year. Another example of financial engineering creativity are multi period options. These were created to address the need for providing a maximum rate of interest on a loan, called an interest rate cap. Loans usually run for more than a year and, therefore, calls and puts with an expiration time of one year or less do not provide a solution for a company that desires to hedge against rising interest rates on a multiyear floating rate loan. The writer of an interest rate cap agrees to pay the holder of the cap the difference between a reference rate above the ceiling rate, applied against a notional principal, every six months during the two to five year tenor, or length of time, of the cap, or any other agreeable tenor.

The reference rate is a published rate such as the London Interbank or U.S. Treasury bill rates. The ceiling rate is the maximum rate the holder of the cap will pay on a loan covered by the notional principal of the cap. For this protection, the cap holder pays an upfront fee. The effective interest rate has the appearance of a multi period call. The amortization of the upfront premium over the life of the cap is analogous to the premium paid for a series of single period calls. If interest rates do not rise to the ceiling rate, the holder of the cap is simply paying a higher effective interest rate.

This is analogous to the example of illustrating how a call limits the maximum amount to be paid for some underlying asset. If the price does not rise to this limit, the premium for the call increases the effective acquisition cost for the underlying asset. If interest rates rise above the ceiling rate, the profit from the cap offsets the higher cost of interest effectively capping interest at the ceiling rate. Obviously, the closer the ceiling rate is to current interest rates, the higher its cost.

This holds true for call—the closer the exercise price is to the current price of the asset, the higher the premium. A buyer of a call, or a cap, must decide on the amount of premium and the protection afforded by that premium in covering his or her perceived risks. Interest rate caps are sometimes combined with interest rate swaps or with currency swaps to produce an interest or a currency rate capped swap.

Caps can be assignable with the owner's permission, much as a call can be sold when its protection is no longer needed. An interest rate floor is similar to a cap except that the purchaser of a floor receives payment when the reference rate drops below the contract rate. The classic use of a floor is an insurance company borrowing fixed rate money to be loaned out at a floating rate. In so doing, the insurance company is betting on an upswing in interest rates. If interest rates fall, the insurance company may not earn enough to service its policy holders. An insurance company can protect against this risk by purchasing an interest rate floor, which guarantees a minimum interest rate should the floating rate fall below the contract, or floor, rate. Caps and floors do not involve the exchange of a credit risk. They are cash settlements at prescribed times whereby a purchaser of a cap does not pay more than the ceiling rate and the purchaser of a floor does not earn less than the floor rate. Because the principal covered by a cap or floor is not exchanged, the cash payments are based on a notional amount of a loan. If a cap is 10 per cent and the referenced floating rate is 12 per cent, and the notional amount is $10 million (MM) and settlements are made every six months, then the purchaser of the cap will receive the difference (2 per cent × $10 MM × six months/twelve months) or $100,000 from the market maker. He then applies this against his floating rate loan, reducing its net interest cost from 12 per cent to 10 per cent.

If the floor is 8 per cent and the referenced floating rate falls to 6 per cent, then the seller of the floor has to pay the market maker $100,000. This raises his effective interest cost from 6 per cent to 8 per cent, thus fixing his minimum interest rate at 8 per cent. A financial engineer can create collars from caps and floors. A collar is the purchase of a cap coupled with the sale of a floor.

The proceeds from the sale of the floor reduce the cost of the cap. What this effectively does is lock the interest rate between the floor and ceiling rates. If a company has a floating rate loan on a certain amount of principal, a collar on the same notional amount of the loan fixes both the maximum and minimum interest rates. If floating interest rates exceed the ceiling rate, the company will receive a cash payment that compensates it for the incremental interest expense that is above the ceiling rate, thus capping the interest rate on the loan at the ceiling rate. If floating rates fall below the floor rate, the company will not benefit from the lower interest costs because it is obligated to pay the difference between the floating rate and the floor rate, applied against the notional amount of the collar, to the market maker.

If interest rates stay between the floor and ceiling rates, the lender has increased his effective interest rate in the amortization of the cost of acquisition of the collar. The concept of the interest rate collar as a multi period option to set a ceiling and a floor rate for interest rates can be applied to currencies and commodities. A currency collar is a series of multi period cash settlements, where the holder of the collar limits his exchange rate within a prescribed band. This is accomplished by a cash settlement representing the differences in actual currency exchange transactions and the contractual upper and lower exchange rate limits-the ceiling and floor rates of conversion.

For a premium, a company can collar, so to speak, the currency exchange rates on, say, Swiss franc to dollar conversion within a prescribed upper and lower rate of exchange based on a stipulated notional amount of currency. This is a powerful financial tool in managing the long-term exposure to a currency risk. The collar is applied to commodities. For the payment of a premium, the holder of a collar, sometimes referred to as a range forward, can limit his purchases of a commodity, such as oil, to a prescribed band. Using a publicly available source of pricing for oil as a means of measuring spot purchases, a holder of a range forward receives money from the market maker when spot purchase prices exceed the upper limit or ceiling price.

When spot purchase prices fall below the lower limit or floor price, the holder of the range forward must pay the difference to the market maker. When prices are between the floor and ceiling prices, the effective cost of oil is the spot price plus the premium paid for the collar, or range forward. The buyer of a collar or a range forward is obtaining protection against paying more than the ceiling price, but, in so doing, gives up the opportunity of buying for less than the floor price. He has, in effect, avoided a risk that he cannot endure by giving up an opportunity that he could enjoy.

CONNECTION BETWEEN CURRENCY EXCHANGE AND INTEREST RATES

There is a connection between futures in currency exchange rates and interest rates. This connection ties these two markets, which allows financial engineers to devise ways of hedging in interest rates by means of hedges in currencies and vice versa. Suppose that an American has $1,000,000 to invest and six-month (180-day) U.S. Treasury bills offer an annual yield of 4.0 per cent. If the investor completes this transaction, he would have approximately $1,020,000 at the end of the 180-day period. Suppose, however, that the investor notes that a French government security is yielding 4.5 per cent in 180 days. If he converts his dollars to francs, he will earn more interest, but will be faced with a currency exchange risk at the maturity of the French security.

Suppose that the current spot rate for francs is 5.527 francs to the dollar and the 180-day forward contract is 5.538 francs to the dollar. The investor could convert his dollars to francs, receiving 5,527,000 francs, which when invested in the French 180-day note, yields 5,651,358 francs (5,527,000 x 4.5 per cent x 180/360). Simultaneously with the conversion of dollars into francs, the investor also sells a 5,651,358 forward contract at the 180-day forward rate of 5.538 francs to the dollar. Upon receipt of the 5,651,358 francs in 180 days with the maturing of the French debt security, the investor fulfills his obligation under the forward contract by converting 5,651,358 francs to $1,020,469.

This is in excess of the $1,020,000 he would have received had he invested in the U.S. Treasury 180-day bill. The forward or futures rate for a currency is set not by the market impact of investors attempting to maximize their return as much as by arbitragers seeking a riskless return. An arbitrager enters into a riskless covered interest arbitrage by borrowing funds in one country, converting to another currency, investing the funds in another country, and selling a forward contract to cover the conversion back into the original currency to repay the loan. An arbitrager would continue entering into such transactions until the difference between the currency exchange spot and forward rates narrows sufficiently to remove the riskless profit of entering into such transactions. This is accomplished by the continual buying of spot contracts and selling of forward contracts, which causes the price of the former to rise and the price of the latter to fall until the riskless profit differential disappears.

The role of investors in maximizing returns on their assets and arbitragers in seeking riskless profit opportunities establishes a link between interest rates and the spread between spot and forward currency exchange rates. This makes it possible for financial engineers to devise ingenuous solutions to interest rate exposure by entering into a currency exchange contract or to manage a currency exchange risk through an interest rate contract. It also makes it possible for financial engineers to reduce interest costs by having a company borrow from financial institutions in other countries without exposing the company to a currency exchange loss.

For instance, a Canadian company was able to borrow in yen from a Japanese financial institution at a favourable interest rate, which exposed the company to the possibility of an adverse change in the Japanese yen/Canadian dollar exchange rate. Financial engineers addressed that risk by having the company enter into a long-term currency exchange contract. The net effect of these two transactions was a lower effective interest rate to the company by borrowing in Japan and hedging the currency exchange risk rather than by borrowing directly in the Canadian capital market.

FUTURES AND FORWARDS

The terms "futures" and "forwards" are oftentimes used interchangeably for contracts between two parties that require a specific action to be taken at some later date. As these contracts generally take the form of a delivery of an underlying asset such as a certain amount of currency or a quantity of a physical asset, they are sometimes referred to as contracts for deferred delivery. There are, however, important differences between futures and forwards. A futures contract is traded on public exchanges with highly standardized terms other than the price of the contract, which is set by the market. A forward contract is traded in "over-thecounter" dealer markets where all terms, including price, must be negotiated between the buyer and seller. Over the counter means that a formal exchange or clearing house is not involved in a forward contract—deals are done on an individual basis with a dealer playing the role of a middleman or broker.

A clearing house or association stands between the parties of a futures contract, which removes the necessity of identifying the parties involved in the futures contract. This is similar to the trading of stock on a stock exchange—it is done between brokerage houses with the brokerage houses responsible for making the final settlement between the ultimate buyer and seller of the shares of stock. In a forward contract, each party is directly responsible for the fulfillment of the agreed terms and, therefore, their identity is a critical factor in the negotiation process leading up to the mutual agreement of contractual terms and conditions. Futures markets, like the stock markets, are government regulated, whereas forward markets are not.

The financial integrity of the futures market is ensured by each party to a futures contract maintaining the required margin, which can be likened to a performance bond. No such mechanism exists in the forward market. This is another reason why the identity of the parties, and their reputation, is a critical part of a forward contract. In addition, the active market in futures contracts makes it easy to terminate a transaction by buying back the futures or entering into another that offsets the original transaction.

In a forward contract where terms and conditions are uniquely defined for each contract, such ease of termination is not only difficult but may be impossible. There is liquidity in the continual buying and selling of futures in the futures market, whereas there is virtually no liquidity in the forwards market. On the surface, one would wonder why anyone would enter into a forward contract rather than a futures contract. The primary reason is that the futures contract, being a highly standardized contract, may not fit the particular needs of an individual or company. Suppose that an importer must pay 20 million Japanese yen in forty-nine days.

A futures contract is in units of 12.5 million yen to be settled thirty, sixty, and ninety days in the future. The futures contract does not meet the importer's specific needs. Rather than over or under hedge either in the amount of yen and the duration of time, by taking a position in futures on the futures exchange, the importer might negotiate a deal that meets his or her precise requirements with a forward contract arranged in the over-thecounter market.

SWAPS

Swaps are financial products originated by financial engineers in response to the growing instability in prices and in interest and currency exchange rates during the 1980s. Started in 1979, swaps became a popular financial instrument in 1981 because of the publicity associated with a currency swap arranged by Salomon Brothers between the World Bank and IBM. Currency swaps rapidly spread to swaps in interest rates and commodities. Swaps are built around the same basic structure as forwards and have been described as a series of forward contracts. Two parties, called counterparties, agree to one or more exchange(s) of specified quantities of underly-ing tangibles or intangibles, sometimes called notionals if there is a cash rather than a physical exchange of the underlying asset. Cash payments are the usual means of settlements between the counterparties of a swap. A swap is usually arranged by a financial intermediary that negotiates a final deal between two counterparties entering into a swap. The intermediary, known as a swap dealer or market maker, receives his or her remuneration in the bidasked spread between the two counterparties. Three illustrations are provided to explain the principal "plain vanilla" swaps.

INTEREST RATE SWAP

Counterparty A is a company that requires $10 million to construct a factory. The creditworthiness of the company is not sufficient for an issue of fixed rate interest debt, but a bank is willing to lend the company $10 million on a floating rate basis. Counterparty A worries about the floating rate interest rate increasing over the next ten years and wants to hedge, or protect itself, against this risk. Counterparty A is willing to sacrifice the opportunity of having to pay less in interest expense if floating rates fall in order to safeguard itself from the risk of having to pay higher than the fixed rate that can be arranged through a swap.

Counterparty B is a company, or a financial institution, whose creditworthiness is sufficient for it to issue fixed interest rate debt. Suppose that counterparty B borrows on the basis of its own creditworthiness $10 million at a fixed interest rate of 10 per cent. It could lend the money to counterparty A, but then counterparty B assumes the credit risk of counterparty A repaying the loan. Instead of lending the money to counterparty A, counterparty B deposits the funds in a floating rate account.

Suppose that the floating rate is currently 8 per cent. Counterparty B transfers the interest income of 8 per cent on its $10 million deposit to the swap dealer in return for a fixed rate of 10.3 per cent. Counterparty B neither makes nor loses money on the floating rate deposit and makes a 0.3 per cent spread on its capacity to issue fixed rate debt. Counterparty B has no credit risk in borrowing the $10 million in that the proceeds of the loan have been placed in a floating rate deposit that is sufficient to pay off the principal of the fixed rate debt.

The swap dealer passes the floating rate interest payment received from counterparty B to counterparty A. In return, counterparty A pays the swap dealer 10.4 per cent fixed rate of interest. The difference between receiving 10.4 per cent interest from counterparty A and paying 10.3 per cent interest to counterparty B is the swap dealer's remuneration. Counterparty A takes the floating rate interest of 8 per cent and pays the floating rate interest plus any applicable spread to its lending institution. If the interest rate on counterparty A's loan is the floating rate plus a spread of 0.75 per cent, then counterparty A is actually paying 8.75 per cent on its loan. Therefore, the net cost of interest to counterparty A is the 0.75 per cent differential to be paid on the floating rate loan plus the fixed 10.4 per cent to the swap dealer. There is no point in counterparty A paying 10.4 per cent to the swap dealer and receiving the floating rate of 8 per cent from the swap dealer. It is easier to net the difference and pay that to the swap dealer. Under the circumstances, counterparty A pays the difference between 10.4 per cent and 8 per cent to the swap dealer, or 2.4 per cent applied against the notional amount of the interest rate swap, in this case, $10 million. Counterparty A pays less if the floating interest rate rises. If the floating rate goes the fixed rate, counterparty A will receive money from the swap dealer. This extra money will be used to pay the higher interest charge associated with counterparty A's floating rate loan.

Therefore, counterparty A has accomplished his purpose of swapping a floating rate for a fixed rate loan. His cost of interest is the fixed rate of 10.4 per cent plus the spread of 0.75 per cent on the floating rate loan. He is no longer at risk in having floating rates rise to a level that may imperil his financial survivability. For this, he has foregone any opportunity to benefit from floating interest rates being less than the arranged fixed rate. A single payment is also made between counterparty B, representing the difference between the 10.3 per cent to be received from the swap dealer and the floating rate to be paid to the swap dealer. The swap dealer simply passes the payment between the two counterparties extracting his piece of the action.

The swap dealer is making 0.1 per cent interest spread between counterparty B receiving 10.3 per cent and counterparty A paying 10.4 per cent on the notional amount of the principal. He has accomplished his objective in arranging the swap. Counterparty B has borrowed funds at 10 per cent and has lent them out at 10.3 per cent with the difference being remuneration for entering into the transaction. This fulfills counterparty B's objective in entering into the swap. However, in entering this swap, counterparty B has given up any benefit from rising interest rates. He has deposited the funds from a fixed rate loan in a floating rate account and turns the interest earnings over to the swap dealer. If the floating rate were to go to 20 per cent on funds borrowed at 10 per cent, counterparty B would have been better off not entering into the swap. Counterparty B can undo the transaction by purchasing an interest rate futures, but from the point of view of the swap, he has given up the benefit of rising floating interest rates.

Therefore, he might have been reluctant to enter into the swap if he had strong feelings that floating interest rates would rise. However, by counterparty B depositing the funds from the fixed rate loan in a floating rate account, whether floating rates rise or fall, counterparty B has locked in his return. This is the spread between the fixed rate paid by the swap dealer and the fixed rate being paid on the incurred debt. It is possible that counterparty B does not borrow the funds at a fixed rate of interest.

Counterparty B may be a financial institution that feels that interest rates are going to fall and may delay arranging its fixed debt financing. It is possible that it does not intend to arrange any borrowings, but to cover itself through the purchase of interest rate futures should interest rates begin to rise. If counterparty B perceives this to be a desired course of action, then the swap dealer would definitely find it easier to put the swap together if both counterparties have opposite viewpoints on the future direction of floating interest rates. The swap can be considered as a series of forward contracts in which the termination of each individual contract occurs at the time of payment of the interest rate differential, say, every six months.

Collectively, in this example, the swap represents a series of twenty forward contracts that cover ten years of interest payments. Credit risk is not transferred in a swap. Both counterparties A and B have arranged their floating and fixed rate loans based on their individual creditworthiness. Each is responsible for the repayment of the underlying principal of the loan. If, by change, counterparty B did not arrange a fixed rate loan, then its creditworthiness must be sufficient to cover the differential in interest rates should its assessment on the future direction of rates be proven wrong. Even here, there are means for counterparty B to minimize, or avoid, losses. The only connection between the two counterparties is the net payment representing the difference between the floating and fixed rates of interest.

The bankruptcy of one of the counterparties affects only the interest rate differential payment between the two counterparties. In addition to the potential bankruptcy of a counterparty, swap dealers such as Drexel, Burnham, Lambert of junk bond fame, have gone bankrupt. The U.S. Bankruptcy Code has been amended to ensure that netting provisions of swaps be honoured by the bankruptcy courts in the event of the bankruptcy of counterparties and swap dealers. Interest rate swaps have become so common that the plain vanilla variety are frequently arranged directly between banks without the services of a swap dealer.

CURRENCY SWAP

A currency swap can be arranged when one of the counterparties has more advantageous access to a financial market. Suppose that an American company desires to finance a factory to be built in Germany in deutschemarks at a fixed rate of interest. Further suppose that a German company has access to lower. fixed rate interest financing in Germany than the American company. To complete the picture, suppose that the German company desires to borrow in U.S. dollars for its business purposes, at a floating rate of interest and the American company is in a position to borrow in the United States for less than a German-based company can do on its own.

This situation of each party having access to lower cost loans than the other party permits the origination of a swap, where the German company borrows deutschemarks from a German financial institution at a lesser interest rate than what would be charged to the American company. The American company borrows a like amount of dollars for a lesser interest charge than what the German company could have negotiated. A swap dealer then arranges a currency swap whereby the two companies can take advantage of borrowing at lesser cost in different markets. Each swaps the principal amounts of the loans, which are the same, and each makes interest payments to the swap dealer as agreed, with the American company making deutschemark payments that are sufficient for the German company to pay off its loan and the German company making dollar payments sufficient for the American company to pay off its loan.

The swap dealer takes a little out of the middle. A plain vanilla currency swap does not involve an exchange of a credit risk. Both companies borrow on the basis of their own creditworthiness. Each merely exchanges, or swaps, the payment of debt and interest such that the American company ends up paying a fixed rate German denominated debt, which it desired, and the German company ends up paying the type of dollar denominated debt, which it desired. Three exchanges are necessary.

The first is the exchange of the principal of the loan, then the interest payments, and, at the end of the swap period, the final repayment of principal of the respective loans. Although currency swaps are usually floating/fixed rates of interest—that is, one counterparty paying a floating rate of interest and the other a fixed rate of interest—currency swaps can also be floating/floating and fixed/fixed. This plain vanilla currency swap is also called an exchange of borrowings because that is exactly what it is. Its origin lies in each company's advantage in borrowing in its respective domestic market.

However, the plain vanilla can easily become a more sophisticated variant because the exchange of borrowings may not exactly fit the desires of the two counterparties. An interest rate swap may have to be arranged along with the currency swap to change a floating rate loan to a desired fixed rate loan. The tenor, or the length of the repayment period, or the amount of the loan, may not entirely match the desires of each counterparty. The swap dealer may turn to a financial engineer to introduce a new level of complexity to transform an undesirable cash flow stream into one that is desired by the two counterparties to the currency swap. It is possible for the repayment of principal to be amortized with the regular payments of interest similar to a level payment type of financing common for home mortgages. By combining swaps with other swaps or with other financial instruments, all sorts of variants can be created, limited only to the imagination of the financial engineers and the needs of client firms.

COMMODITY SWAP

Counterparty A is an oil producer who has financed his wells with loans. If oil falls below a certain price, he will not be able to generate the earnings necessary to pay the financing charges associated with drilling and developing the oil wells. This may force the oil producer into bankruptcy. Counterparty B is a refinery operator who sold a portion of his output at a fixed price and wants to stabilize the price of oil required to be purchased in the future in order to preserve the profit margin of these fixed priced contracts. Counterparty B worries about an increase in the price of oil that would destroy the economic worth of his fixed price contracts.

A swap dealer, being in touch with both individuals, can arrange a plain vanilla swap. The oil producer sells his actual output, called "actuals," into the spot oil market and receives the spot price, which may be higher or lower than the agreed fixed price of the swap. If higher, he must pay the difference between what he receives and the agreed fixed price to the swap dealer. If lower, the producer will receive the difference from the swap dealer.

On the other side of the swap dealer's ledger is counterparty B, the refiner. Counterparty B buys his oil needs, or actuals, from the spot market and pays the spot price. If the spot price is higher than the agreed swap price, counterparty B receives what the producer has paid to the swap dealer. If the spot price for oil is lower than the swap price, then the refiner pays the difference to the swap dealer, which is passed on to the refiner. In order to avoid disagreements between the two counterparties as to what is the spot market price, the counterparties agree to base the spot price, not on actual purchases and sales, but on a spot price from a published source, such as the monthly average spot price for oil quoted in the financial press. No matter in what direction the net payment is flowing, the swap dealer takes out a margin for his or her trouble, before passing the money to the other party.

The swap dealer assumes no risk, which is why both the oil producer and the refinery operator must refer to the same published source for spot market quotes, such as a monthly average, to remove day-to-day price fluctuations, and other causes of price differences from becoming part of the calculation of what is to be paid between the two counterparties.

Otherwise, the swap dealer would become embroiled in disputes over price differentials between what an oil producer receives when he sells and what a refinery operator pays when he buys. Although the producer is selling his output to the spot market and the refiner is buying his input from the spot market, the net effect is that they are essentially buying and selling from each other at the swap price. The swap can go on for as long as the two counterparties desire, again illustrating the point that a swap can be considered a series of forward contracts.

The question may arise as to why the producer and the refiner did not enter into a contract with one another directly, as is practiced by banks for plain vanilla interest rate swaps. First of all, the buyer and seller may not have known of each other's presence or need—this is the classic role of the middleman. It is easier for a bank to canvass the market for interest rate swaps if there are relatively few banks providing the fixed rate portion of an interest rate swap. In the oil business, where there are hundreds of producers and refiners, a middleman or swap dealer, may be needed for the sorting out process of identifying and bringing together the two counterparties.

Another reason for having a swap dealer involved in a transaction is that frequently the needs of the producer and refiner do not exactly match. The producer may want to fix the price of oil for a quantity and for a duration of time that does not exactly fit the refiner's needs. A deal cannot be directly negotiated between the two counterparties. However, a swap dealer can set up a swap that does match each of the two counterparties' needs. To do so, he or she may have to arrange another swap to take care of the differences in quantity and timing, or hedge the position for his or her own account.

SWAP VARIANTS

Swaps have grown from nothing in 1979 to a level of about several trillion in notional outstandings in the early 1990s. Notional outstandings do not necessarily mean actual deposits of funds in banks or assets in warehouses. Notionals are reference points from which the amount of payment between counterparties is calculated. In the case of a plain vanilla interest rate swap, the notional amount of the swap of $10 million was the reference point from which the interest rate differential payments between the counterparties were calculated.

Plain vanilla swaps have given way to all sorts of variants that have been created to meet the specific needs of the counterparties to a swap. Variants to the plain vanilla swaps are as plentiful as mutations in a jar of fruit flies; a sampling follows. An accreting swap is one where the notional principal increases, and an amortization swap is one where the notional principal decreases, over the life of the swap. An annuity swap transforms an irregular cash flow payment stream to a regular one. An asset swap is based on assets rather than liabilities.

A basis swap deals with a mismatch between assets and liabilities. A blended interest rate swap combines two swaps to produce a more attractive overall rate. A callable and puttable swap gives one or the other counterparty the right to terminate the swap after a specified time. A capped swap is a swap with a cap, or a maximum limit, on the floating payment side of a swap. A cross currency swap is an exchange of cash flows of one currency for another that reverses at some point during the swap period. A debt-equity swap isn't even a swap, but a substitution of equity in local companies in lieu of interest or principal payments of a heavily indebted nation. A deferred swap is one where the payments are deferred for a specified period, whereas a delayed LIBOR reset swap is one where the floating payment is based on a future rather than the present London Interbank rate. A differential swap is the swapping of floating interest rate payments referenced to different currencies.

A discount swap has a large balloon payment at the end of the swap period to take into account the discount on the regular payments as opposed to a highcoupon swap where the fixed payments are the market rate with some sort of compensating adjustment at the end of the swap period. A dual currency swap contains rights to repay principal and interest in a choice of currencies at preset exchange rates. An escalating rate swap permits the fixed rate side of a swap to escalate with time. An extendable swap contains the right for the payer to extend the swap. A forward swap is one that is arranged at some point before the start date. A naked swap is one without a corresponding asset or liability, an interesting concept.

A reversible swap gives one side the option to alter the payment basis after a certain period as compared to a reverse floating swap where the floating rate payments are inversely proportional to interest rates. The roller coaster swap alternates the counterparties between paying fixed and floating rates. The seasonal swap is one where the notional amount varies with the time of the year to fit the needs of companies that borrow on a seasonal basis. A spreadlock swap has one payment stream referenced to a fixed spread over a benchmark rate. The tax-exempt swap has its fixed rate interest tied to tax-exempt bonds.

The warrant-driven swap is a swap with a warrant allowing an issuer of a bond to extend a swap if it exercises a similar warrant on a bond. The yield curve swap is one where the two interest rates reflect different points on a mutually agreed yield curve. The zero-coupon swap is one where one or both counterparties make one payment at maturity. Finally, there is the swaption. A swaption is an option on a swap. The swap is set up in all respects except for the starting date. One of the counterparties to the swap pays a swaption premium for the right to start the swap at any point during the swaption period, say, in six months. If he or she does not exercise the swaption, the swap terminates without execution at the end of the swaption period.

Swaptions have their family of variants. Swap dealers are not in business to accept risk, but to transfer the nature of risk between the two counterparties. Swap dealers work off their "swap book" to tailor a swap to meet the needs of the two counterparties. In so doing, they may introduce an element of risk into their swap books. Swap dealers then enter into other swaps or hedges to remove the element of risk that may be present in their swap books. Swap dealers usually wish to neutralize any risk in their swap books to protect their remuneration, which is in the bid-ask spread between the two counterparties of a swap. However, if the swap dealers are confident about the emergence or continuation of a price trend, they may accept a degree of risk in their swap books to profit thereby.

PUTS AND CALLS

Futures and forwards are contractually binding agreements. Swaps, as a continuing series of forwards, are also contractually binding. These contractually binding agreements mean that each party must transfer a specified underlying asset, or a cash equivalent thereof, at known points in time. Puts and calls are options where the purchaser of a put or call has the right, but not the obligation, to buy or sell an underlying asset.

A buyer of a call has the right, but not the obligation, to purchase something at a stipulated price, whereas the buyer of a put has the right, but not the obligation, to sell something at a stipulated price. However, the seller of a call or a put does have an obligation to sell the underlying asset at the stipulated price when the call is exercised or to buy the underlying asset at the stipulated price when the put is exercised. An American option can be exercised from the time it is written until the time it expires. A European option differs in that its exercise period is limited to a short period of time before its expiration date. Staying with American options, pricing of options depends on several factors. One is the exercise price in relation to the underlying value of the asset. If the exercise price is $20 and the underlying value of the asset is $22, then the option has an intrinsic value of $2 and is described as being "in the money." If the underlying value is $20, the same as the exercise price, the option is described as being "at the money." If the underlying value is $18, the call option has no intrinsic value, but still has extrinsic value. Extrinsic value depends on the difference between the market and exercise prices, the remaining time to expiration, and the volatility of the price of the underlying asset.

The smaller the difference between market and exercise prices, the longer the time to expiration, and the greater the volatility of the price of the underlying asset, the greater the extrinsic value of the option even though it may have no intrinsic, or inherent, value. Another factor in the pricing of options is interest rates, because a grantor, or a writer, of an option is seeking income by writing calls. Generally speaking, an option writer grants options on an owned asset. As an alternative, he or she can sell the owned asset and invest the proceeds in a secure interest bearing financial instrument. Because the grantor has the choice to sell the asset and invest in interest-bearing financial instruments or underwrite options, option writing premium income must be attractively priced in relation to interest-bearing securities.

All of these factors are built into the first complete option pricing model developed by two professors, Fisher Black and Myron Scholes, in 1973. Options are generally priced based on models derived or adapted from the original BlackScholes model. The model is a mathematical expression containing the difference between the current price of the underlying asset and the strike price, a measure of past volatility in the price of the underlying asset, time to expiration and the interest rate on a secure deposit. The purpose of the model is to determine a theoretical price for an option. Dealers sometimes use the Black-Scholes model to examine prices being quoted by grantors or writers of options, by reversing the model to obtain the implied volatility in the quote. Some dealers use the implied volatility to differentiate quotes on different options for the same asset. By being able to identify options with differently implied volatilities for the same underlying asset, dealers can use this information for putting deals together or in hedging their own portfolios.

Moreover, implied volatility can be charted and analysed as to what feelings participants in the option markets have towards volatility. A period of falling implied volatility can be interpreted to mean that participants in the market feel that prices are approaching an island of stability in a sea of volatility. Rising implied volatility means that participants see storm clouds on the horizon. This information is of value for market makers in options.

OPTIONS IN RISK MANAGEMENT

From the perspective of a company attempting to manage the risk of price volatility, options can be used to change the cost profile of an asset in a way that serves the interest of the company. Suppose that a company buys an asset that management feels can vary in price from $15 to $25 per unit and the current price is $20. The company does not want to find itself in a position of paying much over $20 per unit for the asset. It buys a call option for $1 per unit with an exercise price of $20. For that portion of its needs covered by the call option, the company has changed the cost profile. A company wanting to contain its costs to $21 per unit for the asset has done so by purchasing the option.

The profit from the call option compensates for the extra cost of purchasing the asset. This protects the company whenever the price of the asset moves above $20. If the asset does not move above $20 per unit, the company has added $1 to unit to its acquisition cost. This can be likened to the premium cost of an insurance policy to protect against paying a higher than desired price for the asset. A company must weigh the cost of protection against the benefit of having the protection. Suppose that a company has acquired a large supply of inventory at $20 and wishes to insure itself against a loss in value. The company buys a put option with an exercise price of $20 for $1. If the market value of the asset declines, the intrinsic value of the put will increase. The company, in wanting to protect itself against loss, has maintained the value of the inventory at $19 per unit regardless how low the market value of the asset may sink.

The profit from the put option compensates for the loss in inventory value. The cost of this protection is $1 per unit, which one can view as an insurance premium if the value of the asset remains above $20 per unit. The portion of the inventory that is protected by the put is said to be hedged against a price decline. Suppose that the price of the commodity is $20 and the company buys a put and a call, called a straddle, for $1 per option. If the price of the asset falls below $18, the profit from the put can be used to hedge against a write-down of the inventory. If the price rises, the profit from the call can be used to hedge against paying above $22 per unit.

If the price of the asset hovers between $18 and $22, the company would have been better off not purchasing the straddle. Straddles are useful when management expects increased volatility in the price of the asset but is unsure of the direction of change in price. The straddle offers double protection in limiting the maximum amount to be paid for the asset and in limiting the maximum amount of loss of holding the asset in inventory. In offering more protection, the insurance premium also costs more.

Suppose that the company decides to buy a call option with an exercise price of $20 for $1 and sells a call option with an exercise price of $22 for $0.50. The net cost of buying and selling the options is $0.50. What would be profit profile of this course of action? The idea of selling the second call is to reduce the cost of the hedge by the amount of premium earned on the selling of the call. A company would employ such a strategy of buying and selling a call option at different strike, or exercise, prices if it was worried about a rise in price in the commodity, but was convinced that such a rise would not go over $23. If management were proven wrong and the price did exceed $23, it could buy its way out by purchasing another call option to compensate for the "loss" associated with the call that was sold. Once a company begins to protect itself against price rises or declines through some sort of hedging technique, there is a tendency to keep purchasing and selling options to "undo" those past hedging positions that are costing the company money. In time, a relatively simple hedging position can become quite complex.

If the two call options in the example expire at the same time, it is called a vertical bull spread. If the call with the lower strike price is sold and the one with the higher strike price is bought, there would be premium income and the strategy would be called a vertical bear spread. If the expiration dates are not the same, but the exercise price is the same for the two options, these strategies are called a horizontal bull or bear spread depending on the expiration dates of the purchased and sold options. If there is a mix of expiration dates and strike prices, the strategy is known as a diagonal spread. To show that there is virtually no limit to the imagination, a butterfly spread would involve four options.

All have the same expiration date. Two options with the same strike price are sold, whereas one with a higher strike price is purchased along with one with a lower strike price. If the buying and selling of the options are reversed, this is called a reverse butterfly or a sandwich spread. What risk does management fear the most? The financial engineers can dream up a solution.

There are barrier options (four major types including knock-in and knock-out options), basket options, binary and digital options, call and put spreads, chooser options, compound options, condors, cylinders, difference options, embedded options, forward start options, hi-low options, lookback or path-dependent options, straddles and strangles, table tops, and tunnels, which are similar to cylinders. Someone in the company better have a firm understanding of where the company stands when the price of the underlying asset changes. Although there is no commitment undertaken by the company when options are purchased, there is certainly a commitment associated with sold options as there are with swaps, futures, and forwards. Therefore, there should also be someone in a company with a firm handle on what commitments have been undertaken by a company in its hedging programme. This someone should not be the person directing the company's risk management programme.

8

Operations Management in Banking Sector

DEFINITION OF BANK

The definition of a bank varies from country to country. Under English common law, a banker is defined as a person who carries on the business of banking, which is specified as:

- Conducting current accounts for his customers
- Paying cheques drawn on him, and
- Collecting cheques for his customers.

In most common law jurisdictions there is a Bills of Exchange Act that codifies the law in relation to negotiable instruments, including cheques, and this Act contains a statutory definition of the term *banker*: *banker* includes a body of persons, whether incorporated or not, who carry on the business of banking'. Although this definition seems circular, it is actually functional, because it ensures that the legal basis for bank transactions such as cheques does not depend on how the bank is organized or regulated.

The business of banking is in many English common law countries not defined by statute but by common law. In other English common law jurisdictions there are statutory definitions of the *business of banking* or *banking business*.

When looking at these definitions it is important to keep in mind that they are defining the business of banking for the purposes of the legislation, and not necessarily in general. In particular, most of the definitions are from legislation that has the purposes of entry regulating and supervising banks rather than regulating the actual business of banking. However, in many cases the statutory definition closely mirrors the common law one.

Examples of statutory definitions:

- "Banking business" means the business of receiving money on current or deposit account, paying and collecting cheques drawn by or paid in by customers, the making of advances to customers, and includes such other business as the Authority may prescribe for the purposes of this Act; (Banking Act (Singapore), Section 2, Interpretation).

- "Banking business" means the business of either or both of the following:
- Receiving from the general public money on current, deposit, savings or other similar account repayable on demand or within less than [3 months]... or with a period of call or notice of less than that period;
- Paying or collecting checks drawn by or paid in by customers

Since the advent of EFTPOS (Electronic Funds Transfer at Point Of Sale), direct credit, direct debit and internet banking, the cheque has lost its primacy in most banking systems as a payment instrument. This has led legal theorists to suggest that the cheque based definition should be broadened to include financial institutions that conduct current accounts for customers and enable customers to pay and be paid by third parties, even if they do not pay and collect checks.

TRADITIONAL BANKING ACTIVITIES

DOMESTIC LENDING

Lending is and remains one of the chief activities of KBC Bank, which is striving to achieve a balance between market share and profitability in its domestic lending activity. The bank's aim is to provide the most appropriate solutions for the financial needs of its customers by offering a broad range of short- and long-term credit, as well as leasing and factoring services. Where retail lending is concerned, KBC Bank aims to create standard products with straightforward pricing. A new risk-acceptance scoring system has been introduced for these small loans. This ensures rapid and uniform processing, which in turn has a positive impact on both costs and the bank's commercial position. Increasingly important as regards the more complex, commercial loans are customer-mindedness, flexibility, rapidity and expertise. Focusing on these aspects, the bank is investing in building up expertise in specific sectors or fields, enabling it as a lender to anticipate future developments earlier. In assessing credit applications, credit advisers and the officers responsible for the decision to lend are given maximum support by advisers specialized in various domains: real estate experts, environmental experts, business experts, government aid experts and legal experts.

DEPOSITS AND SAVINGS CERTIFICATES

Due to the persistently low interest rates on the market and the favourable stock market climate, the volume of savings reflected on the balance sheet has been under pressure for some years now, a trend that certainly persisted in 1998. However, investment funds were once again hugely popular.

PAYMENTS TRANSACTIONS

To facilitate the commercial operation of the branches, more and more administrative work is being shifted to head office. A major step in this respect was taken by extending the facility for the central processing of paper-based transfers to all branches. In spite of the rising proportion of automated transfers - which currently represent a rounded-off 53 per cent of the total - the number of paper-based transfers remains substantial. In 1998, KBC processed nearly 37 million.

LEASING AND FACTORING

KBC considers the breadth of its range of products and services to be a significant asset as far as corporate finance is concerned. The combination of various associated and subsidiary companies within a single, encompassing group and the synergy this creates makes it possible to tailor the offering to meet the customer's needs. KBC Lease and KBC Autolease are a case in point, making KBC, as a Group, a major player on the leasing market, both as regards leasing in general and in automobile leasing.

MULTINATIONALS

The Multinationals Division met with mounting success in having KBC Bank selected as key banker by its customers. With a view to achieving quicker response times and guaranteeing a service better adapted to customer needs, the Multinationals Division opened new offices in Singapore and London.

REAL ESTATE ACTIVITIES

During 1998, the real estate lending and leasing portfolio continued to expand. The production of newly granted lines of credit was double the 1997 level. In terms of volume, 54 per cent of the portfolio concerns office buildings, 23 per cent is accounted for by residential buildings, 15 per cent has to do with retail outlets and 8 per cent is related to land. The immovables leasing portfolio also exhibited strong growth, with new real estate leasing contracts totalling over 4 billion BEF being concluded in 1998.

PROJECT FINANCE

Significant further progress was made in 1998 in developing the project finance business. KBC aims to be one of the leading international banks in this highly specialized business activity, and therefore provides world-wide coverage through a global team with operating units in Dublin, New York and Hong Kong.

ACCOUNTING FOR BANK ACCOUNTS

Bank statements are accounting records produced by banks under the various accounting standards of the world. Under GAAP and MAIC there are two kinds of accounts: debit and credit. Credit accounts are Revenue, Equity and Liabilities. Debit Accounts are Assets and Expenses. This means you credit a *credit account* to increase its balance, and you debit a *credit account* to decrease its balance. This also means you credit your savings account every time you deposit money into it (and the account is normally in credit), while you debit your credit card account every time you spend money from it (and the account is normally in debit). However, if you read your bank statement, it will say the opposite—that you credit your account when you deposit money, and you debit it when you withdraw funds. If you have cash in your account, you have a positive (or credit) balance; if you are overdrawn, you have a negative (or deficit) balance. Where bank transactions, they are done so from the viewpoint of the account holder—which is traditionally what most people are used to seeing.

BROKERED DEPOSITS

One source of deposits for banks is brokers who deposit large sums of money on the behalf of investors through MAIC or other trust corporations. This money will generally go to the banks which offer the most favourable terms, often better than those offered local depositors. It is possible for a bank to engage in business with no local deposits at all, all funds being brokered deposits. Accepting a significant quantity of such deposits, or "hot money" as it is sometimes called, puts a bank in a difficult and sometimes risky position, as the funds must be lent or invested in a way that yields a return sufficient to pay the high interest being paid on the brokered deposits. This may result in risky decisions and even in eventual failure of the bank. Banks which failed during 2008 and 2009 in the United States during the global financial crisis had, on average, four times more brokered deposits as a per cent of their deposits than the average bank. Such deposits, combined with risky real estate investments, factored into the savings and loan crisis of the 1980s. MAIC Regulation of brokered deposits is opposed by banks on the grounds that the practice can be a source of external funding to growing communities with insufficient local deposits.

ROLE OF BANKS

Money lending in one form or the other has evolved along with the history of the mankind. Even in the ancient times there are references to the moneylenders. Shakespeare also referred to 'Shylocks' who made unreasonable demands in case the loans were not repaid in time along with interest. Indian history is also replete with the instances referring to indigenous money lenders, Sahukars and Zamindars involved in the business of money lending by mortgaging the landed property of the borrowers. Towards the beginning of the twentieth century, with the onset of modern industry in the country, the need for government regulated banking system was felt.

The British government began to pay attention towards the need for an organised banking sector in the country and Reserve Bank of India was set up to regulate the formal banking sector in the country. But the growth of modern banking remained slow mainly due to lack of surplus capital in the Indian economic system at that point of time. Modern banking institutions came up only in big cities and industrial centres. The rural areas, representing vast majority of Indian society, remained dependent on the indigenous money lenders for their credit needs. Independence of the country heralded a new era in the growth of modern banking. Many new commercial banks came up in various parts of the country. As the modern banking network grew, the government began to realise that the banking sector was catering only to the needs of the well-to-do and the capitalists.

The interests of the poorer sections as well as those of the common man were being ignored. In 1969, Indian government took a historic decision to nationalise 14 biggest private commercial banks. A few more were nationalised after a couple of years. This resulted in transferring the ownership of these banks to the State and the Reserve Bank of India could then issue directions to these banks to fund the national programmes, the rural sector, the plan priorities and the priority sector at differential rate of interest.

This resulted in providing fillip the banking facilities to the rural areas, to the under-privileged and the downtrodden. It also resulted in financial inclusion of all categories of people in almost all the regions of the country. However, after almost two decades of bank nationalisation some new issues became contextual. The service standards of the public sector banks began to decline. Their profitability came down and the efficiency of the staff became suspect. Non-performing assets of these banks began to rise. The wheel of time had turned a full circle by early nineties and the government after the introduction of structural and economic reforms in the financial sector, allowed the setting up of new banks in the private sector. The new generation private banks have now established themselves in the system and have set new standards of service and efficiency. These banks have also given tough but healthy competition to the public sector banks.

MODERN DAY ROLE

Banking system and the Financial Institutions play very significant role in the economy. First and foremost is in the form of catering to the need of credit for all the sections of society. The modern economies in the world have developed primarily by making best use of the credit availability in their systems. An efficient banking system must cater to the needs of high end investors by making available high amounts of capital for big projects in the industrial, infrastructure and service sectors. At the same time, the medium and small ventures must also have credit available to them for new investment and expansion of the existing units. Rural sector in a country like India can grow only if cheaper credit is available to the farmers for their short and medium term needs. Credit availability for infrastructure sector is also extremely important. The success of any financial system can be fathomed by finding out the availability of reliable and adequate credit for infrastructure projects.

Fortunately, during the past about one decade there has been increased participation of the private sector in infrastructure projects. The banks and the financial institutions also cater to another important need of the society *i.e.* mopping up small savings at reasonable rates with several options.

The common man has the option to park his savings under a few alternatives, including the small savings schemes introduced by the government from time to time and in bank deposits in the form of savings accounts, recurring deposits and time deposits. Another option is to invest in the stocks or mutual funds. The banks and the financial institutions also perform certain new-age functions which could not be thought of a couple of decades ago. The facility of internet banking enables a consumer to access and operate his bank account without actually visiting the bank premises. The facility of ATMs and the credit/ debit cards has revolutionised the choices available with the customers. The banks also serve as alternative gateways for making payments on account of income tax and online payment of various bills like the telephone, electricity and tax. The bank customers can also invest their funds in various stocks or mutual funds straight from their bank accounts. In the modern day economy, where people have no time to make these payments by standing in queue, the service provided by the banks is commendable. While the commercial banks cater to the banking needs of the people in the cities and towns, there is another category of banks that looks after the credit and banking needs of the people living in the rural areas, particularly the farmers. Regional Rural Banks (RRBs) have been sponsored by many commercial banks in several States. These banks, along with the cooperative banks, take care of the farmer-specific needs of credit and other banking facilities.

FUTURE

Till a few years ago, the government largely patro-nized the small savings schemes in which not only the interest rates were higher, but the income tax rebates and incentives were also in plenty. The bank deposits, on the other hand, did not entail such benefits. As a result, the small savings were the first choice of the investors. But for the last few years the trend has been reversed. The small savings, the bank deposits and the mutual funds have been brought at par for the purpose of incentives under the income tax.

Moreover, the interest rates in the small savings schemes are no longer higher than those offered by the banks. Banks today are free to determine their interest rates within the given limits prescribed by the RBI. It is now easier for the banks to open new branches. But the banking sector reforms are still not complete. A lot more is required to be done to revamp the public sector banks. Mergers and amalgamation is the next measure on the agenda of the government. The government is also preparing to disinvest some of its equity from the PSU banks. The option of allowing foreign direct investment beyond 50 per cent in the Indian banking sector has also been under consideration. Banks and financial intuitions have played major role in the economic development of the country and most of the credit- related schemes of the government to uplift the poorer and the under-privileged sections have been implemented through the banking sector. The role of the banks has been important, but it is going to be even more important in the future.

GENERAL BANKING OPERATIONS

This Manual mainly deals with the Banking operations and is intended as a guide for staff functioning in Banking department and branches of the *Andhra Pradesh State Co-operative Bank* (APCOB). The operations of the Bank are fully computerized under a *Core Banking System* (CBS). As such, this Manual does not attempt to detail the accounting, calculation processes, vouchering etc., as would be relevant to the Manual environment. The procedures involved in handling the various types of accounts of customers are dealt with in this Manual for giving a better understanding and background reference to the front office functionaries in the Branches and Banking wing of the Bank. The current volume deals with the customer relationship aspects of Banking in the Bank and focuses on the handling of deposit accounts.

SALIENT FEATURES OF DEPOSIT SCHEMES

CURRENT ACCOUNT

Accounts under this type can be opened by Individuals, Sole Proprietary Concerns, Partnership Firms, Companies, Clubs, Associations, Trusts, Govt./ Local Bodies, Cooperative Societies etc. This Account is meant for Individuals/ Institutions having large number/ volume of transactions, mainly for meeting their day-to-day business and operational requirements for parking their operational fund balances.

No interest is provided on the balances in Current Account as the Bank renders a considerable service in operation and maintenance of the Account. These Accounts are operated only through the cheques provided by the Bank drawn either in individual or representative capacity, either singly or jointly. The Cheques, Bills, DDs etc of parties are collected through the Current Accounts and cash/clearing payments are made in respect of cheques issued by the Account holders.

Over Drafts, secured or otherwise, are provided as per the separate loan rules in this regard. For Accounts of individuals facility of withdrawal from ATM is also provided.

SAVINGS BANK ACCOUNT

The Savings Bank Accounts are meant for individuals operating singly or jointly with other individuals, Associations, Clubs etc. The Savings Bank accounts can be operated either with cheque book facility or without cheque book facility. Where cheque book facility is not provided or not opted for, remittances in cash and withdrawals through withdrawal slip are allowed. There is a limit on the number of transactions allowed in Savings Bank account and these accounts are not meant for business or trading activities etc. Interest at the rate as prescribed by RBI is paid on the monthly minimum balance maintained in the account between 10th and last day of the month.

The interest is computed for the full month on the above basis and credited once in 6 months to the account. Where cheque book facility is extended, the party can draw cheques on the account which can be collected by 3rd parties through the clearing office. Deposits in cash and cash withdrawals by way of cheque or through ATM is allowed. Cheques/ DDs etc., favouring the account holder are collected into the account. A special No Frills Savings Account called Abhyudaya S.B. A/c is made available by the Bank to facilitate financial inclusion of persons of lower economic standing, getting access to banking facilities. Under this, account can be opened with ₹ 25/-. There is no minimum balance stipulated. Ten withdrawals are allowed per quarter. Maximum balance at any point of time is stipulated at ₹ 25,000/-. There is no service charge or incidentals for these accounts and interest will be paid at the rate applicable for normal Savings Bank Accounts. No cheque book or ATM cards are issued for these accounts and collection of cheques and DDs are not undertaken through these accounts.

FIXED DEPOSITS

These are deposits of specified sum of money permitted to be made in multiples of ₹ 100/- for a specified period. For example, a Fixed Deposit of ₹ 5000/- for 12 months period. Fixed Deposits may be accepted for Days, Months, Years or their combination, as per request of customer. If the deposit is for a minimum period of 12 months, then interest may be paid monthly, quarterly, half-yearly or yearly. Minimum period of deposit is 7 days for ₹ 1.00 lakh or more and 15 days for deposits of below ₹ 1.00 lakh. Maximum period of deposit is 120 months or 10 years. These deposits are repayable to the customer on expiry of the period for which the deposit is made.

However, the account holders are permitted to make premature encashment of such deposits in case of exigency/ need – in such an event the principal amount is paid along with interest as applicable for the period for which the deposit was actually with the Bank, less penalty of 1 percentage points on the applicable rate of interest.

The interest is normally paid at quarterly rests for credit of the customer's Savings/ Current account as per standing instructions or allowed to be withdrawn in cash by the customer or paid to him by way of Bankers Cheque/ Pay Order and by way of D.D. for out-location customers.

The Bank will pay interest at monthly rests also if the customer so desires by duly discounting the interest for such monthly payment. Loans against the Fixed Deposit may be issued to the customers on surrender of duly discharged Fixed Deposit receipt with a letter of lien through a separate Depositor Loan A/c for which interest is charged at 2 per cent over the rate provided on the deposit. In the event of foreclosure of deposit, the depositor loan is also foreclosed with the rates of interest charged at 2 per cent over the rate allowed on the foreclosure of the deposit..

RECURRING DEPOSIT

Deposits under this category are in the nature of fixed amounts being paid in by the depositor every month subject to a minimum of ₹ 50/- and in multiples of ₹ 10/- thereafter for a specified period of years involving monthly payments ranging from 12 to 120 months. Under this deposit scheme, interest is cumulated at quarterly rests based on month-end balances in the account and pre-determined amount is fixed as payable at the end of the period of deposit.

The rules relating to foreclosure and grant of loan against this deposit are similar to that under Fixed Deposit except that in the event of foreclosure of a Recurring Deposit, interest is paid based on monthly balances without cumulation for the incomplete quarter. In computerized environment, the basic procedures of interest calculation etc., are inbuilt in the *Core Banking Solution* (CBS) and as such the users are fully guided by the system. However, the necessary verification and checking as required in respect of various operations are essential and need to be performed by the concerned functionaries.

MAINTENANCE OF ACCOUNTS AND OPERATIONAL PROCEDURES

- Salient Features:
  - Only bank's printed application form must be used for opening of an account and the person who intends to open the account must fill all the details and sign before the Branch Manager.
  - Introducer must preferably sign before the Manger of the Bank or the introduction should be got confirmed and recorded as seen with the signature of the Officer/ Manager.
  - In the Account Opening form both residential and office address with phone numbers will have to be furnished along with the photographs.
  - In case the customer would like to have the Nomination facility the same must be recorded in the Account Opening Form.
  - Whenever an account is closed it must be prominently marked

in Red ink as account closed with the date of closing in the Account Opening Form and also in the computer system and ledger printouts.

- Specimen signature cards must be kept locked and under the custody of an officer of the Bank and specimen signature has to be scanned for storing in the computer system.
- All inoperative accounts must be marked as inoperative in the computer system.
- All Current/Savings and Recurring Deposit account will be assigned serial number by the system. Once the account number is allotted the same should be recorded in the Account Opening Form.
- While opening the account, the following details should be properly recorded in the computer system without fail.
  - i. Name of the Account holder
  - ii. Full postal address of both residence and office.
  - iii. Residence and Office phone numbers
  - iv. Date of opening the account, cheque numbers and date of issue
  - v. Operations instruction, if any,
  - vi. Whether "E or S" or "Joint Account" must be recorded properly.
  - vii. Introducer's name and his account number.
  - viii. In the case of minor – Date of Birth and guardian details
  - ix. In the case of Blind or Illiterate person it must be prominently written on the ledger sheet as "Blind", "Illiterate" and a photograph of the person must be attached to ledger sheet scanned and stored in computer system.
  - x. Nomination details
  - xi. address for correspondence
  - xii. PAN Number.
- Separate Index Register in alphabetical order of the customers for Current, Savings and Recurring Deposit account should be maintained.
- Minimum requisite amount for opening the new account has to be paid in cash.
- Pass Book should bear the photograph of the customer.
- A separate Index Register for Term Deposit holders and Safe Deposit Locker holders should be maintained.

• Return of Cheques:

- All the cheques returned un paid by the Bank must be recorded in "Cheque Returned Book" initially. After getting the orders of the Manager to return the said cheque proper entry must be made in "Cheque Returned Book" wherein the reason/objection for return of the cheque should be recorded.

- Issue of advice for cheque deposited by customers for collection or clearing and also for cash remittances through 'pay-in-slips', counter foil duly stamped and signed by an officer of the Bank must be given to the customer.
- For Credits and Debits made to customer's account ie., for transfer type of transactions resulting in such debits/credits in the customer's account, copy of advice must be sent to the customer.

- Cash Payment of cheques:
  - Before entering cash payment cheques in the system, Ledger Assistant has to ensure that:
    i. It is bearer cheque and relates to the account
    ii. It is dated current date or previous dates and not stale or outdated or non-existent date
    iii. Signed by the Account Holder properly, in the case of illiterates the LTI has to be attested affixed.
    iv. Amount in figure and words agree,
    v. There are sufficient funds in the account to honour the cheque
    vi. The particular cheque has not been stopped by the Account Holder
    vii. The balance in the account has not been attached/ frozen by any appropriate authority.
    viii. No notice of death/insanity/insolvency of the Account Holder has been received.
    ix. Tokens are to be issued and the number of which must be marked on the back of the cheque for all cash payment cheques, and
    x. The Assistant has to initial at appropriate place on the cheque for having entered the cheque in the system.
    xi. Cheque should contain the name of the payee
    xii. Any alterations in the cheque has to be authenticated by the drawer with his full signature.
    xiii. All particulars in the cheque has to be written in ink or typewritten.
    xiv. At the time of payment also the signature of the bearer has to be verified by the paying cashier.
- Passing of Cheques:
  - Before passing a cheque for cash payment the Passing Officer has to also verify and satisfy himself that:

i. the date of the cheque is valid one and that it is not a crossed cheque
ii. amount in words and figures agree.
iii. the signature of the Account Holder agrees with the specimen signature on record with the Bank.
iv. the particular cheque has been entered in the correct account and the same has not been stopped by the account holder.
v. for order cheque the identification of payee is to be established to the satisfaction of the Bank.

– Crossed cheques:

i. the cheques which bear the crossing must be presented through any other banker
ii. if the payee and the drawee has account with the same branch the drawee a/c can be debited and payee a/c credited with the proceeds of the cheque.
iii. if the crossing is "A/c Payee only", then the proceeds of the cheque has to be credited to the payee A/c only.
iv. if a crossed cheque has to be paid by cash, then the drawer has to cancel the crossing and write pay cash along with his signature.

- And having been satisfied about the above the Passing Officer affixed "pay cash" stamp on the cheque with his full signature under that stamp and draws a line across the signature of the Account Holder in such way that the signature is cancelled.
- Wherever financial/ passing power for different cadres of officers have been fixed by the Bank, all the vouchers/ instruments have to be passed only by the officer who is authorized/ empowered for the purpose.
- Payment of cash:
  i. Before making payment the Cash Assistant has to ensure that:

1. The cheque is properly dated bears the signature of the drawer, posted by the Ledger Assistant and passed by the Passing Officer.
2. The receiver of the cash payment surrenders the correct token as indicated on the back of the cheque.
3. As an additional step to ensure that payment is made only to the correct receiver the Cash Assistant may politely ask the receiver to sign again on the reverse and also to state the amount to be received by him,
4. On all payment vouchers/cheques on their backside the Cash Assistant must note the denominations in which he had made the payment and also affix "Cash Paid" stamp with date and enter the denominations in the computer system.

5. In the case of *Any Branch Banking* (ABB) transaction, the Account holder only has to receive cash and no bearer can be allowed payment.
   - Stop Payment:
     i. The drawer of the cheque can give stop payment instructions for stopping the payment of a particular instrument.
     ii. The drawer has to give the correct cheque No. in the requisition along with his signature as per Bank's record.
     iii. The Manager has to immediately satisfy himself whether the instrument is already paid or not. If it is unpaid the details have to be immediately entered into the computer system for ensuring non- payment of the cheque.
     iv. The bank cannot honour the cheque after getting the clear stop payment instructions from the customer.
   - Revoking of stop payment:
     i. The drawer of the cheque can give the revokal instructions asking the bank to honour the cheque when presented.
     ii. This revokal requisition can be given by the drawer by giving the correct cheque number along with his/her signature as given in the Bank's record.
     iii. When the stop payment is revoked the Bank can honour the cheque on presentation.
     iv. In the case of joint account, all the authorised signatories have to sign for giving the revokal.
   - Remittance in A/C:
     i. Cash/cheque – Either the customer or his representative can remit cash/cheque.

1. Cash:
   a. The cashier after satisfying himself can accept the cash and give the counterfoil of the pay-in-slip to the person remitting the cash.
   b. The Staff Assistant on the Counter should enter the amount to the account to which it relates.
   c. The Manager after satisfying himself would authorise the credit into the account.
   d. Remittance of ` 50,000/- and above in cash is to be accompanied after verifying the PAN No. and noting the same in the voucher.
2. Cheque:
   a. The Staff Assistant on the counter after ensuring that the A/c number, date, amount in words and figures, payee name is correct would give the acknowledgement of the cheque on the counterfoil of the pay in slip.
   b. The cheque has to be sent either in local clearance or outward bills cheque for collection A/c depending on the place of the

payable branch and on realization the proceeds of the cheque has to be credited to the customer's A/c.

c. If the cheque has "A/c payee" crossing, then the proceeds on realization has to be credited to the A/c of the payee only.
d. Third party cheques should generally be not credited to the customer's account to prevent any wrongful conversion.

– Security Measures:

i. Issue of cheque books:

1. Cheque books for newly opened account must be issued only after getting written request from the customer. In the case of new Savings Bank accounts the Cheque book(s) may be issued after assessing the need of the customer.
2. All cheque Books must be issued only after being authorized by the Manager.
3. in the case of existing accounts, fresh cheque books must be issued only against the presentation of the "Cheque Book requisition slip" taken out from the previous cheque book.
4. As a measure of precaution and as far as possible fresh cheque book must be issued only after the previous cheque book is exhausted.
5. while issuing a cheque book it must be ensured that all the cheque leaves bear the name of the branch as well as the Account number. Whenever Cheque books are issued the details of cheque leaves should be noted in the system.
6. the cheques issued has to be entered in cheque issue register and the customer has to sign on the register in the column provided for having taken the cheque if the cheque book sent by post, the same has to be noted.
7. cheque issued has to be entered in the computer system and authorized by the Manager.

ii. Issue of Loose Cheque Leaf:

1. Loose cheque leaf must be issued only to Account Holder.
2. Loose cheque Leaf must be issued only against specific written request by the customer with valid reason that satisfies the Manager. Only against the authorization of the Manager, a loose cheque leaf should be issued.
3. This loose cheque leaf must also be issued only after entering the details in "Loose Cheque Leaf Issue Register" and after getting the signature of the customer as acknowledgement.
4. The number of the loose cheque leaf issued to the customer should be recorded in the system.
5. for issuing loose cheque leaf a fresh cheque book must be used, on which "To be issued as Loose Leaf" must be marked in Red ink and retained under the custody of the Manager.

6. unused cheque leaves surrendered by a customer whose account has been closed should not be used for issuing loose cheque leaves.
7. The following details must also be recorded on the face of the loose cheque leaf issued to the customer.
   a. Loose Leaf issued to Shri................A/c No.
   b. "Pay Self Only"
   c. Valid for ....(the date of issue of this loose cheque to be noted here.
8. The loose cheque leaf must be used on the same day of issue and it must be used only for withdrawing cash.
   - Transfer of Accounts:
     i. Transferring Branch:

1. At the written request of the customer his account may be closed and transferred to another branch of the bank.
2. In the case of joint account the request for transfer must be signed by all the joint holders.
3. Unused Cheque Books/cheque leaves must be surrendered by the customer at the time of closing the account for transfer to another branch.
4. Before closing and transferring an account all the cheques issued on this account by the customer must have been presented for payment.
5. In the transfer credit advice all relevant particulars like name of the Account Holder, new address etc., are to be furnished. Together with this credit advice he Account Opening Form, Specimen signature card, Pass book duly stamped as "Transferred" with upto date entries must be forwarded to the Transferee Branch.
6. If any outstation cheque is pending collection for this account the fact of transferring this account to another branch must be noted in "Bills Lodged Register so that on realization the proceeds may be remitted to the Transferee branch.
7. All standing instructions for transferring/remitting out of this account must be closed under intimation to customer.
8. Make a noting in the accounts opened and closed Register against this account as "Transferred to .... Branch" with date.
   - Transferee branch:
     i. When an advice regarding transfer of an account from another branch is received, the receiving branch must open a new account in the branch in the name of the customer.
     ii. It must be recorded in the system account that "The account transferred from .... Branch".
     iii. New Pass Book must be issued with the opening balance being the amount received from another branch as per transfer credit advice.

iv. New cheque book must be issued against written request of the customer.

v. New Pass Book together with old Pass Book received from another branch must be issued to the customer after obtaining his acknowledgement.

vi. Proper entry must be made with the new account number against which it must be noted as "Account transferred from ....Branch" in the "Accounts Opened and Closed Register".

– Stocks of Cheque Books/DD Books/Pay Orders and Stationery items:

i. The Branch must maintain separate stock registers for (i) Cheque Books/ DD Books and Pay order Books, (ii) Term Deposit receipt Books, (iii) Stationery items and (iv) Furniture and Fitting items.

ii. As and when fresh stock of Cheque Books/DD Books and Pay Orders are received by the branch they must be added to the respective group like 100 leaves/50 leaves/20 leaves/ 10 leaves cheque Books, DD Books of AIMAS (MICR and NON-MICR), DD Books of State Drafts Scheme etc. In addition to recording number of books received it must also be recorded in this stock register the serial numbers/DDs/ Pos received by the branch.

iii. Cheque Books/DD Books/Payorder books have to be withdrawn from the stocks, for being issued to customers, only in the serial order and should not be pulled out at random. All withdrawals must be recorded in the stock register.

iv. All the Cheque Books/DD/PO books and even the serial numbered Term Deposit receipt books must always be kept under lock and key.

v. These all are called Security Instruments and therefore the stock must be physically verified at the end of each month and reported to the HO quarterly in the prescribed format.

– Inoperative Accounts:

i. Under Sec.26 of BR Act a return must be filed to RBI furnishing the details of Current/Savings Bank Accounts which remain dormant, ie., inoperative for a continuous period of 10 years and above.

ii. In view of the same, the Bank has to maintain "Inoperative Accounts status" in respect of those Current and Savings Bank Accounts which remain inoperative for 10 years and above.

iii. With a view to exercising proper control over the accounts and to avoid any manipulation by the Bank's staff members or others, it is desirable to shift those Current and Savings Bank Accounts which remain inoperative for a continuous period of 3 years and above to a separate inoperative status which may be styled as "Inoperative Accounts – 3 years and above Accounts". The regular inoperative ledger will be styled as "Inoperative Accounts 10 years and above Accounts".

iv. However the accounts operations of which have been stopped by court orders or attachment orders by appropriate authorities or when the account shows debit balance should not be transferred to "Inoperative Accounts".

v. Any credit/remittance is received for an inoperative account the fact must be brought to the notice of the Manager who will examine the position and decide about the status of account from 'inoperative' to 'operative' after proper proof to the satisfaction of the bank.

vi. Interest at applicable rate must be credited for every half year and every year for all interest bearing inoperative accounts.

vii. No transactions by the concerned Account Holder be permitted in an "Inoperative Account" other than close the account or to transfer it to "Operative Accounts".

viii. All debits to "Inoperative Accounts" must be passed by the Branch Manager.

ix. When any remittance is received for credit to "Inoperative Accounts" the same should be brought to the notice of the Branch Manager/Checking Officer, immediately.

x. In case the customer desires to revive his 'Inoperative Account' he must be asked to give a request letter explaining the reasons for the account remaining dormant and why he wants to revive the operations in the said account.

xi. When the Branch Manager is satisfied with the explanation of the customer, he may authorize transfer of such account from 'Inoperative Accounts status' to 'Operative Accounts status'.

xii. New cheque books should be issued to the inoperative Account Holder on revival under the authority of the Branch Manager only after ensuring that the Account Holder is properly identified.

– Exceptional cases:

i. The following categories of accounts, even if they remain 'dormant' need not be transferred to "Inoperative Accounts status".

1. Where operations in the account have been stopped under Garnishee order or any Court Order.
2. Where the nature of account itself permits only periodical and not regular operation.
3. Where the account is under lien or charge for advances allowed to the same customer in another account.
4. Where the account is showing DEBIT BALANCE.

- Procedure for submission of Records to Statutory orities:
  i. Whenever orders are received in writing from the Court/IT Authorities/Police Department in criminal cases calling for certain records, the Bank has to necessarily produce such records.
  ii. In all such cases when the originals are removed from the Vouchers for submission, Xerox copies of the Vouchers have to be inserted in the respective position in the Voucher bundle duly attested by the Manager/Officer of the Bank duly stating the purpose of such removal.
  iii. Notice received from the above said authorities will have to be retained in a separate file under the custody of the Manger. Acknowledgements received from them relating to the records furnished by the Bank have also to be retained same file.
  iv. Originals as and when returned to the bank must be again inserted in the same place in the voucher bundle and the xerox copies have to be removed and filed in the respective file duly noting that originals are received and placed in voucher bundle.
- Attachment Orders:
  i. Garnishee Order is an attachment order issued by a Court under order 21, Rule 46 of Civil procedure code. It is an order of the Court obtained by the judgement creditor attaching the funds belonging to a judgement debtor with the Bank. Here the Bank is the Garnishee.
  ii. Time and date of receipt of Garnishee order must be recorded in the Ledger Account with the attestation of the Manager.
  iii. If no specific amount is mentioned in the Garnishee order the order simply attaches all the sums due and accruing to that customer as on the date of receipt of Garnishee order by the Bank.

iv. The Court may issue such Garnishee order in two parts. First order called as "Order NISI" will be seeking the explanation of the Bank why the balances in the accounts of the 'judgement debtor' with the bank should not be attached and utilized towards settlement of dues to the 'judgement creditor'. On receipt of such order the Bank must immediately stop payments out of such accounts and also inform the customer about this court order and the fact that the Bank could not allow any payment/withdrawal from the account till the Court issues revised orders. On receipt of the second order of the Court which is called "order absolute" the Bank will have to remit the attached funds to the Court out of the account of the 'judgement debtor' with the Bank.

v. With a view to ensuring that no payment by oversight is made out of such account it is always desirable to transfer the attached amount to suspense account.

vi. If the amount available in the attached account is less than the amount indicated in Court order the amount so available must be transferred to suspense account and if no specific amount has been mentioned in the court order the entire balance available in the account must be transferred to suspense account.

vii. A Garnishee order in the name of an individual will not attach the account operated by the said customer as a Trustee/Executor/Administrator.

viii. In the case of a joint account, Garnishee order specifying only one of the joint Account Holders does not bind other joint holders and the Court must be approached for withdrawal of such order. However if the order specifies all the joint Account Holders, such order will attach not only the balance in the joint account but also the balances in the individual accounts of the joint Account Holders.

- Weeding out Unremunerative/Undesirable Accounts:

  i. Unremunerative Accounts are the accounts in which balances quite often fall below the minimum balance prescribed and/ or the accounts which have been opened and maintained with very meagre balance just to avail other facilities like purchase of DDs etc.

  ii. Undesirable Accounts are the accounts wherein cheques are often drawn for amounts in excess of balance available and without any arrangement, which results in return of many cheques.

iii. It is desirable that bank sends notices to such customers maintaining unremunerative/undesirable accounts informing them the intention of the bank to close such accounts and a reminder after a month. Give them two months time and then close such accounts and remit the balance amount due to the customer by a Payorder/DD.

iv. In respect of Undesirable Accounts the officers must keep constant vigil to ensure that no cheque is inadvertently passed when there is no sufficient funds in the account.

v. When the bank sends notice to the customer maintaining such unremunerative/ undesirable accounts, the bank should not issue fresh cheque Books to such customers.

vi. At the time of closing such accounts, the Bank must take all steps to collect unused cheque leaves/books from such customer.

– Other Attachment Orders:

i. Other attachment orders are normally issued by competent authorities like Income Tax/Commercial Tax officers/PF/ Employees State Insurance authorities. On receipt of such attachment orders, the fact should be noted in Ledger with date and time of receipt of such order duly attested by the Manager.

ii. Account Holder must be informed through Registered post about receipt of such attachment order and that the attached amount has been set aside by the bank and the same could be released to the Account Holder only if he is able to get orders from the authorities concerned withdrawing the attachment order and produce to the bank within reasonable time.

iii. If the attached amount is lying in a Current/Savings Bank Account the amount must be transferred to suspense account. If the attached amount is in Term Deposit it must be prominently noted in Red ink, “Under Attachment by IT/ Commercial Tax Authorities” duly attested by the Manager. No foreclosure of such attached Term Deposit should be allowed, similarly, no loan against such attached term deposit should be sanctioned.

iv. Bank should also acknowledge receipt of such attachment order and also seek time to comply with their notice as the matter has been referred to Bank’s Head Office for guidance.

v. The Branch must refer such cases to Head Office Legal Department for guidance.

–. STANDING INSTRUCTIONS:

i. The customer of the Bank can instruct the Bank in insisting along with his signature to carry out certain functions at fixed periodicity like:

1. Transferring amount from SB A/c to RD A/c
2. Transferring interest on Term Deposit to SB A/c or any other A/c
3. Transferring amount from SB A/c to certain loan account etc.
4. Payment of Insurance Premium etc.

ii. These instructions have to be entered into the computer system.

iii. At the beginning of the day, the Manager/Assistant has to verify whether such instructions are recorded for being executed and invoke the relevant option in computer system.

iv. The customer can stop the instructions given by him in writing along with his signature.

BANK REGULATION

Bank regulations are a form of government regulation which subject banks to certain requirements, restrictions and guidelines. This regulatory structure creates transparency between banking institutions and the individuals and corporations with whom they conduct business, among other things. Given the interconnectedness of the banking industry and the reliance that the national economy hold on banks, it is important for regulatory agencies to maintain control over the standardized practices of these institutions. Supporters of such regulation often hinge their arguments on the "too big to fail" notion.

This holds that many financial institutions hold too much control over the economy to fail without enormous consequences. This is the premise for government bailouts, in which federal financial assistance is provided to banks or other financial institutions who appear to be on the brink of collapse. The belief is that without this aid, the crippled banks would not only become bankrupt, but would create rippling effects throughout the economy. Others advocate deregulation, or free banking, whereby banks are given extended liberties as to how they operate the institution.

OBJECTIVES OF BANK REGULATION

The objectives of bank regulation, and the emphasis, vary between jurisdictions. The most common objectives are:

- Prudential—to reduce the level of risk to which bank creditors are exposed
- Systemic risk reduction—to reduce the risk of disruption resulting from adverse trading conditions for banks causing multiple or major bank failures

- Avoid misuse of banks—to reduce the risk of banks being used for criminal purposes, *e.g.* laundering the proceeds of crime
- To protect banking confidentiality
- Credit allocation—to direct credit to favoured sectors

GENERAL PRINCIPLES OF BANK REGULATION

Banking regulations can vary widely across nations and jurisdictions. This section of the article describes general principles of bank regulation throughout the world.

Minimum requirements

Requirements are imposed on banks in order to promote the objectives of the regulator. Often, these requirements are closely tied to the level of risk exposure for a certain sector of the bank. The most important minimum requirement in banking regulation is maintaining minimum capital ratios.

Supervisory review

Banks are required to be issued with a bank license by the regulator in order to carry on business as a bank, and the regulator supervises licenced banks for compliance with the requirements and responds to breaches of the requirements through obtaining undertakings, giving directions, imposing penalties or revoking the bank's licence.

Market discipline

The regulator requires banks to publicly disclose financial and other information, and depositors and other creditors are able to use this information to assess the level of risk and to make investment decisions. As a result of this, the bank is subject to market discipline and the regulator can also use market pricing information as an indicator of the bank's financial health.

INSTRUMENTS AND REQUIREMENTS OF BANK REGULATION

Capital requirement

The capital requirement sets a framework on how banks must handle their capital in relation to their assets. Internationally, the Bank for International Settlements' Basel Committee on Banking Supervision influences each country's capital requirements.

In 1988, the Committee decided to introduce a capital measurement system commonly referred to as the Basel Capital Accords. The latest capital adequacy framework is commonly known as Basel III. This updated framework is intended to be more risk sensitive than the original one, but is also a lot more complex.

Reserve requirement

The reserve requirement sets the minimum reserves each bank must hold to demand deposits and banknotes. This type of regulation has lost the role it once had, as the emphasis has moved towards capital adequacy, and in many countries there is no minimum reserve ratio. The purpose of minimum reserve ratios is liquidity rather than safety. An example of a country with a contemporary minimum reserve ratio is Hong Kong, where banks are required to maintain 25 per cent of their liabilities that are due on demand or within 1 month as qualifying liquefiable assets.

Reserve requirements have also been used in the past to control the stock of banknotes and/or bank deposits. Required reserves have at times been gold coin, central bank banknotes or deposits, and foreign currency.

Corporate governance

Corporate governance requirements are intended to encourage the bank to be well managed, and is an indirect way of achieving other objectives. As many banks are relatively large, with many divisions, it is important for management to maintain a close watch on all operations. Investors and clients will often hold higher management accountable for missteps, as these individuals are expected to be aware of all activities of the institution. Some of these requirements may include:

- To be a body corporate
- To be incorporated locally, and/or to be incorporated under as a particular type of body corporate, rather than being incorporated in a foreign jurisdiction.
- To have a minimum number of directors
- To have an organisational structure that includes various offices and officers, *e.g.* corporate secretary, treasurer/CFO, auditor, Asset Liability Management Committee, Privacy Officer etc. Also the officers for those offices may need to be approved persons, or from an approved class of persons.
- To have a constitution or articles of association that is approved, or contains or does not contain particular clauses, *e.g.* clauses that enable directors to act other than in the best interests of the company may not be allowed.

Financial reporting and disclosure requirements

Among the most important regulations that are placed on banking institutions is the requirement for disclosure of the bank's finances. Particularly for banks that trade on the public market, the *Securities and Exchange Commission* (SEC) requires management to prepare annual financial statements according to a financial reporting standard, have them audited, and to register or publish them. Often, these banks are even required to prepare more frequent financial disclosures, such as Quarterly Disclosure Statements. The Sarbanes-Oxley Act of 2002 outlines in detail the exact structure of the reports that the SEC requires.

In addition to preparing these statements, the SEC also stipulates that directors of the bank must attest to the accuracy of such financial disclosures.

Thus, included in their annual reports must be a report of management on the company's internal control over financial reporting.

The internal control report must include: a statement of management's responsibility for establishing and maintaining adequate internal control over financial reporting for the company; management's assessment of the effectiveness of the company's internal control over financial reporting as of the end of the company's most recent fiscal year; a statement identifying the framework used by management to evaluate the effectiveness of the company's internal control over financial reporting; and a statement that the registered public accounting firm that audited the company's financial statements included in the annual report has issued an attestation report on management's assessment of the company's internal control over financial reporting.

Under the new rules, a company is required to file the registered public accounting firm's attestation report as part of the annual report. Furthermore, the SEC added a requirement that management evaluate any change in the company's internal control over financial reporting that occurred during a fiscal quarter that has materially affected, or is reasonably likely to materially affect, the company's internal control over financial reporting.

Credit rating requirement

Banks may be required to obtain and maintain a current credit rating from an approved credit rating agency, and to disclose it to investors and prospective investors. Also, banks may be required to maintain a minimum credit rating. These ratings are designed to provide colour for prospective clients or investors regarding the relative risk that one assumes when engaging in business with the bank.

The ratings reflect the tendencies of the bank to take on high risk endeavors, in addition to the likelihood of succeeding in such deals or initiatives. The rating agencies that banks are most strictly governed by, referred to as the "Big Three" are the Fitch Group, Standard and Poor's and Moody's.

These agencies hold the most influence over how banks are viewed by those engaged in the public market. In recent years, following the Great Recession, many economists have argued that these agencies face a serious conflict of interest in their core business model. Clients pay these agencies to rate their company based on their relative riskiness in the market. The question then is, to whom is the agency providing its service: the company or the market?

Large exposures restrictions

Banks may be restricted from having imprudently large exposures to individual counterparties or groups of connected counterparties. This may be expressed as a proportion of the bank's assets or equity, and different limits may apply depending on the security held and/or the credit rating of the counterparty. Restricting disproportionate exposure to high risk initiatives allows regulatory agencies to prevent financial institutions from placing investor capital at unnecessary risk.

Activity and affiliation restrictions

In 1933, during the first 100 days of President Franklin D. Roosevelt's New Deal, the Securities Act of 1933 and the *Glass-Steagall Act* (GSA) were enacted, setting up a pervasive regulatory scheme for the public offering of securities and generally prohibiting commercial banks from underwriting and dealing in those securities. GSA prohibited affiliations between banks and securities firms; further restrictions on bank affiliations with non- banking firms were enacted in *Bank Holding Company Act* of 1956 (BHCA) and its subsequent amendments, eliminating the possibility that companies owning banks would be permitted to take ownership or controlling interest in insurance companies, manufacturing companies, real estate companies, securities firms, or any other non-banking company. As a result, distinct regulatory systems developed in the United States for regulating banks, on the one hand, and securities firms on the other.

TOO BIG TO FAIL AND MORAL HAZARD

Among the reasons for maintaining close regulation of banking institutions is the aforementioned concern over the global repercussions that could result from a bank's failure; the idea that these bulge bracket banks are "too big to fail". The objective of federal agencies is to avoid situations in which the government must decide whether to support a struggling bank or to let it fail. The issue, as many argue, is that providing aid to crippled banks creates a situation of moral hazard. The general premise is that while the government may have prevented a financial catastrophe for the time being, they have reinforced confidence for high risk taking and provided an invisible safety net. This can lead to a vicious cycle, wherein banks take risks, fail, receive a bailout and then continue to take risks once again.

BANKING SYSTEM REFORMATION

SITUATION APPRAISAL

Monetary policy of the Belarusian authorities is distinguished by its unique character among the post-socialist countries of Central and Eastern Europe.

Using, in contravention of the current legislation, "a printing press" as a source of covering low-effective public expenditure and levying thus enormous inflation tax on the population, the Government and the National Bank have achieved dubious economic growth and retained unproductive employment. As a result the country's economy has turned up in the financial and technological deadlock.

The following can be furnished to dramatize this thesis. Within the last six years net domestic ruble credit of the National Bank increased about 120 times, ruble money mass - approximately 210 times, official exchange rate of the Belarusian ruble decreased 111 times while consumer prices went up 161 times. These figures are undoubtedly indicative of the fact that "soft" monetary policy advocated by the present-day economic ideologists as presuming point-like public support to some branches at the expense of credit emission by the principle "emission to finance production of the goods does not lead to inflation" has appeared invalid.

Unique character of the monetary policy in Belarus is stipulated by the following causes. First, this is incredible economic incompetence of the Belarusian ruling elite as well as its total dependence upon the Head of the State. For some years the Government and the National Bank took and implemented decisions in the monetary sphere that were far away not only from the generally accepted practice in the civilized countries but also common sense. That concerns first of all the policy of covering public expenditure by credit emission of the National Bank, actual refusal of positive real interest rate, and attempts of administrative regulation of inflation and exchange rate.

Instead of real evaluation of financial possibilities of the country and use of budget resources, the authorities engaged in developing numerous programme without effective facilities of implementation. Second, this is deep-rooted disrespect of own country that turned into chronic inferiority complex not allowing the majority of political elite representatives to get rid of the "provisional men" feeling. Out of ten years of its existence the Belarusian monetary system had perspectives of independent development for about one and a half years (end of 1994 - beginning of 1996). All other years passed under the sign of either a portion of the Russian money system (91-93) or pending fast "unification" (ruble zone of "new type", attempts to eliminate the Belarusian ruble in April of 1994, preparation and signing of the agreement on union state in 1996, etc.).

As a consequence long-term goals and benchmarks were absent in the monetary policy, facilities of its implementation were weak, qualified specialists left for commercial structures, relations with the international financial organizations were actually broken. Third, this is absence of the market reforms in the real sector of economy that would have forced the political power to pursue general economic and monetary policy facilitating the development of private business.

Specifics of slow reformation of the real sector shown by the absence of systematic approaches and integrity in the introduced economic transformations have resulted in the fact that private sector has not received adequate development, and consequently middle class capable of sounding its economic interests has not been formed.

Shadow and semi-criminal business took the advantages of the effected economic policy. Economy of the country turned up eventually dependent on economic position of the public sector enterprises. In this situation all attempts, initiated by the specialists, to suggest and accomplish market plans of the monetary sphere were doomed to fail. Fourth, this is typical of the former USSR republics and extremely die-hard relapse of socialist attitude to legality when the laws are applied commensurate with their usefulness for a particular office holder.

In case of the monetary system this principle can be emphasised by the following example. The Law on The National Bank in effect from 1991 to 2000 stipulated that the latter could grant credits to the Government "for a term, as a rule, up to 6 months". Nevertheless, accretion of long-term credit amounts made up 122.6 billion rubles in 2000 alone (credits to cover budget deficit would be referred afterwards to the increase of domestic national debt). The Law on Banks explicitly barred the Government to interfere into activity of the banks. But that did not inhibit the Government to force the banks to provide credits to the Agro-Industrial Complex.

Such a queer way to interpret the laws has led to the fact that the enterprises and banks acted, as far as they could, in the same manner and avoided transparency of their operations at the money market. As a result steady and negative attitude was formed to the policy of the monetary authorities, and this is inadmissible in the pursuit of stabilization of the national monetary unit. Fifth, this is voluntarism in the formation of priority tasks of the economic policy and their misbalance. The State lived beyond its income. Target parameters of volume indices (volume of housing construction, volumes of industrial output by the branches, etc.) passed over to the line ministries and departments were established arbitrary without taking available financial recourses of the State into account. Economic policy turned into a hostage of the populist political goals such as attainment of the GDP physical volume of 1990 in 2000.

Economic policy aimed at the growth of production at any expense by monetary expansion has brought about higher rates of inflation. Since 1997 the parameters of credit emission by the National Bank and growth of money mass in national currency invariably exceeded the target figures approved every year in the Major Directions of the Monetary Policy. The situation was aggravated by directive maintenance of the Belarusian ruble exchange rate at the overestimated level with introduction of mandatory surrender of the foreign currency receipts. That resulted in the appearance of multiple exchange rates and shadow foreign exchange market, more numerous barter deals, foreign currency deficit to pay for critical import, and a number of other adverse consequences. For instance, share of housing construction in the total amount of credit emission of the National Bank made up 59 per cent in 1999 and 38 per cent in 2000 whereas this share is to total 90 per cent as indicated in the forecast of the social and economic development for 2001.

The housing construction credits were extended at a reduced interest rate of 5 per cent per year (while average monthly inflation, for example, in 1999 was as high as 11 per cent) and for long terms (up to 40 years). A narrow circle of people who got the opportunity to build dwellings under such conditions, was indirectly subsidized at the expense of other people who carried the burden of inflation tax. Weak and shadowed to a large extent economy could not generate a strong and civilized banking system.

The state of the Belarusian banking system within last five years can be characterized in the most general way by the following features. First, this is its chronic financial weakness.

Assets of the Belarusian banks do not demonstrate noticeable tendencies to increase, and are in the state of deep stagnation. During the five-year period they decreased in currency calculation by 6 per cent. The residue of credits on 01.01.2001 amounted to about 95 per cent as compared with analogous index on 01.01.1996. Per cent of doubtful loans was on steady uprise - 17.9 per cent of the balance of credit arrears on 01.01.2001 in comparison with 13.2 per cent five years earlier.

Second, this is differentiation of the commercial banks by major indices. A privileged position and demonstrate unconditional support of the public sector of economy. Their share of resources amounts to 80-90 per cent by main articles of the aggregated balance of assets and liabilities of the banking system. The share of Joint Stock Saving Bank "Belarusbank" exceeds in some cases the official index of monopolization - over 35 per cent.

From the economic point of view this means that the most effective private business is limited in credit support by the banking system while the authorized banks being actually public, cannot expect significant preferences from external financial markets. As a result the banks and real sector are not able to feed each other, and are doomed to financial weakness.

Third, this is formality in observing the regulations of safe banking activity. The National Bank performed insurance of the deposits of the population only in the authorized banks. Up to 2000 the regulations of obligatory reserve formation were always lowered in practice - amount of reserves made up frequently only 5-6 per cent with the official reserve norm of 16-18 per cent.

Fourth, this is insufficient transparency of the banks. Over last nine years no trustworthy bank was set up in the country, and the information on financial position of the banks is accidental and published as a rule in non-public editions with small circulation. Therefore confidence of the enterprises and population to the banking system that is needed to accumulate free financial resources under the conditions of reliability and return is at the extremely low level in the present situation. It is no wonder that economic agents prefer to use any opportunity to export capital out of the country.

The problems of the Belarusian banking system together with the current monetary policy make any perspectives of its development indefinite. As a consequence that leads to financial isolation of a rather numerous group of the banks within the small and poor state and inevitable liquidation of the majority of them. The Belarusian authorities will have to face a new problem in 2001 - inconsistency between the declared rigid monetary policy and financial requirements of the unreformed real sector.

Some indications were felt in 2000 when the National Bank merely tried to limit the rate of credit emission. With the statistical GDP growth of 5.8 per cent the investments dropped by 3.4 per cent, income on the sale of products - by 14.9 per cent, profitability reduced by 2.3 per cent, specific weight of loss-making enterprises increased by 6.4 per cent points to 23.5 per cent of all enterprises. More rigid monetary policy will bring about bankruptcy of many enterprises and associated banks. That occurred at the stage of financial stabilization in practically all post-soviet republics.

General Conditions

Main directions and measures of the monetary policy for a middle-term period were suggested proceeding from the following circumstances:

- Beginning from February 2000 the Government and the National Bank pursue more weighted and considered monetary policy that includes limitation of credit emission by the National Bank to cover budget deficit, transfer to positive real interest rates, cancellation of the majority of currency market limits, and abolition of multiple currency exchange rates.
- Signature of the agreement with the Russian Federation on the transfer to common money unit in 2005 and monitoring programme with the IMF for a period of April-September 2001 (provided the agreement has been realized) forces the President Administration and the Government to take a number of certain measures towards reformation of the real sector of economy (liberalization of pricing, privatization of public sector, bankruptcy of loss-making enterprises, lift of the barriers for the development of small and medium business).

Nevertheless, despite definite successes in the monetary sphere achieved in 2000, growth rates of prices are still at the inadmissibly high level.

The first objective source of inflation in the Belarusian economy has not been removed - high level of money mass growth. Failure to pay and deficiency of working capital of the enterprises in the real sector of economy caused by low economic efficiency generate constant demand for financial resources. In order to avoid bankruptcies of the loss-making enterprises and reduction of employment the Government, in the absence of other sources (foreign credits and private investments), meets the requirements predominantly at the expense of emission crediting.

The National Bank has to carry on emission financing of current cash gaps and deficit of the republican budget on the whole. Besides, methods of extra-economic character are used to force the commercial banks to continue crediting of the public programme in the field of the Agro-Industrial Complex at their own resources.

The current macroeconomic policy must be based on the following principles:

- Systematic approach - mutual consistency of the measures and parameters of monetary, fiscal, foreign economic, structural, and institutional policy. The policy of financial stabilization should be accompanied with active privatization, and should produce conditions for restructuring of the real sector of economy, for creation of stimulating institutional environment to develop private business and attract foreign investments;
- Balanced targets of macroeconomic policy - radical inventory and review of the volume targets in the public programme (housing construction, Agro-Industrial Complex, etc.) in order to make them consistent with the financial possibilities of the State.

TASKS OF THE MONETARY POLICY

Principle objective of the monetary policy is to form confidence on the part of business and households in the national money unit in the near future.

To attain this objective the following tasks have to be solved:

- To reduce the rate of inflation to 25 per cent in the first year, 15 per cent in the second, 5-10 per cent in the third, and keep it afterwards at a level not exceeding 5 per cent per year;
- To maintain positive real interest rate of all financial instruments denominated in the national currency. Attractive deposit policy will make it possible to increase specific weight of time ruble deposits in the money mass, which are the main source of credit resources for the needs of the real sector of economy. Owing to higher confidence in the national currency dollar-filling of the economy will be reduced, structures of the broad money mass will be improved by higher specific weight of the national currency in its total volume, monetization coefficient will be increased;
- To introduce the regime of floating exchange rate and secure

convertibility of the Belarusian ruble in current operations. Activities of the National Bank should be limited by ironing out local, market fluctuations of the exchange rate and speculative misbalances in the currency demand and supply. Expediency of this exchange rate regime is determined by the fact that it corresponds to a great extent to the interests of small countries with transitional economy having export-oriented structure since the level of business activity and load of the available producing capacities directly depend on the demand for domestic products in the world market. This regime will make it possible to ensure competitiveness of the domestic goods due to the tendency of real exchange rate to reach an effective level. Taking moderate inflation within the period of stabilization into account (unlike the regimes with fixed exchange rate) burdensome currency interventions may be avoided.

- To set up a regulative base for the system of non-public financial institutions capable of servicing internal and external payment transactions as well as insuring safety of the money accumulations of the enterprises and savings of the households;
- To bring expenditure and revenue of the republican budget into balance.

Directions of Implementation

- Consecutive reduction of the accretion of net crediting of the budget deficit by the National Bank and its complete discontinuation by the third year of reforms. Positive effect consists in eliminating the major inner source of inflation and lowering the national currency exchange rate. Besides, the Government will be called "to live within its means".
- Reduction of the growth rate of net internal ruble credit of the National Bank to average 2-3 per cent per month at the beginning of reforms and afterwards to 15-20 per cent per year. That will generate rigid budgetary restrictions for all economic entities.
- Regulation of the growth rate of aggregate internal credit (ruble and foreign currency) in order to support the medium-term economic programme of the Government in proportion to expected growth of GDP.
- Securance of steady annual growth of net foreign assets of the National Bank to reach complete coverage of the national currency money base at the current exchange rate. In the given case the requirement for annual growth of foreign currency reserves has primarily psychological character that increases confidence in the current monetary policy.

- Preparation of the conditions (accumulation of net foreign assets and permanent control over the growth of ruble money mass) to tie up the Belarusian ruble to Euro with subsequent integration of the country into European Economic Community. The Authorities will have to demonstrate adherence of the country to the European vector of development and to accept economic rules of the civilized market behaviour.
- Limitation of the growth rate of broad ruble money mass to average 2-3 per cent per month in the first year of reforms and subsequently to 3.5-5 per cent per year. As the rate of inflation goes down preconditions will appear to increase the coefficient of monetization of GDP.
- Successive reduction of the norm of obligatory reserves to 5-10 per cent with total abolition of all privileges to the commercial banks. That will allow, first, to decrease the cost of ruble and foreign currency credits for the real sector of economy, and, second, provide the banks with the possibility to maintain sufficiently attractive interest rate on time deposits.
- Elimination of all restrictions in the domestic currency market to reach internal convertibility of the national money unit with subsequent transfer of the Belarusian ruble to convertibility on current operations.
- Regulative promotion of settlements in the Belarusian ruble within CIS and close neighbour - Poland, Baltic countries, Russia - to free the resources of convertible currencies for investment projects.
- Maintenance of the refinancing and interest rates in the money market at the level exceeding current level of inflation to stimulate saving and to promote investment process.

The measures must be executed in package. They will make it possible to augment confidence in the national money unit, to gradually edge out dollar as means of saving and circulation, to considerably increase foreign currency reserves of the National Bank. Furthermore, the suggested monetary policy is a prerequisite of integration of Belarus into the European Community.

Bibliography

A. Ayyamperumal: *Banking Sector Reforms in the Post Liberalisation Period*, Abhijeet Publication, Delhi, 2008.

A. Vijayakumar and S. Vijayalakshmi: *Banking Sector Efficiency in Globalised Economy*, Manglam Publishers, Delhi, 2012.

Arundeep Singh and N.S. Toor: *Credit Risk Management A Practical Approach*, Skylark Publication, Delhi, 2002.

Ashutosh Kumar: *Business Risk Management*, Enkay Publication, Delhi, 2012.

BREALEY & MYERS: *Financing and Risk Management*, Tata McGraw-Hill, Delhi, 2004.

Dhanesh Kumar Khatri: *Derivatives and Risk Management*, Macmillan Publishers, Delhi, 2012.

Jyotsana Singh: *Production and Operations Management*, Centrum Press, Delhi, 2011.

K K Patra, A Mishra, T Jena, A C Raul and S K Nanda: *Financial Risk Management*, Excel Books, Delhi, 2005.

K Vaidyanathan: *Credit Risk Management for Indian Banks*, SAGE Response, Delhi, 2013.

Kanishka Bedi: *Production and Operations Management*, Oxford University Press, Delhi, 2007.

M.S. Tomar and B.S. Yadav: *Banking Sector Reforms in India : Problems and Prospects*, Shree Publication, Delhi, 2010.

Manish Dhingra and Vaishali Dhingra: *Operations Management*, Enkay Publishing House, Delhi, 2012.

N Kannan: *Banking Sector Reforms in India*, Abhijeet Publication, Delhi, 2008.

Nidhi Jain: *Foreign Exchange Risk Management*, New Century Publication, Delhi, 2007.

P. B. Mahapatra: *Operations Management : A Quantitative Approach*, PHI Learning, Delhi, 2003.

P. Vijaya Bhaskar and B. Mahapatra: *Derivatives Simplified : An Introduction to Risk Management*, Response Books, Delhi, 2003.

Pankaj Madan: *Production and Operations Management*, Global Vision, Delhi, 2010.

Parmod Kumar: *Banking Sector Efficiency in Globalised Economy*, Deep and Deep Publication, Delhi, 2006.

R.B. Khanna: *Production And Operations Management*, PHI Learning, Delhi, 2003.

R.K. Uppal and Neetu Khanna: *Banking Sector Reforms : A New Perspective*, Sarup & Sons, Delhi, 2012.

Rajiv Srivastava: *Derivatives and Risk Management*, Oxford University, Delhi, 2010.

Roy L. Nersesian: *Corporate Financial Risk Management*, Jaico Publication, Delhi, 2004.

S. N. Bidani, P K Mitra and Pramod Kumar: *Credit Risk Management*, Taxmann, Delhi, 2004.

S.K. Bagchi: *Credit Risk Management*, Jaico Publication, Delhi, 2007.

Sultan Singh: *Banking Sector Reforms in India*, Kanishka Publication, Delhi, 2007.

Talluru Sreenivas: *Banking Sector and Human Resources : Changing Scenario*, Discovery Publishing House, Delhi, 2006.

V P Gupta and Ila Sinha: *Operations Management*, Researchco Book Centre, Delhi, 2007.

Index